Social Inequalities, Media, and Communication

COMMUNICATION, GLOBALIZATION, AND CULTURAL IDENTITY

Series Editor: Jan Servaes, Ph.D.
City University of Hong Kong

The *Communication, Globalization, and Cultural Identity* series explores and complicates the interlinked notions of "local" and "global" by integrating global dependency thinking; world-system theory; local, grassroots, interpretative, and participatory theory; and research on social change.

In the current world state, globalization and localization are seen as interlinked processes, and this marks a radical change in thinking about change and development. It also marks the arising of a new range of problems. One of the central problems is that the link between the global and the local is not always made clear.

The debates in the field of international and intercultural communication have shifted and broadened. They have shifted in the sense that they are now focusing on issues related to "global culture," "local culture," "(post)modernity," and "multiculturalism," instead of their previous concern with "modernization," "synchronization," and "cultural imperialism." With these new discussions, the debates have also shifted from an emphasis on homogeneity toward an emphasis on differences. With this shift toward differences and localities, there is also an increased interest in the link between the global and the local and in how the global is perceived in the local.

Titles in series are:

Technological Determinism and Social Change: Communication in a Tech-Mad World, edited by Jan Servaes

Communicating Global to Local Resiliency: A Case Study of the Transition Movement, by Emily Polk

Social Inequalities, Media, and Communication: Theory and Roots, edited by Jan Servaes and Toks Oyedemi

Social Inequalities, Media, and Communication

Theory and Roots

Edited by
Jan Servaes
and Toks Oyedemi

LEXINGTON BOOKS
Lanham • Boulder • New York • London

Published by Lexington Books
A imprint of The Rowman & Littlefield Publishing Group, Inc.
4501 Forbes Boulevard, Suite 200, Lanham, Maryland 20706
www.rowman.com

Unit A, Whitacre Mews, 26-34 Stannary Street, London SE11 4AB

British Library Cataloguing in Publication Information Available

Library of Congress Cataloging-in-Publication Data

Names: Servaes, Jan, 1952- editor. | Oyedemi, Toks, editor.
Title: Social inequalities, media, and communication : theory and roots / Jan Servaes and Toks Oyedemi.
Description: Lanham : Lexington Books, [2015] | Series: Communication, globalization, and cultural identity | Includes bibliographical references and index.
Identifiers: LCCN 2015044193 (print) | LCCN 2015046583 (ebook) | ISBN 9781498523431 (cloth : alk. paper) | ISBN 9781498523448 (Electronic)
Subjects: LCSH: Digital divide. | Equality. | Information technology—Social aspects. | Information technology—Political aspects. | Mass media—Social aspects. | Mass media—Political aspects.
Classification: LCC HM851 .S5656 2015 (print) | LCC HM851 (ebook) | DDC 303.48/33—dc23
LC record available at http://lccn.loc.gov/2015044193

∞™ The paper used in this publication meets the minimum requirements of American National Standard for Information Sciences—Permanence of Paper for Printed Library Materials, ANSI/NISO Z39.48-1992.

Printed in the United States of America

To Bryce, Fiona, Lisa, Myra, Patchanee, Tayo,
and the millions of people who strive for a
sustainable future that is just and equitable,
whilst living within the limits of supporting ecosystems.

Contents

Figures

Tables

Abbreviations

AOSIS	Alliance of Small Islands States
ANC	African National Congress
BCC	Behavior Change Communication
CDA	Critical Discourse Analysis
CfD or C4D	Communication for Development
CDSC	Communication for Development and Social Change
CSO	Civil Society Organization
CSSC	Communication for Sustainable Social Change
CTCs	Community Technology Centers
DEIC	Dutch East India Company
DIDIX	Digital Divide Index
ECA	Ethnographic Content Analysis
FAO	Food and Agriculture Organization
FGD	Focus Group Discussions
GAID	Global Alliance for ICT and Development
GATS	General Agreement on Trade in Services
GDI	Gender Development Index
GDP	Gross Domestic Product
GEAR	Growth, Employment and Redistribution
GEM	Gender Equity Measure
GHS	South Africa's General Household Survey
GMMP	Global Media Monitoring Project
GNH	Gross National Happiness
GNP	Gross National Product
GSE	General Self Efficacy
HDI	Human Development Index
HPI	Human Poverty Index
ICT	Information and Communication Technologies

ICTD	Information and Communication Technologies for Development
IMF	International Monetary Fund
ISA	Ideological State Apparatuses
IT	Information Technology
ITU	International Telecommunications Union
MDGs	Millennium Development Goals
M&E	Monitoring and Evaluation
NEET	Not in Education, Employment, or Training (youngsters)
NGO	Non-Governmental Agency
NICT	New Information and Communication Technologies
NIDS	South Africa's National Income Dynamics Study
NTIA	US National Telecommunications and Information Administration
NWICO	New World Information and Communication Order
OECD	Organization for Economic Cooperation and Development
OPEC	Organization of Petroleum Exporting Countries
PAR	Participatory Action Research
PBS	Public Broadcasting Service
PCDA	Postcolonial Critical Discourse Analysis
PPP	Purchasing Power Parity
PSA	Public Service Advertisement
PT	Postcolonial Theory
R&D	Research and Development
RDP	South Africa's Reconstruction and Development Program
RME	Research, Monitoring and Evaluation
RTC	Right to Communicate
SAPT	South African Post and Telecommunications
SDGs	Sustainable Development Goals
SIDS	Small Island Developing State
SPO	Turkish State Planning Organization
TOP	Technologies Opportunities Programs
TÜBİTAK	The Scientific and Technological Research Council of Turkey
UDHR	Universal Declaration of Human Rights
UK	United Kingdom
UN	United Nations
UNCSTD	United Nations Commission on Science and Technology for Development
UNCTAD	United Nations Conference on Trade and Development
UNDP	United Nations Development Programme
UNESCO	United Nations Educational, Scientific and Cultural Organization
UNFCCC	United Nations Framework Convention on Climate Change

US	United States
WB	World Bank
WCC	World Council of Churches
WFTO	World Fair Trade Organization
WTO	World Trade Organization

Acknowledgments

This book project started as a "big idea" sometime in March 2014. We gradually developed that big idea into a Call for Chapters and circulated it in our respective online networks. The response was overwhelming, resulting in our mailboxes being flooded with hundreds of e-mail inquiries and expressions of interest. Eventually, we gathered about 75 abstracts, of which 35 were selected for the next round: an invitation to draft a chapter. After each submitted chapter went through peer review, twenty-seven were considered acceptable after revisions. Of all these, twenty-two chapters will be published in two volumes. The review and selection process was not always easy. We had to disappoint a number of people who were eager to contribute. However, our decisions were mainly based on the quality of the content, the strength of the argument, and the "newness" of the proposed or applied methodology or theory. We deliberately tried not to select on the basis of "status" of the author or the "prestige" of the affiliation she or he represents. We are therefore proud to state that most of the published contributions come from creative and emerging "new critical voices" in our field.

We wish to thank and congratulate, not only the authors of the published chapters, but everybody who has been involved in this challenging, interesting, and important project. It is good to realize that so many are still concerned about global issues of injustice, inequality, and human rights, and willing to engage in creative and critical ways to advocate for more just, equal, social, and humane objectives.

We also wish to acknowledge and thank Julia E. Kirsch, Vice President/Publisher, Brian Hill, Associate Editor, and Eric Kuntzman, Assistant Editor, at Lexington Books, a division of the Rowman & Littlefield Publishing Group, for their support and assistance.

Introduction

Is In/Equality Thinkable?

By Toks Oyedemi and Jan Servaes

Social inequality is a global phenomenon. It is a basic component of human societies. The unequal distribution of economic, social, and cultural capitals has an impact on every sector of human life.

While the nature and pattern of inequality in societies are shaped by particular historical contexts, social structures, economic and cultural configurations, the various forms of inequalities—economic, political, cultural, technological, and social—manifest themselves in race, gender, ethnicity, religion, and, in general, the social stratification they create in society. Issues of poverty, gender inequality, class struggle, racial discrimination, economic imbalances, and other social fractures continue to shape the social analysis of participation, exclusion, and inclusion in society.

Contestations between neoliberalism, rights and participation influence arguments about unemployment, poverty, and social inclusion. This has lately been exemplified by social uprisings and protest movements in Africa, America, Asia, Europe, and the Arab world, with actors agitating for equitable representation and participation to better their well-being and prospects in life. Analyses of inequalities in society often reveal social conflicts based on class, gender, religious, geographical, economic, racial, and ethnic fractures. However, as David Grusky and Manwai Ku (2008) observe, the rising interest in inequality is not merely fueled by moral obligation and the realization that social inclusion is a fundamental social good, but increasingly by the awareness of its consequences and threat to the world community.

Alongside this realization, media and communication events, technologies and industries are increasingly shaping global and local cultures. The digital technology revolution has spurred many developments in communication and culture. The commercial availability of the Internet, the explosion of digital satellite television content platforms, innovations in mobile communication technologies, and the increasing proliferation of media and communication contents across many platforms have shaped a global society where engagements with media and communication have become an essential aspect of life (Hamelink 2015; Mansell and Raboy 2014). This then raises many critical questions: What are the implications of social inequalities on media and communication? How does class analysis provide understanding of media contents and media ownership? Who gets to use these technologies, and who is excluded? How do issues of racial representation and discrimination shape identity, culture, and participation in the media? How does gender analysis reveal representation, marginalization, and inclusion of people in media realities? Who owns and controls these technologies and how does the control shape economic and social participation of those outside the ownership class? In what ways do capitalism and neoliberal ideologies determine patterns of exclusion and inclusion in the media? How are media and communication tools effective in addressing social concerns around development and social change? And, moreover, another puzzling question is "how the proponents of the inclusion thesis expect that—if information is a key resource and if access to such a resource has historically always been skewed—it could be any different today" (Hamelink 2015: 149).

IS EQUALITY POSSIBLE?

What mostly concerns scholars is how social inequality shapes distorted experiences of existence and well-being across the world. Acknowledging the existence of social inequality seldom raises the critical question: Is equality possible? This question, undoubtedly, takes us to the domain of philosophical and sociological discourses that present contesting theorizations of inequality and equality.

In his critical review of John Rawls' *A Theory of Justice*, Robert Nisbet (1974) warns of philosophes who in "pursuit of equality" tend toward a radical critique of the social order with a vision for social utopia. Nisbet argues that what is desired is not so much equality of any kind as individual or collective freedom to pursue goals to the limit of capacity and desire. However, in a capitalist society "freedom" is often equated with the freedom to participate in the capitalist marketplace, and the history of human societies shows that the ability to participate is often determined by factors like education, levels of income, race, gender, geography, class, social and political power. The result is that some in society are "better placed" to participate in various social and economic activities for their well-being, than others. This is the core critique of social inequality.

Discourses of social inequalities aim to reveal how social fractures in society manifest in unequal life experiences. The goal of these discourses is not the social utopia of an absolute equality in society. Equality means different things depending on social, political, and economic interpretations. Within these interpretations are contesting arguments about the (im)possibility of equality in society. The ontological ideology of equality is that all people are naturally equal. This is noted in the axiom that "all men are equal before God," and are created equal with natural rights. This ideology has been embraced in constitutional declarations of statehood. Take, for instance, the assertion in the US *Declaration of Independence* (1776), "that all men are created equal, that they are endowed by their creator with certain unalienable rights, that among these are life, liberty and the pursuit of happiness." But often this equality is mitigated by social and economic contexts. Human beings are not equally endowed naturally, and the social condition of a person's birth may shape that person's social and economic experiences for the rest of her or his life.

James Bryce in his 1898 essay, *Equality,* identified four kinds of equality: civil, political, social, and economic equalities (see also Flew 1982). *Civil equality* indicates equality before the law, equal legal rights to freedom of speech, to personal safety, to the holding and disposal of property and other civil rights issues. But as admirable as civil equality is, history of human societies show that certain groups, due to class, power, race, gender, wealth, and income, experience unequal dispensation of civil rights. *Political equality* describes equal rights of citizens to participate in the democratic process through electoral procedures of voting for persons and being voted for. But in many nations of the world attaining equality through political rights has been hampered by so many levels of social inequalities. Much of the history of South Africa or the United States shows that political equality was not a desired goal, and violence has been used against people with the purpose of maintaining political inequality. In these nations race and gender were used to deprive many people, in the case of South Africa, most of its people, equal political rights.

Social equality portends that all people have equal social status with implications on social rights, such as civil and political rights. It describes the absence of social hierarchy and social ranks and that all should treat the other as equal. This equality operates in the realm of social intercourse, however the unequal possession of natural traits, unequal levels of education and intellect, and the unequal distribution of economic and political power have implications for social relations. As James Bryce (1898) acknowledges, differences of intellect and education produce differences of tastes and association, and differences in wealth allocation produce differences in social habit that affect social relations. Pierre Bourdieu (1979) critically engages this in *Distinction* by exploring how the tastes for certain cultural products or artifacts—music, arts and food—relate to social and cultural capital or class. For Bourdieu individual taste, lifestyles, and habits are culturally and socially linked to social groups or class to produce a "*habitus*," a shorthand expression for much of the socialization that individuals of particular groups undergo. Class, caste, ethnicity, gender, income, and property ownership often define location in a social structure with a resultant implication on inequality.

How can one realistically talk of *economic equality*? Is the equal possession of property or wealth attainable, that one is not richer or poorer than his/her neighbor? The condition of birth, education, intellect, natural endowment, social class, and so forth provide resources that equip some to accumulate wealth and property more than others. The equalization of economic resources is not the goal; the objection is the extreme forms of economic inequality. Only few people in society have been able to use their social class and social network to create immense wealth. Consequently, this accumulation of wealth and property increasingly resides in the "invisible hands" of the "happy few" who control the social and economic configurations of society. In the current capitalist dispensation the ownership structure of industries is in few hands, income inequality in many nations is increasing, and tax policy tends to favor the extremely wealthy. Figures and data to illustrate this are there for the taking. One good source to start from would be the annual Human Development Reports, published by the United Nations Development Program (UNDP). In his critique of economic inequality in the United States, Joseph Stiglitz (2011; 2012) notes that 1 percent of the people take nearly a quarter of the nation's income, which allows them to control the financial and legislative system of the nation. He argues that inequality is *self-perpetuating*, that it is produced by the vast amount of political power the wealthy hold to control legislative and regulatory activity. Corporate wealth has never been greater than it is today, and this is an issue of rising concern. Corporate CEOs have never earned more than they earn now. And the disparity between CEO income and the rest of the corporation's employees has never been larger. All this has been detailed in French economist Thomas Piketty's (2014) best-selling book, *Capitalism in the Twenty-First Century*. Piketty says the rich few are getting far richer while most of the rest of us are getting poorer.

Sadly, to confirm this, former Treasury Secretaries Robert Rubin, Henry Paulson, and Timothy Geithner were asked about the issue of income inequality during a conference in Beverly Hills. They basically laughed over it (Carter and Walsh 2015). While in office, all three men advocated Wall Street–friendly policies that helped bolster pay for top bankers and the wealthy. Overall worker wages have been stagnant for decades and falling for most American workers since 2007 (Gould 2015).

Nothing new here, as this fact was already forewarned over a century ago: "The holders of vast fortunes acquire undue power, they have undue influence with rulers, they may corrupt legislators, they may pervert the power of a state to serve their selfish ends" (Bryce 1898: 467). Drawing from the work of James Bryce in this current analysis of social inequality and equality is very poignant for two reasons. First, Bryce, considered a liberal scholar, politician, and diplomat possessed critical skills as both an intellectual and a political figure, thereby straddling both the theoretical and the practical legislative applications of the concept of equality. Second and more interestingly, he wrote his critical and idealistic essay on equality in 1898, but a large part of the oeuvre of his scholarship on race reveals a completely different thinker. He did not believe in equality of races. His opinions on (in)equality of races is noted in some of his works, such as his 1902 lecture delivered at Oxford on *The Relations of the Advanced and Backward Races of Mankind*, the 1897 *Impressions on South Africa,* and his 1888 *The American Commonwealth.* As a result, his thinking and opinion contributed to the ideological narrative and policy approach of imperial Britain during his time. In defending the inequality of races, he noted in *The Relations of the Advanced and Backward Races of Mankind*:

> Now for the future of mankind nothing is more vital than some races should be maintained at the highest level of efficiency, because the work they can do for thought and art and letters, for scientific discovery, and for raising the standard of conduct, will determine the general progress of humanity. If therefore we were to suppose the blood of the races which are now most advanced to be diluted, so to speak, by that of those most backward, not only would more be lost to the former than would be gained to the latter, but there would be a loss, possibly an irreparable loss, to the world at large. (p 36)

It is precisely because of such historical narrative of race, and sexist ideologies of gender that scholarship of social inequalities is very critical. Studying social inequalities in society reveals how issues, such as race, gender, and ethnicity intersect with economic resources and political capital to keep some groups in society at a disadvantaged position.

The capitalist economic system perpetuates this inequality, and often when this system tyrannizes a class of people, and they object and react, their objections are not often seen as reactions to the exploitative nature of capitalism and its attendant inequality, but rather as attitudes typical of indolent and unproductive classes. For instance Bryce stated about Black South Africans, "The male Kafir is a lazy fellow who likes talking and sleeping better than continuous physical exertion, and the difficulty of inducing him to work is the chief difficulty which European mine-owners in South Africa complain of" (Bryce 1899: 89).

A similar history can be drawn from the discussion on *culture and communication rights*. The concepts "freedom of information," "free flow of information," "freedom of opinion," "freedom of expression," and "freedom of the press" have always been at the base of the Western way of thinking. They, among other things, were explicitly referred to in the American Constitution of 1776 and during the French Revolution. Article 12 of the American *(Virginia) Bill of Rights* (1776) states that "the freedom of the press is one of the great bulwarks of liberty and can never be restrained but by despotic government." In the French *Les Droits de l'Homme et du Citoyen* of 1789 it is stated that "the free expression of ideas and opinions is one of the most precious human rights; every citizen should be able to speak, write, and print freely; this freedom can only be restricted in those cases determined by law" (our translation). Though the freedom of word and expression have always been subject to fundamental restrictions, they nevertheless are part of the European and American ways of thinking, which led to freedom of printing and a free press. These rights, the *civil or freedom rights*, can be said to be the *first generation of human rights*. A second generation of human rights was inspired by socialist revolutions at the turn of the century, and emphasized *the economic and sociocultural rights of people*. The right to work, education, shelter, and the right to participate in cultural life, belong to this *second generation* of human rights. The first and second generations of human rights were reformulated as binding international law in two conventions that were adopted in 1966 and came into effect in 1976: the International Covenant on Economic, Social, and Cultural Rights, and the International Covenant on Civil and Political Rights. The *third generation* of human rights—the *solidarity or collective rights*—emerged through anti-colonialist revolutions emphasizing national self-determination and nondiscrimination. Solidarity rights pertain primarily to certain collective concerns, such as peace, development, ecological balance, culture, and communication. The Report of the World Commission on Culture and Development, chaired by Javier Pérez de Cuéllar (1995), started from this third generation of human rights. It argued that development divorced from its human or cultural context is growth without a soul. This means that culture cannot ultimately be reduced to a position as a mere subsidiary of economic growth. The report went on to argue that "governments cannot determine a people's culture: indeed, they are partly determined by it" (De Cuéllar 1995:15). The basic principle should be "the fostering of respect for all cultures whose values are tolerant of others. Respect goes beyond tolerance and implies a positive attitude to other people and a rejoicing in their culture. Social peace is necessary for human development: in turn it requires that differences between cultures be regarded not as something alien and unacceptable or hateful, but as experiments in ways of living together that contain valuable lessons and information for all" (De Cuéllar 1995: 25) (for more details, see Servaes 2004).

ANOTHER TYPE OF EQUALITY?

Further to the current discourse on equality, arguments have been made for another type of equality—equality of opportunity, which in capitalist dispensation implies fair and open competition for resources. It indicates that everyone has the opportunity to accumulate property, wealth, and social status, and that life-chances opportunities and location in social structure are determined on equal competitive terms for all members of society. The study of social inequalities reveals that giving fair and equal chance to all does not guarantee that everyone will succeed as every other, or produce equal outcomes. Social stratification and social-economic dynamics in society still shape opportunities. The ideologies of equal opportunity and justice (justice as fairness as in John Rawls' articulation in *A Theory of Justice*) are often adopted as principles guiding social policies in addressing inequalities (Sachs 2012).

Therefore, Amartya Sen (1992) argues that, since humans are different in the environment they live, in physical characteristics, in communities they belong to, and in opportunities available to them, income inequality fails to reveal how these human diversities affect inequalities. For instance a disabled person *functions* differently in society than an able-bodied person will, even if they receive the same income. Sen defines functioning as what an individual may value doing or being, whether it is relevant to "*well-being*" in a society. Functioning may range from achieving basic health wellness, participating in a community, attaining educational qualifications or whatever an individual values or hopes to achieve. *Capability* refers to the ability to achieve functioning (well-being). It includes the set of opportunities available to an individual to achieve functioning, it is the freedom and rights of an individual to achieve well-being. Expanded to social inequalities, the capabilities approach addresses the issues of social justice, basic rights as a set of fundamental entitlements for all citizens, and opportunities available for citizens to function in society. The absence of all these exacerbate social inequalities.

THE NATURE OF SOCIAL INEQUALITIES

There are variations of inequalities in society. *Economic inequalities* reveal the imbalances in income and wealth within and between nations. Studying wage allocations among workers, individual and household earnings, and disposable income allow scholars to measure the pattern of income inequality among population in a nation. Current critique of income inequality draws on the analysis that few people control a big chunk of income and wealth of a nation. In the United States, for instance, the richest 1 percent of the population own more wealth than the bottom 90 percent. In 2010, 93 percent of the additional income created in the United States went to the top 1 percent (Kristof 2014).

In the classical critique of capitalism, Karl Marx and Friedrich Engels (1948: 25) observed that "private property is already done away with for nine-tenths of the population; its existence for the few is solely due to its non-existence in the hands of those nine-tenths." Studying income inequalities provides a critical approach to examine wealth and property accumulation and centralization, tax and labor market policies, and the workings of the financial industry. *Gini-coefficient* measurement is commonly used to study income inequalities among individuals and groups in society. Gini-coefficient uses a numerical metric between 0 and 1, with 0 reflecting a situation of economic equality where everyone has same income and 1 as complete inequality where one person has all the income and the rest have none (IndexMundi 2015; World Bank 2015). The concern about economic inequalities is the social and cultural effect and impact that they have on society. Rising crime, unemployment, fractures in social relations, and lack of access to many social and cultural resources have been directly linked to economic inequality. Most of the countries with the highest indexes, and thus the most inequality, were in Africa and Latin America. Eastern and Northern Europe were highly represented in the most equal countries at the other end of the spectrum. The United States and China fell in the middle of the list (Kiersz 2014).

There is also *political inequality*, which relates to the allocation of power in society. Political inequality reveals why and how certain groups in society influence political decision making in society. Despite claims of equal democratic processes for all people, certain individuals and groups have greater influence on the makings of the democratic process and the decision-making procedure that eventually shape a favorable bias of legislative or policy decision toward them. The discussions about civil equality and civil rights show that ability to participate in political process is still unequal in many societies. Take for instance the current debates regarding voting rights in the United States, fifty years after the voting rights legislation, rights groups are still challenging aspects of the voting process that is discriminatory.

Social inequalities studies broadly provide a contextual and demographical analysis to inequalities; they reveal how economic and political inequalities are experienced by people based on human attributes. Social inequalities are inequalities based on race, ethnicity, gender, education, geography, and so forth, with regard to how they give rise to social status, class, prestige, and conditions of well-being. Scholarly studies abound on how racial inequality shapes economic, social, and cultural experiences of minority populations and people of color. Manza (2009) notes different racial and ethnic groups are found in most contemporary societies, whether and how racial difference matters for the pattern of inequality depends on public policies regulating economic and political life. Social inequalities, he argues, are historically contingent. Drawing examples from the United States, he notes that African-Americans and Latinos experience discrimination in the labor market, a racially segregated housing market, police harassment with higher rates of incarceration in the criminal justice system. The historical nature of social inequalities and the implication on current life chances in the United States form the critical essay by Ta-Nehisi Coates (2014) in *The Case for Reparations*. He notes "two hundred fifty years of slavery. Ninety years of Jim Crow. Sixty years of separate but equal. Thirty-five years of racist housing policy. Until we reckon with our compounding moral debts, America will never be whole." Critical studies of social inequalities allow for the examinations of variations, such as gender inequalities, educational inequalities, rural-urban inequalities, digital inequalities, and so forth.

The various forms of inequalities are *not* self-contained. There is a relationship among the different forms, as inequality in one area may affect and exacerbate inequalities in other areas. Economic inequality may affect access to cultural goods, such as digital technologies, ability to access health care services, and ability for quality education. This intersection is the essence of scholarship on inequalities and the policy approach to addressing them. Analysis of social inequalities moves us away from an economic deterministic approach to inequalities, it connects issues of social relations, class, race, taste, culture, way of life, sexuality, sexual identities, incarceration, ethnicity, legal and justice system, cultural representation and re-presentation, poverty, and so forth to broader patterns of social stratification and socioeconomic dynamics in society (for more details, see Hirst 2001; Marger 2013; Melamed and North 2010; and Sernau 2014).

SOCIAL INEQUALITIES, MEDIA, AND COMMUNICATION

Alongside the imbalances and inequalities identified earlier, media and communication events, technologies and industries are increasingly shaping global and local cultures. The digital technology revolution has spurred many developments in communication and culture. The commercial availability of the Internet, the explosion of digital satellite television content platforms, the innovations in mobile communication technologies, and the increasing proliferation of media and communication content across many platforms have shaped a global society where engagements with media and communication have become an essential aspect of life (Robbins 2005; Wyatt et al. 2000).

The analysis of social inequalities from a media and communication perspective takes us into the cultural and transcultural realm (Appadurai 2013; Hepp 2015). Culture in a capitalist society is not merely *culture* but also *products*. Cultural practices as industry has led to a global network of media and communication conglomerates with tentacles spread globally. Cultural practices have become products that are created, packaged, and marketed. The intersection of culture and economics subsequently leads to issues of *communication power* (Castells 2013)—to control the cultural industry and to shape culture. As a result culture is packaged for its market values, in this process cultures are represented and re-presented in ways that suit market dictates.

The discussion about the digital divide cannot be avoided either. In assuming that bridging the divide would be the end of inequality, conventional digital divide accounts often "close their eyes to sociologically rooted individual and systemic indicators that should be considered when defining divides" (Tsatsou 2011). However, development organizations and industries seem to be slowly moving away from these discourses. For instance, the United Nations Development Programme's (UNDP 2012) report "Mobile technologies and empowerment: enhancing human development through participation and innovation" relinquishes the digital divide problematic. Partly, this has to do with their claim that technology diffusion, speared by the mobile phone, has reached the world's poorest populations, supposedly creating more cross-country convergences than divides in what the report (UNDP 2012) describes as "a new wave of democratization of access to innovative information and communication channels, propelled by state-of-the-art technologies and diminishing barriers to entry" (p. 8). But more strikingly, the report critiques the technological determinist assumption that "access equals participation" and social change. It states that "In the 1990s, closing that divide became the main target of most development initiatives, essentially focusing on access to ICTs and overlooking other critical and underlying development goals" (UNDP 2012: 12). Waiving decontextualized approaches that consider technology merely a "thing," the report claims that "alone, mobile phones will neither pull people out of poverty, nor propel democratic governance. They must be part and parcel of broader development agendas" (UNDP 2012).

Questions then arise about: Who control the cultural industry and who is excluded? How does this ownership structure shape participation in the media, how do issues of race, class, sexuality, and gender shape inequality patterns in the media and communication landscape? Who can access media and communication platforms? How can communication platforms be used in addressing issues of inequalities that characterize development and social change agendas? How can the production and regulation of transcultural communication be assessed "in terms of transmedial interdependencies of communication across cultures" (Hepp 2015: 230)?

These are some of the questions that this book seeks to address through the contributions of scholars from many regions of the world.

The first volume of this book, which you are currently reading: *Volume 1: Theory*, engages the various historical and theoretical approaches to social inequalities and their relevance for a contemporary analysis of media and communication. This volume explores scholarly analysis of theories and the conceptual framings of social inequalities in relation to media and communication. It examines class analysis and postcolonial theories in relation to media and communication realities. It also provides analysis of social inequalities with regards to technologies.

The second volume of the book, available as *Volume 2: Praxis*, connects specific thematic and theoretical issues to practical case-based assessments of social inequalities and communication.

THEORETICAL STUDY OF SOCIAL INEQUALITIES AND COMMUNICATION

This volume starts with a theoretical analysis of social inequalities. Drawing from works of Karl Marx and Friedrich Engels, Anthony Giddens, Pierre Bourdieu, Amartya Sen, and many others, Toks Oyedemi presents and discusses the structuralist, culturalist, and postmodernist approaches to inequalities. This theoretical discourse is then related to the framing of inequalities in access to communication technologies, specifically how these theoretical approaches influence the framing of digital inequalities, and the policy narratives developed to address technology gaps. Massimo Ragnedda and Glenn Muschert introduce Max Weber's theory of stratification to clarify how social stratification in the digital age is reproduced online. This allows for the examination of digital inequalities as extension of traditional forms of inequality, and to explore if new forms of inequalities are emerging. This chapter argues that notions of digital divides should be approached not only from the economic structure's point of view (within the state and between states) typical of a Marxist analysis, but also the broader axes of stratification such as the social conditions of stratified relations, to understand the influence of class, status, and power in creating the digital gap identified as the basis of digital inequalities. Focusing also on the other two forms of stratification, namely "status" and "party," Ragnedda and Muschert clarify the importance of status in a postmodern (network) society in relation to new social and digital inequalities;

the influence of social class and political affiliation upon digital divides; and, finally, the importance of prestige in digital participation or exclusion.

As the neoliberal model of development becomes hegemonic and global inequalities increase, disagreements between North and South regarding environmental issues also become deeper and the possibility for resolving these is subverted by the close connection between environmental decisions and economic development, corporate interests and a categorical commitment to a free market economy. Nevertheless, Eunice Castro Seixas argues, this hegemonic framing of environmental and "sustainability" issues does not represent the entire picture since it silences alternative voices and perspectives. Postcolonial approach allows the study of North-South (mis)communication about development and social change. Postcolonial and decolonial approaches invite us to ask the questions of "Who has the right to speak about development and how?" "Whose voices are being suppressed?" and most important: "How can we give visibility to 'subaltern'/alternative voices?" and "How can we construct alternative ways of thinking about development and of promoting environmental justice?"

In this section of the book, *Ruth Sanz Sabido* also proposes the use of Postcolonial Critical Discourse Analysis (PCDA). She argues that media representations should be analyzed by taking postcolonial power relations into account. The combination of postcolonial theory and critical discourse analysis stems from the observation that both have certain aims in common. Although they are completely independent from each other, both theories are concerned with the concept of "power" and, in their own particular ways; both seek to expose oppression and power inequalities. One of Sabido's main findings, based on a detailed PCDA of the representations of Palestine in the British press since 1948, is that media representations have evolved over time, depending on the dominant political discourse in each sampled period. The diachronic evolution of these representations demonstrates that meanings and ideological positions are not fixed. This finding is also supported by parallel insights regarding the use of news sources, the historical contextualization of the conflict in the news coverage, as well as data about visible and invisible entities in the conflict. The postcolonial approach to this conflict restores the largely neglected historical connection of the British Mandate to its proper place in understanding the significance of these representations.

CLASS ANALYSIS OF MEDIA AND CULTURE

Understanding social inequalities through class analysis provides a critical framework to examine the experiences of members of social groups in relation to socioeconomic and cultural issues. Class analysis often intersects with race and gender to unveil deeper social fractures. This is illustrated in this section of the book by Debra Clarke through a Canadian case study. Clarke examines the significance of class and gender inequalities within political communication generally and, in particular, with respect to television journalism, which continues to be a primary vehicle of political communication. A central concern is to trace how social inequalities are manifested in the dynamics of news production and news reception, and in such a way that television journalism, and political communication more generally, effectively contribute to the political exclusion of major social groups such as women and the working class.

The association of class-group contestation, citizenship, identity, media, and the state is critically examined by *Nova Gordon-Bell*. She explores the nature of class-group contestations in Jamaica since independence, the rise of a predominantly black Anglophone elite oligarchy and the relegation of the predominantly Creole-speaking Afro-Jamaican to the periphery.

Redefining culture as "hegemonic ideology" and class as groups acting to preserve, destroy or transform society, Gordon-Bell explains how Jamaican media have reinforced the dominant tropes and rituals of Jamaican identity and citizenship while profiting from group resistance on the periphery. In the face of increasing competition, Jamaican media struggle to maintain critical ideological nonnegotiables on behalf of elite classes while maintaining their relevance to others. Having become a platform for ideologies from the periphery that are commercially viable, but also the antithesis of Anglophone elite constructs of "the Jamaican," local media must still represent and signify this other "Jamaica" as undesirable and aberrant. The media rely heavily on the state, therefore, to shield it from counter-hegemonic pressures for a more democratic representation of Jamaica. This chapter argues that it is through its control of the state that the elite oligarchy acts as final ideological (cultural) arbiter in class-group contestations. Paradoxically, therefore, social inequality and elite oligarchy in the island is facilitated by the island's political systems which maintain a "form" of democracy that has yet to dismantle the frameworks of society and power inherited from the British colonial experience.

With the media becoming a platform for ideologies from the periphery that are commercially viable but also the antithesis of Anglophone elite constructs of "the Jamaican," local media must still represent and signify this other "Jamaica" as undesirable and aberrant, while relying heavily on the state, therefore, to shield it from counter-hegemonic pressures for a more democratic representation of Jamaica.

Examining the media from the lens of class analysis also allows for a study of the representation of groups in society. The third chapter in this section, written by Fulya Sen and Furkan Sen, examines the media representation of class issues in Turkey based on the media coverage of work-related rights. It demonstrates that the mainstream media under the control of the government are far from understanding and practicing the true concept of public responsibility with the inability to deal with issues of inequality based on the societal class structures found in Turkey. Using three cases of social disputes, Sen and Sen show the invisibility of class identity in mainstream news media, and the absence of coverage of structural problems or social welfare rights in the news texts of both alternative and mainstream media.

TECHNOLOGICAL DETERMINISM AND SOCIAL CHANGE

The concepts of digital divide and digital inequalities have brought to global attention the pattern of inequalities regarding access to and use of digital technology tools. But the history of technology is equally a history of inequalities. Access to technological innovations has been shaped by social inequalities in their diffusion. Concomitantly, the historical trajectories of social inequalities in human societies tend to shape access to many resources and utilities, including technology. In this section of the book—that could also be considered as an addition to another book in this series, that is, Servaes 2014—an examination of the forms of capitalism and their impact on social inequalities and the resultant effect on skewed penetration of technology is presented.

To understand technology and inequalities a critical examination of theoretical narratives is important, considering that these narratives tend to shape policy approaches in addressing technology inequalities. As a result, the various theoretical narratives that describe a technological deterministic approach carry with them neoliberal capitalist tendencies. Theories and concepts gathered under the title of "information society," such as "global village," "post-industrial society," "service economy," "network society," and "information age," provided a discursive basis for the restructuring of capitalism in the 1970s and afterward. These narratives moved beyond the realm of theory and shaped social reality with influence in policy processes of many nations. Consequently, this has a crucial role in the articulation of these countries to neoliberalism with a mystified technology and social change perceptions that conceal social inequalities. *Banu Durdağ* eloquently dissects this narrative in the case of Turkey's technological and social policies. She clearly explains how this narrative, which played a role in the articulation processes of developing countries to the neoliberal policies, still underpins the creation of mystified technology and social reality perceptions that obscure social inequalities, from unequal distribution of resources, poverty and unemployment to identity and gender discrimination, especially in Turkey's projections of technology and social progress.

Next, Ilse Marien, Rob Heyman, Koen Salemink and Leo Van Audenhove move the analysis of technology and social inequalities beyond the socio-demographic characteristics in relation to patterns of technology access, adoption, usage, and skills to the premise of the voluntary engagement with ICTs. They examine the concept of *digital by default* where services are digitized at an ever-faster pace in many sectors, such as in finance, employment, and educational opportunities, and where digital products and applications are succeeding in rapid cycles. The problem is that public and private institutions are implementing the majority of these digitization processes without an in-depth consideration for those who are being victimized and set aside. This implies that the crucial question of research on digital inequalities is not who chooses to engage with ICTs and who does not, as if it were predetermined by choice, but instead at which levels the digitization of society in all its forms is reinforcing or creating mechanisms of social exclusion.

From a South African perspective, Toks Oyedemi explores how racial capitalism shaped colonial and apartheid patterns of inequalities, and how the current democratic capitalism of post-apartheid South Africa is shaping a new form of inequalities. The argument is made that this trajectory of inequalities manifests in the distorted access to many social and economic resources, including communication technologies.

THEORY VERSUS/AND PRAXIS

Lastly, the concept of power becomes very critical again in explaining the relationship between theory and praxis. In the eleventh chapter of this first volume, Kala Ortwein, Sarah Rowe and Olga Shapovalova draw a distinction between academic institutions and the realm of bottom-up grassroots activism situated outside of academia. They ask whether action can be implemented without a theoretical understanding of complex issues, or not? And, if action can be conducted without theory, to what extent is theory relevant? Although they question the accessibility and applicability of some theoretical practices, they acknowledge the potential for theory to be an underlining principle in many nonacademic and academic pursuits. The Indian anthropologist Arjun Appadurai (2013) summarizes this dilemma in a succinct way:

> Research is normally seen as a high-end, technical activity, available by training and class background to specialists in education, the sciences, and related professional fields. It is rarely seen as a capacity with democratic potential, much less as belonging to the family of basic rights. All human beings are, in a sense, researchers, since all human beings make decisions that require them to make systematic forays beyond their current knowledge horizons.

> This is especially the case in a world of rapid change, where markets, media, and migration have destabilized secure knowledge niches and have rapidly made it less possible for ordinary citizens to rely on knowledge drawn from traditional, customary, or local sources. Further, as the institutions and values of democracy sweep the world, knowledge (both abstract and empirical) is the coin of the realm, and the capacity to distinguish knowledge from rumor, fact from fiction, propaganda from news, and anecdote from trend, is vital for the exercise of informed citizenship" (Arjun Appadurai 2013: 269).

Bringing together hermeneutics, phenomenology, psychoanalytics, and Marxism—with excursions to Butler, Gadamer, Marx, Merleau-Ponty, Kristeva, and Jung—Kala Ortwein, Sarah Rowe, and Olga Shapovalova explore the ways in which praxis leads theory, and the ways theory leads praxis. Using the example of "vulnerability", an argument is made about the frames that scholars and activists frequently use to describe vulnerable bodies. This then allows for the examination of how various types of vulnerability can be understood, explained, and reformed in academic and nonacademic spheres.

In other words, Ortwein, Rowe, and Shapovalova attempt to explicate these murky and cyclical approaches, ultimately leading to conclude that praxis and theory both lead, aid, and work together in fascinating ways. It is only through a complementary interaction of both praxis and theory that social change can occur. Or, as Julian Agyeman (2013: 168) aptly summarizes the "chicken and egg" problem of building both a movement and a vision: "Without a vision, movement-building is fragmented and slow. Without a movement, visions are narrow and competing, rather than shared."

VOLUME II: PRAXIS

We sincerely hope that this first volume provides enough food for thought and appetite for the second one, which is more focused on case studies and applications. The Table of Contents reads as follows:

Poverty and the Media

Chapter 1: Dialogic Journalism: Bringing marginalized communities into the implied audience.

Chapter 2: All people are equal, but some people are more equal than others: How and why inequality became invisible in the British press.

Chapter 3: Britain's Hidden Hungry?—The portrayal of food bank users in the UK national press.

Chapter 4: The Invisible Hand Begs for "Sadaka": Does the Media Legitimize Poverty via Islamic Alms in Turkey?

Technology and Inequalities

Chapter 5: Social Inequalities in Digital Skills The European framework and the Italian case.

Chapter 6: Breaching the Divide: "Hole in the Wall" Computer Kiosks for Education and Development in Urban Bangladesh.

Women, Empowerment, and the Media

Chapter 7: Hill Women's Voices and Community Communications about Climate Change: The Case of Henvalvani Community Radio in India.

Chapter 8: Citizen Media and Empowerment. An analysis of three experiences of media re-appropriation carried out by women in the popular insurrection of Oaxaca, Mexico (2006).

Representations of Race, Sexuality, and Gender in the Media

Chapter 9: Harassed, marginalized, and childless: Gender inequality in the Australian news media—A feminist analysis.

Chapter 10: Cross-National Coverage of Rape and Rape Culture: A Community Structure Approach.

Chapter 11: Multiculturalism as a Disempowering Paradigm: The Canadian Case.

REFERENCES

Agyeman, J. (2013). *Introducing Just Sustainabilities. Policy, Planning and Practice.* London: ZED Books.

Appadurai, A. (2013). *The future as Cultural Fact. Essays on the Global Condition.* London: Verso.

Bourdieu, P. (1979). *Distinction.* Cambridge, MA: Harvard University Press.

Bryce, J. (1898). Equality. *The Century,* Vol 56 (3) pp. 459–469.

Bryce, J. (1899). *Impressions of South Africa.* London: Macmillan.

Bryce, J. (1902) *The relations of the advanced and the backward races of mankind.* Oxford: Clarendon Press.

Carter, Z. and B. Walsh (2015). "Three Rich Treasury Secretaries Laugh It Up Over Income Inequality." *Huffington Post*, Retrieved on September 4, 2015, from http://www.huffingtonpost.com/entry/geithner-rubin-paulson-income-inequality_55e9eabde4b093be51bb73c3.

Castells, M. (2013). *Communication Power*. Oxford: Oxford University Press.

Coates, T. (2014) The case for reparations. *The Atlantic.* Retrieved on August 17, 2015, from http://www.theatlantic.com/features/archive/2014/05/the-case-for-reparations/361631/.

De Cuéllar, Javier Perez (ed.) (1995). *Our Creative Diversity*. Report of the World Commission on Culture and Development. Paris: UNESCO.

Flew, A. (1982). Four Kinds of Equality. *Reason Papers* No. 8 pp. 17–35.

Gould, Elise (2015). "2014 Continues a 35-Year Trend of Broad-Based Wage Stagnation." *Economic Policy Institute*, February 19, 2015. http://www.epi.org/publication/stagnant-wages-in-2014/.

Grusky, David B., and Manwai C. Ku. (2008). "Gloom, Doom, and Inequality" in *Social Stratification: Class, Race, and Gender in Sociological Perspective*, 3rd edition, edited by David B. Grusky, Manwai C. Ku, and Szonja Szelényi. Boulder CO: Westview Press pp. 2–28.

Hamelink, C. (2015). *Global Communication.* Los Angeles CA: Sage.

Hepp, A. (2015). *Transcultural communication.* Chicester: Wiley Blackwell.

Hirst, Charles (2001). *Social Inequality: Forms, Causes, and Consequences*. New York: Allyn and Bacon/Pearson Education.

IndexMundi (2015). *GINI Index—Country Ranking.* http://www.indexmundi.com/facts/indicators/SI.POV.GINI/rankings.

Kiersz, Andy (2014). Here Are The Most Unequal Countries In The World. *Business Insider.* http://www.businessinsider.com/gini-index-income-inequality-world-map-2014-11#ixzz3kvcUZTIO.

Kristof, N. (2014). *An Idiot's Guide to Inequality.* Retrieved August 17, 2015, from http://www.nytimes.com/2014/07/24/opinion/nicholas-kristof-idiots-guide-to-inequality-piketty-capital.html?_r=0.

Les Droits de l'Homme et du Citoyen (1789) https://fr.wikipedia.org/wiki/D%C3%A9claration_des_droits_de_l%27homme_et_du_citoyen_de_1789.

Mansell, R. and Raboy, M. (eds.) (2014). *The handbook of global media and communication policy*. Chicester: Wiley Blackwell.

Manza, J. (2009). Inequality and society: An introduction. In J. Manza and M. Sauder (eds.). *Inequality and Society: Social science perspective on social stratification*. New York: W.W. Norton & Co.

Marger, Martin (2013). *Social Inequality: Patterns and Processes*. New York: McGraw-Hill.

Marx, K., & Engels, F. (1948). *The communist manifesto*. New York: International Publishers.

Melamed, David and Michael S. North (2010). "The Future in Inequality." *Social Psychology Quarterly*. 73 (December 4): 346–347.

Nisbet, R. (1974). The pursuit of equality. National *Affairs* 35, pp. 103–120.

Piketty, T. (2014). *Capital in the twenty-first century*. Cambridge, MA: Harvard University Press.

Robbins, Richard (2005). *Global Problems and the Culture of Capitalism*. New York: Pearson Allyn and Bacon.

Sachs, B. (2012). The limits of fair equality of opportunity. *Philosophical Studies* Volume 160 (2) pp. 323–343.

Sen, A. (1992). *Inequality reexamined*. Cambridge, MA: Harvard University Press.

Sernau, S. (2014). *Social Inequality in a Global Age*. Los Angeles: Sage.

Servaes, J. (2004). "Human rights, participatory communication and cultural freedom," in Lee, P. (ed.), *Many Voices, One Vision. The Right to Communicate in Practice*, Southbound-Penang, WACC-London, pp. 149–162.

Servaes, J. (ed.) (2014). *Technological Determinism and Social Change. Communication in a Tech-Mad World*. Lanham: Lexington Books.

Stiglitz, J. (2011) Of the 1%, by the 1%, for the 1%. Retrieved August 17, 2015, from http://www.vanityfair.com/news/2011/05/top-one-percent-201105.

Stiglitz, J. (2012). *The Price of Inequality: How Today's Divided Society Endangers Our Future*. New York: Norton.

Tsatsou, P. (2011). Digital divides revisited: what is new about divides and their research? *Media, Culture & Society* 33(2): 317–331.

United Nations Development Programme (UNDP) (2012). *Mobile technologies and empowerment: enhancing human development through participation and innovation.* http://www.undp.org/content/undp/en/home/librarypage/democratic-governance/access_to_informationande-governance/mobiletechnologiesprimer.html.

US *Declaration of Independence* (1776) http://www.archives.gov/exhibits/charters/declaration_transcript.html.

US *Virginia Bill of Rights* (1776) http://www.archives.gov/exhibits/charters/virginia_declaration_of_rights.html.

World Bank (2015) Gini index. http://data.worldbank.org/indicator/SI.POV.GINI

Wyatt, S., Henwood, F., Miller, N. and Senker P. (eds.) (2000). *Technology and In/Equality. Questioning the information society*. London: Routledge.

Part I

IN SEARCH OF THE THEORETICAL ROOTS FOR A STUDY OF SOCIAL INEQUALITIES AND COMMUNICATION

Chapter One

Framing Social and Digital Inequalities

A Structuralist, Culturalist, and Postmodernist Review

Toks Oyedemi

The commercial and public availability of the Internet in the early 1990s brought to contemporary prominence two dominant narratives that are historically core thrusts of discourses about technology and society. One, there is the celebratory rhetoric around the potential of the Web to liberate human thoughts, improve human sociability, provide easy access to information, encourage collaboration, and improve knowledge sharing. Two, there are concerns about what this new technology means for participation, equity and social inequalities in society (Castells 2002, Mansell 2002, Servaes, 2014, Servon 2002, van Dijk 2005, Warschauer 2003).

For about twenty years *"digital divide"* remains a global concept that describes the inequalities in access to the Internet. Coined in the US National Telecommunications and Information Administration's (NTIA) 1995 ground-breaking report entitled "Falling Through the Net: A Survey of the 'Have Nots' in Rural and Urban America," "digital divide" has become a universal term for uneven access to digital resources. For two decades studies have revealed that inequality of online access is a reflection of a larger pattern of social inequalities in society, where socioeconomic status defines access to many resources including technology (Mossberger, Tolbert, and Stansbury 2003, DiMaggio & Hargittai 2001, Van Dijk 2005, Hargittai & Shafer 2006, Hargittai 2008, Hargittai & Walejko 2008).

Engaging digital inequalities from a broader frame of social inequalities thus becomes relevant to the study of access and uses of digital communication technologies. Consequently, studying the nature and pattern of social inequalities is a relevant academic exercise in the social analysis of technology penetration. How social inequalities are defined, identified, analyzed, and framed has implications on how inequity in access to resources is framed and addressed in policy narratives. The study of social inequalities follows a trajectory of different theoretical and historical approaches. The task here is to engage a theoretical analysis of the structuralist, culturalist, and postmodernist approaches to inequalities and how they influence the framing of digital inequalities, and the policy narratives developed to address technology gaps.

STRUCTURALIST APPROACH TO SOCIAL INEQUALITIES AND DIGITAL INEQUALITIES

Structuralist Framing of Inequalities

Karl Marx's analysis of society based on class structure is seminal to the structuralist approach to inequality. This approach develops from class theory, and focuses on class classification to measure and define inequalities in society. To Marx (1948) the structure of society is based on the conflict between two major class structures: the bourgeoisie and proletariat. As he notes with Friedrich Engels, "the history of all hitherto society is the history of class struggle" (p. 9), this class antagonism defines the nature of inequality in the classic Marxian approach. The bourgeoisie is the ruling class, the possession class, and the class that owns the bulk of means of production. The proletariat is the working class, the labor class, whose livelihood is based on their labor, employment, and wage from the bourgeoisie.

The relations in society, according to Marx and Engels, are predicated on the productive forces developed through division of labor. As they note in *The German Ideology,* "the nature of individuals thus depend on the material conditions determining their production" (1974: 42). The cycle of production and development of private property define the social intercourse in society; whereas the survival of the poor and the working class is dependent on their labor—their productive capacity, the survival of the bourgeoisie is dependent on private ownership of property.

The structure of society is based on this inequality and the antagonism between the propertied class and the labor class. In their critique of private property in *The Communist Manifesto,* Marx & Engels (1948: 25) assert that "private property is already done away with for nine-tenths of the population; its existence for the few is solely due to its non-existence in the hands of those nine-tenths." Class antagonism is strengthened with the development and growth of industries that provide immense benefit for agglomeration of capital by the bourgeoisie class. But for the modern laborer on the other hand, he or she "sinks deeper and deeper below the conditions of existence of his own class. He becomes a pauper, and pauperism develops rapidly than population and wealth" (ibid: 21).

The concept of individuality is also critical in understanding Marxist class theory as it relates to social inequalities. Marx asserts in *The Grundrisse* that society is not defined as a group of individuals, but rather by the pattern of connections and relations that define the existence of these individuals:

> Society does not consist of individuals; it expresses the sum of connections and relationships in which individuals find themselves. It is as though one were to say: from the standpoint of society there are neither slaves nor citizens: both are men. Rather they are so *outside* society. To be a slave or to be a citizen are social determinations, the relationships of Man A and Man B. Man A is not a slave as such. He is a slave within society and because of it (Marx 1857).

To Marx, these connections and relationships that define the existence of individuals in society are constructed based on capitalist exchange in an economic continuum of property, labor, production, and wage. This economic continuum is encapsulated in the classifications of the bourgeoisie and proletariat, which define class theory in the Marxian approach.

Marx Weber develops the Marxian class theory from it dichotomous approach toward a pluralist model. He identifies the limitation of economic determinism in Marxian class theory and develops the theory beyond economic relations and capital production. In *Class, Status and Party*, Weber (1958) outlines three types of social structure. The first structure is the economic structure; this involves the propertied class as against the laborers in typical Marxian approach. The second is the social structure; this is related to what he terms "status honor" which operates on the assumption that a specific "style of life" can be expected from those who wish to belong to a class. It also operates on ethnic and caste segregation. Consequently, Weber extends class theory beyond economic determinism to include ethnic and caste exclusion and inclusion as basis of inequalities and class in society.

The third structure is political, which he termed "party"; the core element of party is power. The acquisition of social power may exist without class or status as in through violence. For Marx, social power is an economic/ materialist phenomenon, which is gained through the possession of material object. Weber uses this framework of class, status and party to discuss the open and close relationship in his "closure model." This model explains the process of participation (inclusion) and exclusion in society. Participation may be gained through class, status, or party. These elements can conversely be used as tools of exclusion in society.

However, Weber's extension of the Marxian class theory was not a particularly revolutionary discourse on class and inequalities. Centuries earlier, Jean-Jacques Rousseau's 1754 *Discourse on the Origin of Inequality* argues the development of property ownership led to the establishment of political institution, government, and law to protect the property of the rich, and the beginning of wars among humans. Precisely, "there arose rivalry and competition on the one hand, and conflicting interests on the other, together with a secret desire on both of profiting at the expense of others. All these evils were the first effects of property, and the inseparable attendants of growing inequality" (1973: 87). In addition to property ownership Rousseau identifies some values as elements of inequality. These include, envy, liberty, nobility, power, personal merit, public esteem, and recognition—self or public. So while recognizing the role of property ownership and riches in construction of inequality in society, Rousseau also identifies some human values as basis of inequality. He declares:

> It is to this desire of being talked about, and this unremitting rage of distinguishing ourselves, that we owe the best and the worst things we possess . . . if we have a few rich and powerful men on the pinnacle of fortune and grandeur, while the crowd grovels in want and obscurity, it is because the former prize what they enjoy only in so far as others are destitute of it; and because, without changing their condition, they would cease to be happy the moment the people ceased to be wretched (p. 101)

Weber's extension of Marxian class theory to include status and honor resonates with Rousseau's discourse. Giddens (1973) also notes that the Weberian critique and model of class theory is not sufficiently radical. In his discussion of class theory Giddens offers *structuration* of class relationship. His observation is that the blind spot in the class theory concerns the process at which economic classes become social classes. *Structuration* of class relationship explains the degree to which mobility closure exits in relation to specific market capacity (i.e., the measure of mobility in class structure).

Giddens identifies a mediate structuration of class relationship and a proximate structuration of class relationship. The mediate refers to class in relation to the degree of market capacity. This involves three basic elements: ownership of property, educational and technical qualification, and possession of manual labor. The proximate structuration of class relationship refers to the "localized" factors, which shape class structure, such as division of labor, authority relationship, and distributive grouping. The structuration of class relationships leads to the foundation of a basic three-class system: upper, middle, and lower classes. Giddens argues that where ethnic differences serve as a disqualifying market capacity as in those in the lowest-paid occupation, and chronically unemployed there is the existence of an underclass.

Parkin (1979) in his critique and analysis of the class theory takes a neo-Weberain approach by developing the closure model to "exclusionary closure model," which explains the attempt by one group to secure for itself a privilege position at the expense of some other groups through a process of subordination. Exclusionary closure model operates on two levels: property ownership (the bourgeoisie class), and credentialism—the use of academic and professional qualifications and credentials as means of monitoring entry to key positions, in society. There is also collectivist exclusion based on communal factors like religion and individualistic exclusion based on meritocracy.

The class theories that define structuralist approach to inequality can be criticized for their emphasis on class antagonism, economic determinism, emphasis on structures, and rigid divisions. Social inequalities in society are not merely feasible on drawn lines of categories or structures, but on a multidimensional approach that overlaps many identifiable categories. The structuralist approach to inequality focuses on categorization of class to measure and address inequality. Class is seen as a bundle of endowments—for example, educational level, working conditions, status, employment, and reward packages (such as income). This leads to the use of capital reward, income, to measure inequality. The form of measuring inequality in this approach focuses on income inequality between and within countries, it draws on income based on average income (GDP) per capita and purchasing power parity (PPP). It uses *Gini Coefficient* calculation to measure global inequality and household income inequality, and ratios of extremes that compare few richest countries to few poorest countries or few richest segments of population to few poorest segments of the population (Grusky & Ku 2008).

The framework in addressing inequalities in this approach is based on economic narrative and bureaucratic universalism (Grusky & Ku 2008). The economic narrative places emphasis on competitive market to address inequalities and discrimination. It draws on many neoliberal policy agendas to improve market efficiency and encourage competition in the market-place in order to "level the playing field." Bureaucratic universalism focuses on achieving equality through universalistic criteria. For example, modern personnel practices of promotion, hiring, and firing are based on credentials and meritocratic approach, and the assumption that competition opens opportunity for equality (Grusky & Ku 2008).

Structuralist Approach to Digital Inequalities

The concept of "digital divide" exemplifies the structuralist approach to ICT gaps. This concept remains one of the poignant descriptions of access gaps to technology. Digital divide became a popular concept as a result of the US government's study of telecommunication access conducted by the National Telecommunication and Information Administration (NTIA) in 1995. The report of this study highlighted the gaps in access to information and communication technologies in the United States. Following a structuralist approach, access gap to technologies is seen in terms of separation between classes, those with access and those without. It illustrates access gap as categorical and structural divides between the information rich and the information poor, between the "haves" and the "have-nots" along groupings of race, socioeconomic, geographic, and educational levels. While a category of people live in the information society, others live in the other divide.

Apart from classification of ICT access by categories, digital divide also defines technology gap as a problem of access. To bridge this divide is to provide access to people. As Servon (2002) notes, because the problem was narrowly construed as a problem of access, policies and programs are also narrowly focused on access. O' Hara and Stevens (2006) concur; they claim that since the problem of technology gaps was framed as a problem of access, the solution was to place computers strategically, and "problem solved!"

Studies conducted in this approach adopt a bivariate methodological analysis of access, usually comparing access between two categories. Examples of this approach include studies of access and gender category, rural-urban divide, developing-developed countries, race groups, and economic groupings usually structured according to income. Income levels and technology access is a popular trend in measuring the divide in technology penetration; this follows on structuralist income inequality approach to social inequality.

Policy strategies in this approach focus mainly on two agendas: providing access to the unconnected, and adopting neoliberal market strategies to the access issue. State intervention in bridging the divide focuses on providing public access. Community Technology Centers (CTCs), telecenters, and public libraries became access points for the unconnected. Personal, home-based individual access as a policy was relegated in favor of public access. Policy programs geared toward access includes E-Rate, which provides funding for equipment purchase and infrastructure, but no funding for training, Technologies Opportunities Programs (TOPs) and Community Technology Centers (CTCs). Servon (2002) cites an example of this approach to "bridge the digital divide" in the US, when the governor of the state of Maine allocated about $65 million to provide laptops to seventh-grade students, but no funding was allocated for training. Scholars have argued that this approach of providing physical contact to technology as a way of bridging the divide was a result of neoliberal market definition to social issues, which usually interprets public interest in market terms (Aufderheide 1999, Horwitz 1990, Stevenson 2009).

With a neoliberal approach to social issues, the narrative is of market efficiency. In order to encourage access, the public (consumers) must be provided with choice, and only a competitive market can provide such choice. Eventually, introducing competition in the telecommunications sector becomes the policy approach to access and public interest. This was the same ideology that drove the formulation and implementation of the US Telecommunications

Acts of 1996 with a resultant effect on the US telecom market and the global telecom landscape (Aufderheide, 1999). This ideology eventually led to the deregulation of the communications industry and the eventual mergers and acquisitions trend that followed.

Horwitz (1990) in studying the deregulation process in the American telecommunication sector identifies the irony of regulation in this process. He questions that if the need for regulation in the first place was to avoid the abuse of market power by telecom corporations, why deregulate the sector? Because with deregulation comes massive abuse of market power. Stevenson (2009) in her study of the discourse of "digital divide" argues that the rhetoric of digital divide was beneficial to the neoliberal state. The rhetoric defines the problem as physical access, which benefit a neoliberal agenda, that moves technology gap issue from the concept of universal service, that implies state intervention in encouraging household access, to universal access that favors public access, leaving individual access to the dictate of the market.

Taking a cue from a structuralist approach to inequality that identifies class classifications in studying social inequalities with an economic approach of state-capital-labor continuum, a structuralist approach to technology gaps focuses on access divide between groups and categories of population with a market approach to policy. It adopts a technology determinist and economic reductionist approach. The problem with this approach is that it limits access to physical access without paying deeper attention to the contours of digital skills and use patterns. As a result, very limited studies were conducted around issues of technology skills and uses in the early study of digital divide, and in areas such as the disabled and ICT gaps. This approach also focuses policy on a market narrative, which leads to corporations targeting services in urban and economic areas and neglecting rural areas and inner cities. Despite all these shortcomings, this approach undoubtedly provides a robust method to unveiling access gaps in certain population groups, such as the rural population and the low-income groups, which an individual-based approach to access gaps may not reveal thoroughly.

CULTURALIST APPROACH TO SOCIAL INEQUALITIES AND DIGITAL INEQUALITIES

Culturalist Framing of Inequalities

The culturalist perspective of inequality offers a cultural rationale for the class approach. It expands class theory beyond a structuralist approach that reduces class structure and fractions to economic functionalism. The approach here is that classes are not just based on structural conditions, but are also socially constructed closed groupings in which distinctive culture emerges. This culture thus influences attitude, taste, behavior, and membership in class. The works of French sociologist Pierre Bourdieu and American sociological theorist James Samuel Coleman are influential in this approach.

Bourdieu (1984, 1986) offers a critique of the classical model of class analysis noting the reductionist tendency of economism in it and develops a theory of capital beyond the economic connotation. According to Bourdieu (1986), it is impossible to account for the structure and functioning of the social world unless capital is engaged in all its forms beyond the one form recognized in economic theory. Bourdieu develops a theory of "forms of capital" to include economic, cultural, and social capitals. The theory expands Weber's closure model in "class, status and party" further to unveil the different social and cultural properties that define class fractions. In Bourdieu's analysis, capital can be:

- *Economic capital*: which retains its structuralist and economic meaning by being immediately and directly convertible into money or property rights.
- *Cultural capital*: in certain conditions this may be converted into economic capital, but it is institutionalized in the form of
  1. Embodied cultural capital, which is capital acquired through socialization, inculcation and assimilation. It is embodied in individual personality such as self-presentation, language, and linguistic capabilities.
  2. Objectified cultural capital is exemplified by material objects. These are tools such as books, paintings, machine (computers), and instruments. To own these tools, one needs economic capital, and embodied capital to utilize them.
  3. Institutionalized cultural capital: examples are educational qualifications and certificates bestowed by institutions.
- *Social capital*: this is manifested in membership in group and organization, networks of influence and relationship.

These forms of capital tend to enhance social location in class hierarchy in society, and the lack of them can contribute to social inequalities. These forms of capital lead to class-specific cultures that are defining features of inequality system. Bourdieu's social analysis of different capitals provides a synthesis of classical Marxian approach and the Weberian "status honor." Bourdieu (1984) develops an extensive analysis on the connection between cultural disposition and class; his discourses on class and culture explore how cultural competence revealed in the nature of cultural goods consumed relates to a social class. For instance, he explores how the tastes for certain cultural products or artifacts—music, arts, and even food relate to social and cultural capitals, like educational capital or a class. For Bourdieu, taste in cultural practices such as newspaper reading, art, museum visitation, food, drink, and music is social marker that separate distinct social classes or class fractions.

Coleman (1988) is one of the earliest theorists to use the term social capital and relate this to how it affects many social sectors, particularly in education. In his research on high school completion, he argues social capital (social networks) leads to formation of human capital, and it plays a critical role in high school completion. Through empirical study, he found that the lack of social capital in family and in community is a contributing factor to high school dropout.

Althusser (1971) engages the concept of ideology to extend Marxian reproduction of labor power with social and cultural perspectives. His concept of ideology discuses the reproduction of labor power, but extends it to the reproduction of submission to the ruling ideology embedded in social and cultural practices. Through the use of what he calls "Ideological State Apparatuses," he implies that society is structured by socially and culturally constructed locations of power by certain sectors of society, whose ideology "governs" the rest of society. The Ideological State Apparatuses (ISA) include the religious, educational, family, legal, political, communications (press, radio, television, etc.), and cultural (literature, arts, sports, etc.) systems. Althusser's postulation is that these state apparatuses are location of power and can be used to describe the layers of inequality between the location of power and subordination in society.

This bears resonance with Antonio Gramsci's concept of *hegemony*. Gramsci (1968) describes cultural hegemony as implying a situation where in a culturally diverse society a social class rules and dominates over the rest of the society. The dominance of one social group, usually a ruling class is implemented not only through economic domination but also through socially and culturally constructed ideologies. The ideas of this class come to be seen as the standard; they are seen as universal ideologies, perceived to benefit everyone while only really benefiting the ruling class. This hegemony may be maintained through social and cultural institutions, practices, and technologies.

Forms of measuring inequalities in culturalist approach tend to focus on measuring life expectancy across countries, adult literacy, enrollment in the three levels of education: primary, secondary, and tertiary, and access to social and cultural good/resources. The theoretical approach in addressing inequality in this approach is a cultural narrative, which argues for resources that lead to equality-enhancing practices. These are practices that enhance a "taste" and disposition for equality through education, social networks, and sociocultural practices. Political narratives in this approach follow direct political action to address inequality, for example, in liberal welfare regime, the use of anti-discriminatory legislation to reduce inequality of opportunity and create more opportunity for lower class, as in affirmative policies.

Culturalist Approach to Digital Inequalities

Bourdieu's cultural theories have been adopted as theoretical framework to analyze inequality in many social sectors. For example, Abel (2008) engages cultural capital and social inequalities in health and Kvasny (2006) applies Bourdieu's cultural approach to study the cultural reproduction of digital inequalities. Kvasny is critical of the reductionist nature of the concept of digital divide, and argues that access should be seen within the framework of digital inequalities, which reflects the nature of social inequalities in society and the effects they have on access to digital technologies. The issues of poverty, illiteracy, unemployment, and social networks are factors that affect digital access. Her study of ICT access is relevant for cultural approach to digital inequalities. She studies a community technology center in a predominantly poor African-American community where half of the residents have less than a high school education, and found that Community Technology Centers (CTC) initiative is set up as a technological fix, and instead of redressing the "digital divide" it may unwittingly reproduce inequality. She argues that mere physical access and training in the CTC are not enough; access must go beyond the quantitative indicators of how many people have access to computer or to the Internet. Her findings reveal there are broader social, economic, technical, cultural, and historical factors that both enable and constrain people's ability to engage with technology.

Jan van Dijk (2005, 2012) is also critical of the structuralist approach to access as applied to the notion of digital divide, and instead offers a cultural perspective. His culturalist approach indicates that inequality in society is not solely based on class defined by some economic capabilities, but it is based more and more on complex social and cultural issues. Likewise digital divide connotes that a chasm exist between those with access and those without, it assumes the problem is a solely technological and economic one, and makes the divide looks like absolute inequalities. Van Dijk develops a framework to expand the notion of digital inequalities by adopting a resource approach, which enumerates critical resources that are necessary for *different kinds of access*:

1. Temporal resource (time to spend on different activities).
2. Material resources (income, and other physical technological resources).
3. Mental resource (knowledge, technical skills).

4. Social resources (social network, position, and relationship).
5. Cultural resources (cultural assets—status and credentials).

Engaging these resources is important in holistic study of access to technologies. To van Dijk, these resources have implications on different kinds of access to digital technologies:

1. Motivational access (motivation to use digital technology).
2. Material access (physical access—possession of technology devices and permission to use them).
3. Skills access (possession of digital skills).
4. Usage access (number and diversity of applications, usage time).

This conceptual framework expands the discourse of access beyond the dominant meaning of "haves" and "have-nots" in the digital divide tradition.

DiMaggio and Hargittai (2001) and Servaes (2014) also argue that attention should be shifted from the concept of digital divide to a more socially and culturally meaningful digital inequalities. They assert this does not only refer to inequality in access but also inequality among those with formal access (especially with regard to the Internet). They identify five critical dimensions of digital inequalities:

1. Inequality in technical apparatus: an inferior/outdated apparatus limits the benefits one can tap from the Internet.
2. Inequality in autonomy of use: how much control do people have over their use pattern? Home, work, and public access offer different use benefits.
3. Inequality in skill: competence is related to individual capacity to use digital technologies.
4. Inequality in the availability of social support: social support/network is useful in the way people develop digital competence.
5. Variation in use: Income and cultural capital, especially education, can influence the use of digital technologies for enhancement of human and social capital, and political participation.

Similarly, Mossberger, Tolbert and Stansbury (2003) attempt to reframe the issue of digital divide, as other scholars have done, beyond the issue of physical access. They, like many other critics, are critical of the policy approach to access that focuses on public access and market operations in bridging the access divide. They argue for a more comprehensive approach that focuses on home access and use divide. Because of the benefits and externalities derived from ICT, they urge government intervention based on public good, and not market dictates. They offer a deeper rationale for government intervention, by drawing on the concept of equity, which moves the debate about access to a higher level of pursuing equal opportunity for all citizens. Beside access divide, they also identify skills divide, economic opportunity divide (how technology enhances economic opportunity), and democratic divide (political /civil participation online).

In sum, the focus of the culturalist perceptive to digital gaps focuses on various patterns of divides: skills, access, and use divides. Methodological approach in measuring access also shifted from mere quantitative indicators to measuring use pattern. For example, in the United States of America, the Pew Internet and American life projects measure the pattern of use in different contexts, according to gender, age, race, et cetera. It measures not only access to technologies but also what people use them for. The National Telecommunications and Information Administration (NTIA) fourth report (2000) also looks at the role of cultural capital (education) and ICT access, and the fifth report, *A Nation Online,* looks at Internet use. Policies in the culturalist approach address issues of skills development and training.

POSTMODERNIST APPROACH TO SOCIAL INEQUALITIES AND DIGITAL INEQUALITIES

Postmodernist Framing of Inequalities

A basic tenet of postmodernism is the rejection of a universal truth that is valid for all peoples, classes, cultures, races, and groups; instead it emphasizes individuality, and relative truth of each person. Hence, the fragmented, fractured, relative and personal experiences shape individual truth relative to society. This paradigm offers an approach to social inequalities that provides a shift from class-based analysis to a multidimensional and individual model. The core elements are that the class concept should be abandoned altogether and focus should be on individualization of inequality rather than class-based analysis. The argument here is that income inequality is not enough to measure the range of conditions that lead to inequality. Inequality can be measured through many dimensions—geography, health, human diversity, digital culture, education, imprisonment, and so forth. Current discourses of inequality focus on issues of social justice, human rights, participation, citizenship, and freedom of life choices. Inequality in this approach is not based on categorical differences, but rather on differential life chances and opportunities. There is a move from the collective and groupness that define class theory to individualization that defines current ideology of inequality. Issues such as globalization, migration, gender (e.g., women empowerment, and gay rights are openly discussed than in previous eras), and technology are contributing to the shift in the discourse of social inequalities. Notable works in this approach include, Pakulski and Waters (1996), Beck and Lau (2005), Sen (1990), Giddens (2007), Stiglitz (2008), Firebaugh (2008), and Tilly (2005).

Pakulski and Waters (1996) argue in *The death of class*, that the "economisms" and "groupness" propositions of class theory do not address the fragmented nature of current form of society and the patterns of current inequalities that arise from oppression, postcolonial racism, issues of human rights, sexual preference, gender discrimination, environmental degradation, citizen participation, identities, and individualities. They argue that the economic structure of class theory is deficient in tackling the structure of society based on postindustrialization and post modernization. This is an era of wide redistribution of ownership and proliferation of individual and small ownership, the globalization of market, the increasing growth of financial markets and wealth as compared to industrial and agrarian property ownership.

Beck and Lau (2005) refuse to accept postmodernity as a term to describe new epoch, instead opting to describe it as "second modernity." In the notion of second modernity, the binary struggles and classification of class theory is inappropriate to describe the current structure of society. The structural relation of economics, work, labor, and state is giving way to a culture of individualization. Categorical boundaries are becoming unclear. Beck and Lau (2005) adopt the concept "self-culture" to describe the movement away from class categories to a cultural and political dynamics of one's own life in relation to the society.

The basic tenets of self-culture and social inequalities include 1) *Demographic* criteria—growing number of single-person household, single-parent household; 2) *Freedom*—the increasing focuses on reforms to address personal freedom to attain basic rights, citizenship, the rule of law, and opportunities; 3). *Self-organization*—enshrined in the notion of participation, the rights of citizen to take charge of what they deem personally important—politically and socially. For instance, participation is not just a question of voting, but complaining, campaigning, organizing, and advocating. Self-culture sharpens inequality and makes inequality more visible.

Sen (1992) introduces the concept of "functioning and capability" to tackle social inequalities. Arguing that income inequality of the structuralist paradigm is deficient in measuring the range of inequalities that people confront. He notes, for instance, that human diversity reveals social inequalities than income inequality. Since humans are different in the environment they live, in physical characteristics, in communities they belong to, and in opportunities available to them, income inequality fails to reveal how these human diversities affect inequalities. For instance a disabled person functions differently in society than an able-bodied person will, even if they receive the same income.

Sen defines functioning as what an individual may value doing or being; it is relevant to well-being in a society. Functioning may range from achieving basic health wellness, participating in community, attaining educational qualifications or whatever an individual values or hopes to achieve. Capability refers to the ability to achieve functioning (well-being). It includes the set of opportunities available to an individual to achieve functioning; it is the freedom and rights of an individual to achieve well-being. Expanded to social inequalities, capabilities approach addresses the issues of social justice, basic rights as a set of fundamental entitlements for all citizens, and opportunities available for citizens to function in society. The absence of all these exacerbate social inequalities.

Giddens (2007) in the postmodernist approach focuses on social justice with regards to the "excluded" individuals, the highly vulnerable, the unemployed, and the poor. Arguing that the old class division is now determined by individual differential life-chances. Giddens directs attention to unequal opportunities as contributing factors to social inequalities, and noting the redistributive policy of welfare regime in addressing this. Giddens notes that social justice focuses on the fight against poverty, access to education and training, employment, a welfare system, and limiting income inequalities.

Generally the theoretical discourse in addressing inequality in the postmodernist approach argue that class identities, ideologies, and organizational approach are becoming less useful and new theories and approaches—perhaps more cultural than structural with attention to individuality should be developed.

Forms of measuring inequality in this approach combine the forms in the structuralist and culturalist approaches. It focuses on the human development index which is a multivariate index based on GDP per capital, Purchasing Power Parity (PPP), life expectancy at birth, enrollment in educational institutions, adult literacy rate, gender equity, access to basic human needs: housing, food, health services, and water; access to cultural and social resources (including telecommunications).

The postmodernist approach basically reveals that inequality is multidimensional and conventional studies of socioeconomic and cultural inequality hardly exhaust all forms and layers of inequality.

Postmodernist Approach to Digital Inequalities

There is a shifting paradigm in the framing of ICT gaps. Increasingly many scholars are reframing the issue away from the term "digital divide" to terms that reflect a multidimensional approach to digital inequalities. This includes concepts such as digital entitlement (Mansell, 2002), technology and social inclusion (Warschauer, 2003), digital citizenship (Mossberger, Tolbert and McNeal, 2008), digital literacy (Servaes, 2014) and digital inequality (DiMaggio and Hargittai, 2001). These concepts link access to technology to wider and multifaceted ideology of society inclusion. Many rights-based issues such as participation, equity, equality, social justice, human rights, citizenship, entitlement, and empowerment become lenses at which to engage digital inequalities.

Tilly (2005) identifies four critical recent bases of contemporary inequalities, namely: financial capital, information, science, and media for storage and transmission. The role of digital technology as value, producing resource is obvious in his calibration of social inequalities. In this regard, access and use of information and communication technologies are value-producing opportunity that redresses the problem of inequalities, and lack thereof exacerbates inequalities.

Garnham (1999) and Mansell (2002) adopt Sen's capability approach to the study of ICT gaps. For Garnham access to communication technologies is a form of entitlement especially in welfare states. In communication policy, this civic entitlement is raised under the policy rubric of universal service and access in telecommunications, and public interest and service in broadcasting. Drawing on Sen's "capability and functioning" approach, Garnham then argues that the communication entitlement of a citizen provides the capability to function in society. Because the market cannot solely provide this entitlement, it warrants government intervention. Functioning as a citizen means achieving well-being, and communication technologies provide the capability for citizens to achieve aspects of this functioning.

Mansell (2002) echoes Garnham's argument by directing the focus to what she calls "digital entitlement." She argues that access should be seen as entitlement and rights of every citizen, and the enhancement of citizen's capability to function. She argues further that if the benefits of digital media offer the capabilities for citizens to participate effectively in society, and access is unavailable to a majority of citizens, then there is a need for a rights-based approach to policy. Her suggestions are twofold: that policy should favor tool kits that foster acquisition of skills for creating and sharing digital information, and a need for a rights-based policy rather than policy that focuses on legal issues and regulation about bridging the divide that work on a supply side of the industry and encourages market power of firms.

Mossberger, Tolbert and McNeal (2008) draw on citizenship rights to argue the notion of digital citizenship. According to Mossberger et al., digital inequality gaps should be addressed from the ability of an individual to be a digital citizen. A digital citizen is defined as someone who uses the Internet regularly and effectively, that is daily use. This contrasts with the methodological approach adopted in measuring access and use in the digital divide paradigm, which measures access based on physical access and occasional use. Implicit in the notion of digital citizenship are issues of belonging, capability, participation, citizenship rights, entitlement, social justice, social inclusion, frequent use of technology, and skills acquisition.

Drawing on liberal ideology of individual rights, freedom and equality, and civic republican ideology of communal and public good, Mossberger et al., argue for a citizenship rights approach to broadband access, while noting the ascriptive hierarchical qualities (of race, education, gender, geography) that define those without access. They adopt a multivariate approach in measuring digital gaps; this combines various social issues and elements of population to measure access, as compared to the bivariate approach of most digital divide studies. In line with this approach, Fuchs (2009) finds out that income inequality is not the only reason for lack of access, there are socio, cultural, political issues that hinder digital access.

Warschauer (2003) engages the role of technology in social inclusion. The social inclusion framework focuses on social development and the integration of ICT into communities, institutions, and societies. This shift to social inclusion framework works on the following premises: 1) that there is a new information economy and network society that has emerged, (2) ICTs play a critical role in this new economy and society and (3) that access, broadly defined, can help in the inclusion of population in this new society. To achieve this social inclusion, Warschauer offers four resources that are necessary in order to promote the goal of social inclusion:

1. Physical resources (devices and conduits)
2. Digital resources (contents, e.g., health, education, etc., and language)
3. Human resources (literacy and education)
4. Social resources (community and institutions—building social capital).

Hargittai (2008) asserts that access is not the sole measure of digital inequalities; digital abilities and use also have the potential to contribute to social inequalities. Evident in this discussion is the multidimensional method of a postmodernist approach to digital gaps. This approach shifts access from public access to home and household access, and daily use rather than occasional use. Broadband and mobility access (WiFi) become important, there is increasing emphasis on skills, and access is framed as rights, social justice, equality and entitlement for citizens to be able to achieve "functioning," and participate in society through digital means (Oyedemi, 2014).

CONCLUSION

All the three approaches have their potentials and challenges for addressing ICT gaps. The structuralist approach of class structure helps to identify groups in society that are still unconnected to ICT, but faces the challenge of seeing access in bipolar lens of "haves" and "have-nots" leading to an economic reductionist approach to policy. The culturalist approach addresses this economism and offers social and cultural aspects to access gaps, and as a result draws attention to pattern of use, and how cultural and social issues affect access. Policy in this approach tends to address skills and use pattern, and specifically draws on political narrative in policy direction, such as liberal welfare approach of universal service, as against economic, market, and industry-oriented universal access.

The postmodernist approach offers a different perspective, since inequality is multidimensional—can be social, political, physical, cultural, and so forth, digital gaps should be confronted from a broad principle that encapsulates the multidimensional nature of inequalities. Universal concepts of human rights, social justice, participation, freedom, and equality are used to argue the rationale for every citizen, irrespective of physical and geographical attributes, to have access to the current platform of communication. This approach has an appeal that is effective in a theoretical explanation of digital gaps, and a rationale for policy intervention about digital inequalities.

REFERENCES

Abel. T. (2008). Cultural capital and social inequality in health. *Journal of Epidemiology & Health* 62: pp. 1–5.

Althusser, L. (1971). *Lenin, philosophy and other essays.* New York, NY: Monthly Review.

Aufderheide, P. (1999). *Communication policy and the public interests: the Telecommunications Act of 1996.* New York, NY: Guilford Press.

Beck, U & Lau, C. (2005). Second modernity as a research agenda: Theoretical and empirical explorations in the "meta-change" of modern society. *British Journal of Sociology*, Vol. 56, pp. 525–557.

Bourdieu, P. (1984). *Distinction: A social critique of the judgment of taste*. London: Routledge.

Bourdieu, P. (1986). "Forms of capital." In J. Richardson (Ed.). *Handbook of theory and research for the sociology of education.* New York, NY: Greenwood Press.

Castells, M. (2002). *Internet galaxy: reflections on the Internet, business, and society.* New York: Oxford University Press.

DiMaggio, P. & Hargittai, E (2001). From the "Digital Divide" to "Digital Inequality": Studying Internet use as penetration increases. Retrieved January 24, 2014, from https://www.princeton.edu/~artspol/workpap15.html.

Firebaugh, G. (2008). The new geography of global inequality. In D. Grusky (Ed.). *Social stratification: Class, race, and gender in sociological perspective.* 3rd edition (pp. 1044–1056). Boulder, CO: Westview Press.

Fuchs, C. (2009). The role of income inequality in a multivariate cross-national analysis of the digital divide. *Social Science Computer Review*, Vol. 27, No 41, pp. 41–58.

Garnham, N. (1999). Amartya Sen's "capabilities" approach to the evaluation of welfare: Its application to communication. In A. Calabrese & J. Burgelman (Eds.).

Communication, citizenship and social policy: Rethinking the limits of welfare state. NY: Rowman & Littlefield Publisher.

Giddens, A. (2007). *Europe in the global age.* Cambridge, UK: Polity.

Giddens, A. (1973). *The class structure of the advanced societies*. New York: Harper and Row.

Gramsci, A. (1968). *Prison notebooks.* London: Lawrence & Wishart.

Grusky, D & Ku, M. C. (2008). Gloom, doom, and inequality. In D. Grusky (Ed). *Social stratification: Class, race, and gender in sociological perspective,* 2–28. Boulder, CO: Westview Press.

Hargittai, E. (2008). The digital reproduction of inequality. In D. Grusky (Ed). *Social stratification: Class, race, and gender in sociological perspective,* 861–892. Boulder, CO: Westview Press.

Hargittai, E & Shafer, S (2006). Differences in actual and perceived online skills: The role of gender. *Social Science Quarterly,* Vol. 87 (2) pp. 432–448.

Hargittai, E & G. Walejko (2008). The participation divide: Content creation and sharing in the digital age. *Information, Communication and Society. 11*(**2**): 239–256.

Horwitz, R. (1990). *The irony of regulatory reform: The deregulation of American Telecommunications.* New York: Oxford University Press.

Kvasny, L. (2006). The cultural (Re)production of digital inequality, *Information, Communication and Society,* Vol. 9, No. 2, pp. 160–181.

Mansell, R. (2002). From digital divides to digital entitlements in knowledge societies. *Current Sociology* 50, 407–426.

Marx, K. (1857). *Grundrisse* Retrieved: https://www.marxists.org/archive/marx/works/1857/grundrisse/ch05.htm.

Marx, K., & Engels, F. (1948). *The communist manifesto.* New York: International Publishers.

Marx, K., & Engels, F. (1974). *The German ideology.* London: Lawrence & Wishart.

Mossberger, K., Tolbert, C. J., & Stansbury, M. (2003). *Virtual inequality.* Washington, DC: Georgetown University Press.

Mossberger, K., Tolbert, C. J & McNeal, R. S (2008). *Digital citizenship: the Internet, society and participation.* Cambridge, MA: MIT Press.

Oyedemi, T. (2014). Internet access as citizen's right (?): Citizenship in the digital age. *Citizenship Studies*, DOI: 10.1080/13621025.2014.970441 (Print: 2015, Vol. 19 No. 3/4).

Pakulski, J., & Waters, M (1996). *The death of class.* Newbury Park, CA: Sage.

Parkin (1979).

Rousseau, J. (1973). *The social contract and discourses.* (G. G. H Cole, Trans). London: J. M. Dent & Sons. (Original work published 1754).

Sen, A. (1992). *Inequality reexamined.* Cambridge, MA: Harvard University Press.

Servaes, J. (ed.) (2014). *Technological Determinism and Social Change. Communication in a Tech-Mad World.* Lanham: Lexington Books.

Servon, L. J. (2002). *Bridging the digital divide.* Malden, MA: Blackwell.

Stevenson, S. (2009). Digital divide: a discursive move away from the real inequalities. *The Information Society.* 25: 1–22.

Stiglitz. J. (2008). Globalism Discontents. In D. Grusky (Ed.). *Social stratification: Class, race, and gender in sociological perspective*. 3rd edition. Boulder, CO: Westview Press.

Tilly, C. (2005). Historical perspectives on inequality. In M. Romero, & E. Margolis, (Eds.). *The Blackwell companion to social inequalities* (pp. 15–30). Malden, MA: Blackwell.

Van Dijk, J. (2005). *The Deepening divide: Inequality in the information society*. Thousands Oaks, CA: Sage.

Van Dijk, J. (2012). *The Network Society. Social Aspects of New Media*. London: Sage.

Warschauer, M. (2003). *Technology and social inclusion: Rethinking the digital divide*. Cambridge, MA: MIT Press.

Weber, M. (1958). Class, status and party. In H. H. Gerth., and C. Wright Mills, (Eds.) *From Max Weber: Essays in Sociology*. New York: Oxford University Press.

Weber, M. (2008). Class, status, party. In D. Grusky (Ed.). *Social stratification: Class, race, and gender in sociological perspective*. 3rd edition (pp. 114–124). Boulder, CO: Westview Press.

Chapter Two

Theorizing Digital Divides and Inequalities

Massimo Ragnedda and Glenn W. Muschert

INTRODUCTION

Inequalities that exist in the digital sphere are certainly entangled with inequalities present in the "social sphere." The aim of this chapter is to sketch a concept of stratification and inequalities in the digital sphere, the goal of which is to clarify whether the digital divide simply extends traditional forms of inequality, or whether it also includes new forms, which might include counter-trends that alleviate traditional inequalities and/or which form new modalities of inequality.

The discussion will proceed from a theoretical perspective using Max Weber's theory of stratification, in order to clarify how social stratification in the digital age is reproduced online. The main idea is that inequalities in the digital sphere are based on features that, just as in the social sphere, go beyond the economic aspects of inequality. Indeed, what we argue is that to understand digital inequalities, the discussion should not focus on class dynamics (economic aspects), but also status/prestige (cultural aspects), and group affiliations (political aspects). As in "real life," *social stratification in the digital sphere* is the result of this complex interplay of three factors. Indeed, as relevant to inequalities the material and ideological realms traditionally studied in nineteenth- and twentieth-century sociology, Weber's insights provide an opportunity to revise Marxist conceptions of class that give primacy to structured economic inequalities (i.e., class dynamics). While the relevance of class cannot be denied, a nuanced approach to stratification might also include aspects of social stratification in the digital sphere which relate to differential rewards experienced by groups and individuals in such areas as market influence, political power, and social status/prestige.

This complexity is precisely why we adapt Weber's perspectives on stratification to contemporary dynamics observed in digital spheres. With this idea in mind, we explore from a theoretical point of view, the social inequalities in the age of the Internet, focusing beyond the economic role of social class, to encompass two broader dynamics of stratification described by Max Weber: that is, "status" and "party." Thus, we assume that the basic principles of social stratification should be sought not only in the economic sphere, but also in the spheres of political culture and politics.

Our aim is thus threefold: 1) to initiate a scholarly discussion of the importance of status and group affiliation in a postmodern society specifically in relation to digital inequalities; 2) to explore the importance of prestige in digital participation/exclusion; and, 3) to explore the influence of group affiliation (Weber's notion of "party" or political power) on digital participation/exclusion. These key distinctions Weber identified about inequality continue to be relevant in a digital age, although this perspective has thus far remained underdeveloped.

SOCIAL STRATIFICATION AND SOCIAL INEQUALITIES

Social inequalities are usually described as the unequal distribution of opportunities, rewards, goods, wealth, education, healthcare, and punishments for different socially defined categories of persons within a group or society. Each society exhibits inequalities among individuals and groups, and as these are the sedimentation of social history, they give rise to social strata in the practice of social relations, notably regarding access to social rewards such as money, prestige, and power. Social inequality in preliterate societies, characterized by a low division of labor and mainly unstructured, was much lower than in today's complex societies. Sociology, more than any other discipline, has attempted to explain the origin of such inequalities. Among the various approaches we can mention here, the three that have dominated the debate among sociologists, and which have influenced the debate beyond the discipline, are the classical statements (and subsequent scholarly traditions) of Emile Durkheim, Karl Marx, and Max Weber. The idea is to apply these approaches in order to understand and explain the inequalities in the age of the Internet. The goal is to identify digital stratification and digital inequalities and read it through these theoretical lenses.

Durkheim explained inequalities in terms of their "*functionality*" for the larger social system, based on the different functions necessarily carried out by individuals in a variety of social circumstances. Presumably, more skilled citizens were to carry out the more complex function and this would give rise to different social strata. In the functionalist view, social stratification is necessary for the development of different skills, talents, training, and capacities, with each role being rewarded differently. This differentiation among individuals and groups then gives rise to the division of labor without which social order (i.e., society) could not persist. In the Durkheimian perspective, society requires inequalities, some of which are legitimate and some of which are not, depending on how it is interpreted within its relevant social context.

Karl Marx, on the other hand, mainly focuses on the *class* to describe and explain the social stratification and social inequalities. Briefly, according to Marx, the class of an individual is determined by elements of a structural nature. Specifically, as defined in *The Communist Manifesto* ([1974] 1848), in capitalist society is the possession of the means of production the key variable to determine the membership of the class. The whole social superstructure is based on the economic dimension or structure. However, the binary division, based upon the control over the means of production, between bourgeoisie (capitalist class) and proletariat (working class), have been extensively criticized and considered outdated in the postindustrial society. As society has evolved, it is evident that also social class has evolved. However, it could be argued that possession of the means of production, even in a postmodern society is important to define social class. Moreover, it could be argued that this perception of social class is reproduced in the digital sphere and social class influences the access, the skills, and the use of the Internet.

However, while the economic factors are extremely important in understanding the social structure, Marx seems to overestimate this element excluding other components of social inequalities, such as prestige and power.

Finally, according to Weber, the complex interplay of these elements (*status and party*), in addition to the economic aspects, form the social stratification. Thus, from a Weberian perspective, social stratification could be described as the relatively stable organization of society into groups with different ways of enjoying the opportunities and rewards offered by the society. The Weberian approach to social stratification seems to offer a better understanding of social inequalities. This is why we will mostly focus on this approach to evaluate, discuss, and understand digital inequalities. However, all these three approaches have been formulated long time before the advent of the new ICTs. It is important, at this point, to explain how social inequalities are produced or reproduced in a digitally organized society.

Each of the classical sociological traditions of social stratification offers insight into digital inequalities, however in the following section we will clarify the contributions and weaknesses of the Durkheimian and Marxist traditions, and ultimately will argue for a new Weberian discussion. Given its relatively nuanced conceptualization and multiple dimensions (i.e., class, status, and politics), a Weberian approach to stratification allows not only for a "thick description" of the mechanisms of social inequalities in the digital sphere, it also suggests potential to answer a troubling question that has thus far remained unanswered in the digital divide field. That is, it is unclear whether these traditional forms of inequality simply replicate themselves in the digital sphere, or whether the digital divide operates under its own dynamics. The question remains: do social inequalities in traditional (so-called "real life") dimensions of economic, status, and political relations simply replicate themselves (or extend intact) into the digital sphere? Or, does the digital sphere bring with it *new modalities of inequality*, and therefore new potentialities as well as challenges? Since more aspects of social life are migrating and expanding online, systems of structured inequalities are now reproduced in the digital sphere, the question becomes how social inequalities and social stratification are replicated in the digital sphere. The idea of this chapter is to start a scholarly debate whose goal is to explain digital inequalities in relation to dynamics social *class* (lifestyle and market influence), social *status* (prestige and culture), or *power* (political impact or authority).

READING DIGITAL DIVIDES

In order to attempt to answer this crucial question, we need to introduce the so-called digital divide, a phenomenon since always at the centre of Internet studies (Bonfadelli 2002; Katz & Rice 2002; Mossberger, Tolbert, & Stansbury 2003; Servaes 2014; van Dijk 2005), and inevitably tied with the concept of social inequalities. The digital divide has been studied since the mid-1990s from different perspectives and approaches. The idea of inequalities in access to—and use of new ICTs (and in particular the Internet) across different population segments and countries has been at the center of many studies in the last decades (National Telecommunications and Information Administration 1995; DiMaggio, Hargittai, Russell Neuman, & Robinson 2001; Norris 2001; Ragnedda & Muschert 2013; Witte & Mannon 2010). Because of the centrality of the Internet, researchers have focused on the gaps in adoption and use of the new ICTs. Castells, for instance, argues that "the differentiation between Internet-haves and have-nots adds a fundamental cleavage to existing sources of inequality and social exclusion in a complex interaction that appears to increase the gap between the promise of the information age and its bleak reality for many people around the world" (2001: 247). So, in its basic terms, the digital divide describes inequalities in the access to the ICTs. However, the access to the ICTs is not the "only divide" among users and citizens, and it is not the only divide that creates social and digital inequalities. This is why the analysis proposed by Castells, in some ways still valid, has been reformulated and addressed, over the time, in different ways (Servaes 2014; Sparks 2013; van Dijk 2006). Indeed, the literature goes beyond this simple and binary divide between Internet-haves and have-nots, including other divides that exacerbate digital inequalities and digital exclusion. Van Dijk, (2005) and van Deursen & van Dijk (2013), for instance, focus on numerous divides including ICT-skills, physical, motivational, and use purpose. These divides should be seen in addition to the "simple" access (or lack thereof) to the new technologies of communication, as the first study of the digital divide made by the US Department of Commerce's National Telecommunications and Information Administration (NTIA) in July 1995 have made. This misleading binary idea has been progressively dismissed and further integrated with several sociological patterns that include economic, social, geographical, gender, education, and prestige divides, connecting the phenomenon of social inequalities to the new digital inequalities (DiMaggio et al. 2004; Sparks 2013).

The initial technocratic approach to the digital divide as social and cultural phenomenon that underlines inequality in providing access to technology is outdated in an era characterized by a massive use (at least in the industrialized societies) of the Internet (Tondeur, Sinnaeve, van Houtte, & van Braak, 2011). It sounds more pertinent analyses the digital divides in relation to the different ways in which ICTs are used (Hargittai & Hsieh, 2010), and in relation to the ICT experiences and the capacities in using technologies among citizens with different socioeconomic backgrounds (Hargittai 2002, 2010). So, while the gap in access to the Internet has steadily declined in the course of the last decades, noteworthy differences persist in terms of Internet usage and differential skills (Hargittai and Hinnant 2008; Selwyn 2004; Van Dijk 2005; Zillien and Hargittai 2009).

Indeed, there are differences in connection speeds, and where one accesses the Internet, such that a person with reliable broadband who access the web at work, home, and on a mobile device would presumably be in a better position than one accessing the web via dial-up with limited access. Similarly, a person with great skill in navigating the web would be at comparative advantage in accessing information, as would a person with greater resources of time to spend online. Thus, *the digital divide may be measured in a variety of ways*, and along a continuum including the following aspects: access vs.

non-access; number of sites of access; varying skill at using digital tools; the amount of time spent online; the variety of activities accomplished online; the motivation in using the Internet; and how frequently a person goes online. All these factors inevitably create digital inequalities in the digital sphere. All these factors influence the way in which citizens engage with ICTs (van Dijk 2005) and, at the same time, are influenced by the unequal access to socio-economic, cultural, and personal resources.

At this point, we apply the three previous theoretical approaches in analysing the social stratification to the digital age. We start with the functionalist approach "to read" digital stratification. According to this approach we might find that the digital divide is mainly based on the digital skills and, more importantly, that such digital divide and digital inequalities may be useful and functional to the rise of new talents and capacities, differently rewarded. These different skills and different remunerations create a new digital stratification that may encourage and thrive on inequalities in the age of the Internet. However, are the skills required in social life different than the skills required online, or are they equivalent extensions of such? That is, would an exploration of digital skills reveal that the Internet and other digital spheres are structured similarly as offline society, and so therefore reproduce the inequalities based on different skills and rewards? As we have seen, many scholars argue that digital skills are important in understanding and analyzing the digital divide. What is unclear is whether these digital skills are directly tied with the offline skills, or if they are something different and disconnected. In the first case, indeed, the digital inequalities could be seen as the reproduction, in digital space, of the inequalities pre-existing in the society. In the second case, however, digital inequalities have their own dynamics not necessarily connected with the social world. The difference is worth noting. In the first case, new ICTs are reproducing and reinforcing social inequalities, solidifying the social structure based on the division of labor. In the second case, digital inequalities are created by the new digital skills created by new digital technologies. Because digital skills seem tied with social structures and since the Internet requires a form of digital stratification based on different skills/talents, we may assume, at least in part, that digital inequalities are reproducing and reinforcing previous inequalities. However, a functionalist approach to social inequalities may underestimate other social patterns that influence the rise of strata, such as social status and inherited positions. That is why, even underlying its theoretical and useful insights, we will not use this theoretical approach.

Neither will we use the Marxist approach, because it mainly focuses, as we have seen, on the economic structures and class conflicts. A Marxist approach underlines the formation of dominant groups in the digital sphere and, above all, shows the capital accumulation dynamics that reproduce social inequalities in the digital world (Fuchs, Mosco, 2012). According to Graham (2001) we are living in digital dark ages in which the knowledge economy is seen as alienation. *The digital sphere tends to reproduce the relation of power that characterizes social inequalities in the real life.* While Marx's concept of class highlights the existence of objectively structured economic inequalities in society, we assume that the basic principles of social stratification should be sought not only in the economic sphere, but also in the spheres of politics and culture.

Weber revises Marx's analysis arguing that social stratification relates to the access of different groups and individuals in social rewards such as money, power, and prestige. This seems to be particularly true in the digital sphere. We are assuming that while the economic sphere is still important and valid to analyze the new inequalities, it sounds more pertinent and insightful to analyze such inequalities from a broader perspective. Weber's potential contribution to digital divide and in digital inequalities studies is on two planes: First, Weber argues that there are a variety of economic factors relevant to the formation of class relations. In addition to the access (or lack thereof) to the means of production, skills, and credentials (or qualifications) can be dominant features of many professions. Those with access to and control over such qualifications enjoy a "market situation" more advantageous than those without such control. The Weberian approach provides a richer understanding of inclusion and exclusion that goes beyond a narrower class-based analysis.

FROM SOCIAL INEQUALITIES TO DIGITAL INEQUALITIES

As we have seen above, social inequalities present in the social structures are not presumably disconnected with the digital inequalities present in the digital sphere. Digital inequalities are, indeed, embedded in social structures (van Dijk 2005; Helsper 2012), and thus digital and social inequalities must be deeply *intertwined*. Bonfadelli (2002), for instance, argues that previous social inequalities not only affect digital divides but reinforce and exacerbate pre-existing social inequalities. Furthermore, several patterns, which characterize and shape the social structure (such as education, skills, income, occupation, and gender influence) the access and the use of the Internet (Rice & Katz 2003; van Deursen & van Dijk 2013). Analyzed from this perspective it seems that social inequalities already existing in the society are *reproduced and reinforced* online. However, we argue that there exists a kind of recurring cycle between social and digital inequalities. Namely, social inequalities are the root of digital inequalities, seen as the different skills at using information sources and opportunities that are the major cause of digital divide (Selwyn 2004; Hargittai and Hinnant 2008); however, at the same time digital divides increase and reinforce social inequalities already present in a stratified social sphere.

However, so far, it is not clear if the digital divide influences social stratification or, reflexively, social stratification influences the development of the digital divide, and if the digital divide is reproducing or limiting social inequalities.

To better explain this point we draw upon two well-known theories: "the Matthew effect" and the "theory of the knowledge gap," both of which, when applied to the digital age, argue that digital technologies are increasing the divide and the social inequalities, instead of limiting the gap. Briefly, the "Matthew effect," first introduced by sociologist Robert K. Merton almost a half century ago (1968), argues that "the rich get richer and the poor get poorer," though in his particular exploration this referred to the world of scientific inquiry. Merton applied a verse taken from the Gospel of Matthew: "For unto every one that hath shall be given, and he shall have abundance: but from him that hath not shall be taken even that which he hath" (Matthew 25, 29). Merton's idea was that well-known scientists usually get more recognition than anonymous researchers, even if their research and findings are rather similar. If we applied this concept to the digital divide (Helsper 2012; Pearson 2009; van Dijk 2005), we can see that pre-existing inequalities are *amplified* in the digital sphere. The rich, in terms of skills, income, and abilities get more advantages from the Internet than those poorly skilled users (DiMaggio, Hargittai, Celeste, & Shafer 2004). Thus, following this vein we can argue that social inequalities are not only replicated, but also amplified in the digital sphere.

Delving yet deeper in this vein, the knowledge gap hypothesis, first theorized by Tichenor, Donohue, & Olien (1970), before the advent of the Internet, argued that information and knowledge are not equally distributed in society. Briefly, the main assumption of this theory is that "as the infusion of mass media information into a social system increases, segments of the population with higher socioeconomic status tend to acquire this information at a faster rate than the lower status segments, so that the gap in knowledge between these two segments tends to increase rather than decrease." In other words socio-economic status influences the way in which we acquire information and knowledge and thus the gap, in terms of knowledge, between high socio-economic status and lower status will increase. This, despite the fact that both statuses will improve in knowledge because of the further information acquired. Some researchers (Bonfadelli 2002; Rogers 2003; Selwyn 2004; van Dijk 2005) applied this suggestive hypothesis to the digital divide, arguing that while both statuses will benefit from rich opportunities offered by new ICTs, those individuals and groups of highest status will gain more and sooner, thereby widening the pre-existing gap. In accessing and using resources offered by the Internet, those with a high socioeconomic status will get first and more efficient access to the opportunities offered by the ICTs. Consequently, it could be argued that the Internet has indeed *exacerbated* existing inequalities, rather than decreasing them.

The gap between "information rich" and "information poor" or between "users" and "losers" has been widened further by the new media and, more importantly, seems to reflect the ongoing inequalities in the social sphere.

However, it must be said that digital inequalities may evolve over time and some inequalities could be reduced or deleted. As van Dijk and Hacker (2003) argue, it would be in error to think about the digital divide as a static phenomenon, as inequalities are continually moving. The advent and adoption of new ICTs create new opportunities for social mobility, a process through which changes in the level of prestige of the subject can be realized. Indeed almost everybody who has access to the Internet may use it to improve their status and prestige. The Internet, for instance, may enhance individual social capital by offering new opportunities (Kraut et al. 2002; Zhao 2006). However, according to several studies, the digital divide may also increase the inequalities in social capital (Quan-Haase and Wellman 2004, Katz and Rice 2003; Hargittai 2002). This *complex interplay* of social capital and the Internet usage, has been at the center of several studies (Agarwal, Animesh and Prasad 2005; Goldfarb 2006; DiMaggio et al. 2004). However, other studies (e.g., Haythornthwaite & Wellman 2002; Witte & Mannon 2010) have shown that different indicators of economic well-being influence the use of the Internet. Again, it seems that previous and stratified inequalities influence the use of the Internet and, in so doing, influence digital inequalities. Moreover, not only do those in advantageous economic situations use digital resources more and more effectively, but it is also the case that citizens whose occupational position is more "prestigious" demonstrate a similar dynamic.

The difference in usage of the Internet may notably influence life chances, a concept used by Weber to indicate the chances that individuals have of gaining access to scarce and valued outcomes. The concept was further elaborated by Giddens, who explained it as "the chances an individual has for sharing in the socially created economic or cultural 'goods' that typically exist in any given society." New digital technologies offer *new opportunities* to improve people's social lives and, in so doing, can affect social and digital inequalities. The Internet's potentiality to transform lives remains crucial and access could open the doors to important societal resources, such as education, healthcare, social services, et cetera, thereby improving quality of life.

How does access and effective use of digital technologies influence access to opportunities in "real" life? Weber argued that it is the market which regulates the life chances enjoyed by individuals, and in turn we argue that in a society increasingly organized via digital networks, life chances are still determined within the market, but that this process is heavily influenced by the digital skills, authentications, and social capital resources. As Weber moved beyond Marx's binary distinction between property owners and non-owners to focus also on prestige and skills, in an analysis of stratification in digital society we should move beyond the distinction the Internet haves and have-nots, by developing social theory of digital inequalities integrated within the social structures of inequality. As Weber, skills and assets only have value in the context of a market; hence, digital skills as well have value in the context of market of life chances (both digital and "real life"). Several studies have shown how specific online activities may offer users more opportunities to enhance their life chances (e.g., Hargittai and Hinnant 2008; Kim and Kim 2001; Mossberger et al. 2003; Van Dijk 2005; Zillien and Hargittai 2009). Interestingly enough, several studies have shown, that the use of new ICTs for "capital enhancing" activities are influenced by skills (Hargittai 2010; Zillien and Hargittai 2009).

CONCLUSION

The Weberian approach allows for a more fine-graded set of distinctions in how social (and digital) inequalities exist and interact. Beyond the simple binary conceptions of access vs. no-access or high skill vs. poor skill, the inclusion of Weberian concepts allows for a more complex picture of how the digital divide co-exists and interacts with social inequalities. This relatively "thick description" allows us to see that it is not only economics which drive digital divides, but that there is also a high level of relevancy to dynamics of status, prestige, certifications/professional legitimacies, and political influence. In addition, the concept of life changes (a combination of potentialities and hindrances) playing out in the marketplace of social life is also very useful.

As more activities of social life move and/or expand into the digital world, we expect the influence of the digital divide to have an increasing effect on social inequalities, both within the digital sphere but also beyond. While new technologies, theoretically speaking, may provide opportunities for everybody to improve their life chances (and subsequently to overcome hindrances to life chances), it seems that this possibility is not in fact equally realized. Indeed, it is mainly those individuals and groups who enjoy better social positions, typically along with better digital skills, and with a better social capital and social networks, who are most likely to exploit the potentialities offered by digital new technologies. In so doing social inequalities are reproduced (or exacerbated) by the advent of digital skills, even if, for some, the possibility to overcome such inequalities potentially emerges.

REFERENCES

Agarwal, Ritu, Animesh Animesh, and Kislaya Prasad (2005). Social Interactions and the Digital Divide: Explaining Regional Variations in Internet Use, *Robert Smith School Research Paper* 06–024.

Bonfadelli, H. (2002). "The Internet and Knowledge Gaps: A theoretical and Empirical investigation." *European Journal of Communication,* 17, 65–85.

Castells, M. (2001). *The Rise of the Network Society: The Information Age: Economy, Society, and Culture*. Hoboken: John Wiley & Sons.

DiMaggio, P., Hargittai, E., Russell Neuman, W., & Robinson J.P. (2001). Social Implications of the Internet. *Annual Review of Sociology*, 27(1), 307–336.

DiMaggio, Paul, Eszter Hargittai, Coral Celeste, and Steven Shafer. "From Unequal Access to Differentiated Use: A Literature Review and Agenda for Research on Digital Inequality," in: Neckerman K (Eds), *Social Inequality*. New York: Russell Sage Foundation, 2004.

Fuchs, C. & Mosco, V. (eds.). (2012). Marx is back—the importance of Marxist theory and research for critical communication studies today. *tripleC—Open Access Journal for a Global Sustainable Information Society,* 10(2), 127–632.

Goldfarb, Avi. "The (Teaching) Role of Universities in the Diffusion of the Internet," *International Journal of Industrial Organization* 24, 2 (2006): 203–225.

Graham, Philip W. (2001) The digital dark ages: The knowledge economy as alienation. In Brown, H., Lovink, G., Merrick, H., Rossiter, N., The, D. & Wilson, M. (eds.). *The fibreculture reader: Politics of a digital present.* Melbourne: Fibreculture Publications.

Hargittai E. and Hinnant, A. (2008) Digital inequality: differences in young adults' use of the Internet. *Communication Research* 35(5): 602–621.

Hargittai, E., & Hsieh, Y.P. (2010). From Dabblers to Omnivores: A Typology of Social Network Site Usage. In Z. Papacharissi (Ed.), *A Networked Self* (pp. 146–168). London: Routledge.

Hargittai, Eszter. "Second-Level digital divide. Differences in people's online skills," *First Monday*, 7, 4 (2002).

Haythornthwaite, C., & Wellman, B. (2002). The Internet in Everyday Life: An Introduction. In B. Wellman & C. Haythornthwaite (Eds.), *The Internet in Everyday* Life (pp. 3–41). Oxford: Blackwell.

Katz, J.E. & Rice, R.E. (2002). *Social Consequences of Internet Use: Access, Involvement and Interaction*. Cambridge, M.A: MIT Press.

Katz, James and Ronald E. Rice. "Comparing Internet and Mobile Phone Usage: Digital Divides of Usage, Adoption, and Dropouts," *Telecommunication Policy*. 27, 8–9 (2003): 597–623.

Kim, M. and Kim, J. (2001) Digital divide: conceptual discussions and prospect. In: Kim W, Ling TW, Lee YJ, et al. (eds) *The Human Society and the Internet*. New York: Springer, pp. 136–146.

Kraut, Robert, Sara Kiesler, Bonka Boneva, Jonathon Cummings, Vicki Helgeson, and Anne Crawford. "Internet Paradox Revisited," *Journal of Social Issues* 58, (2002): 49–74.

Merton, Robert K. (1968). The Matthew Effect in Science. *Science* 159 (3810), 56–63.

Mossberger K, Tolbert, C.J. and Stansbury, M. (2003) *Virtual Inequality: Beyond the Digital Divide*. Washington, DC: Georgetown University Press.

Pearson J.L. (2009) *The Matthew Effect, the Digital Divide and the American Dream*. NMEDIAC, 6(1). http://www.ibiblio.org/nmediac/summer2009/MatthewEffect.html (accessed November 7, 2014).

Quan-Haase, Anabel, and Barry Wellman. "How does the Internet Affect Social Capital?" in: M. Huysman and V. Wulf (eds.), *Social Capital and Information Technologies*. Cambridge, MA: MIT Press, 2004.

Ragnedda, M. & Muschert, G.W. (Eds.) (2013). *The Digital Divide: The Internet and Social Inequality in International Perspective*. Oxford: Routledge.

Rice, R. E. & Katz, J. E. (2003) "Comparing Internet and Mobile Phone Usage: Digital Divides of Usage, Adoption and Dropouts," *Telecommunications Policy* 27(4): 597–623.

Rogers, E. M. (2003). *Diffusion of Innovations*. New York: Free Press.

Selwyn, N. (2004). Reconsidering Political and Popular Understandings of the Digital Divide. *New Media & Society*, 6(3), 341–362. doi:10.1177/1461444804042519.

Servaes, J. (ed.) (2014). *Technological Determinism and Social Change. Communication in a Tech-Mad World*. Lanham: Lexington Books.

Sparks, C. (2013). What Is the "Digital Divide" and Why Is It Important? *Javnost—The Public*, 20(2), 27–46. doi:http://javnost-thepublic.org/article/2013/2/3/.

Tichenor, P., Donohue, G. & Olien, C. (1970). "Mass Media Flow and Differential Growth in Knowledge." *Public Opinion Quarterly*, 34, 159–170.

Tondeur, J., Sinnaeve, I., van Houtte, M., & van Braak, J. (2011). ICT as cultural capital: The relationship between socioeconomic status and the computer-use profile of young people, *New Media & Society*, 13(1), 151–168.

van Deursen, A.J.A.M. & van Dijk, J.A.G.M. (2013). The digital divide shifts to differences in usage. *New Media and Society*, 16, 507–526.

van Dijk, J.A.G.M. & Hacker, K. (2003) The Digital Divide as a Complex and Dynamic Phenomenon, *The Information Society: An International Journal*, Vol. 19, Issue 4, 2003, 315–326.

van Dijk, J.A.G.M. (2005). *The Deepening Divide: Inequality in the Information Society.* London: Sage.

van Dijk, J. A. G. M. (2006). *The Deepening Divide: Inequality in the Information Society*. Thousand Oaks, CA: Sage.

Witte, J.C., & Mannon, S.E. (2010) *The Internet and Social Inequalities*. New York: Routledge.

Zhao, Shanyang. "Do Internet Users Have More Social Ties? A Call for Differentiated Analyses of Internet Use?" *Journal of Computer Mediated Communication* 11, 3 (2006): 844–862.

Zillien N and Hargittai E (2009) Digital distinction: status-specific Internet uses. *Social Science Quarterly* 90(2): 274–291.

Chapter Three

North-South "Miscommunication" about "Sustainable Development" and Social Change

Contributions from Postcolonial and Decolonial Theories

Eunice Castro Seixas

INTRODUCTION

As the neoliberal model of development becomes hegemonic and global inequalities increase, disagreements between North and South regarding environmental issues also become deeper and the possibility for resolving these is subverted by the close connection between environmental decisions and economic development, corporate interests, and a categorical commitment to a free market economy. Nevertheless, this hegemonic framing of environmental issues does not represent the entire picture since it silences alternative voices and perspectives. Postcolonial and decolonial approaches invite us to ask the questions of "Who has the right to speak about development and how?"; "Whose voices and alternatives are being suppressed?" and most important: "How can we give visibility to these 'subaltern'/alternative voices?" and "How can we construct alternative ways of thinking about development and of promoting environmental justice?" More than a theoretical framework, decolonial thought represents a meta-theory aiming to radically modify the categories and concepts of Western Philosophy (Tlostanova 2011) and build an alternative "geopolitics of knowledge" from the subaltern epistemic place, that is, the experiences of the "Global South" or the perspective of coloniality (Mignolo 2003, Grosfoguel 2008). This is also the proposal of an "Epistemology of the South" (Santos 2002; 2011–2012) based on three premises: 1) "that the understanding of the world is much more wider than the western understanding of the world"; 2) "that the world's diversity is infinite," and 3) "that there isn't a general theory that can adequately cover all this diversity of the world" (Santos 2011–2012: 17). Building on these premises, an epistemology of the South has to be open to other frameworks and social/economic/ecological models besides Western science. Santos proposes a double work of *sociology of absences* and *sociology of emergences*. The sociology of absences allows us to understand the present as an "incomplete past" by rendering visible the experiences that were silenced or excluded from history. This implies analyzing the legacies of the "modern matrix of coloniality of power, knowledge and being" (Maldonado-Torres, 2007) throughout history and how this matrix still influences the way we speak for instance, about development, environment, and inequality, the language and the categories we use. The sociology of emergences allows us to understand in which way the present we live in is an "unfulfilled present" and thus to "take care of the future," that is, to widen the horizon of possibilities and alternatives (Santos 2002; 2011–2012; Servaes 2013). This chapter builds on these approaches and concepts to discuss the issue of North-South communication about inequality in the context of "sustainable development" and climate change, taking as a case-study the UN Climate Summit of 2014.

UN CLIMATE SUMMIT: MISTRUST, POWER, AND DISCOURSE

At the UN Climate Summit in September 2014, several of the participating countries made initial statements in which they: 1) affirmed the importance of addressing climate change as well as the importance of the UN Climate Summit; 2) presented themselves as devoted to taking actions about climate change and as morally responsible actors in complying with the international commitments and 3) either appealed or demanded that other countries honored their current commitments under the Convention and Kyoto Protocol. Some more powerful countries also stated some conditions for their compliance to the international agreements and attempted to affirm their own approach on climate change governance. In all cases there was a clear mistrust about the other countries' sincerity in complying with their commitments that was nonetheless discursively used in different ways depending on power issues.

For example, the statement made by *China* at this UN Climate Summit reveals a double positioning: as a country that takes its *own* measures against climate change but also fulfills its international obligations.

> China attaches high importance to addressing climate change. As Chinese president Xi Jinping pointed out, responding to climate change is what China needs to do to achieve sustainable development at home as well as to fulfill its due international obligation as a responsible major country. This is not at others' request but on their own initiative. China was the first among developing countries to formulate and implement a national climate change program. Recently,

> we adopted the national plan on climate change to make sure we will meet the target of cutting carbon intensity by 40 to 45 percent by 2020 from the 2005 level. We are committed to taking proactive steps to promote energy conservation, emissions reduction, low-carbon development and ecological progress. In 2013, carbon intensity in China was down by 28.5 percent from the 2005 level. That was equivalent to a reduction of 2.5 billion tons of CO2 emissions.[1]

Throughout this statement there is the assumption that China does not need lessons from other countries regarding tackling the threat of climate change. It is subsequently argued that "China was the first among developing countries to formulate and implement a national climate change program," and examples are given of progress made toward reducing carbon emissions. Thus, China, one of the major world polluters, was presenting itself as a "responsible major country," one that is actively and on its own initiative addressing the problem of climate change, hence constituting itself as an example among developing countries. The issue of trust and of being "truthful to our commitments" is repeatedly stressed in this statement and linked to a moral issue of great importance to the "Chinese people." This serves as a reminder of the unfulfilled commitment made by developed countries to give a "financial support of 100 billion US dollars and technology transfer to developing countries by 2020," thus presenting these "developed" countries as morally flawed. It is a clear discursive strategy of positive self-presentation and negative other-presentation.

The case of *Germany* is the reverse. Here one finds the same discursive strategies of positive self-presentation and negative other-presentation in terms of an ethical discourse, but the "other" are now the "developing and emerging economies." Thus, this statement portrays Germany as a leader in addressing the climate change threat, with "ambitious targets," but at the same time stating the conditions for the pursuit of these goals, specifically, "that developing and emerging economies do their part too." Categories here are important because they define the global order and point to the issue of responsibilities in climate change governance. In this statement the category of "industrialized countries" (instead of "developed") and the addition of the category of "emerging economies" are clear indicators that the previous categorization of countries in "developing" and "developed" countries is no longer appropriate. Indeed, at the Lima Climate Change Conference in December 2014, these categories (which at Kyoto distinguished between Annex 1 "developed" countries and non-Annex 1, "developing countries," binding the former to reduce GHG emissions by an average of 5.2 percent during the period 2008–2012) have formally disappeared, being substituted by the principle of "common but differentiated responsibilities," which nonetheless leaves many doubts about how it should be put into practice.

> Germany is leading the way with ambitious targets.
> By 2020, we want to reduce our carbon emissions by at least 40 percent compared to 1990 levels.
> By 2022, we will have phased out nuclear power.
> And by 2025, we will have increased the share of renewable energy to at least 40 percent.
> But we can only limit global warming to below two degrees if developing and emerging economies do their part, too. We will give them massive support.
> In Copenhagen in 2009, the industrialized countries made a commitment to mobilize, from 2020, an annual 100 billion US dollars.
> Germany stands by this commitment. We are already the world's second largest donor of climate finance. Over the last decade, we have quadrupled official funding—to a level of about 1.8 billion euros.
> I will work to ensure that Germany's contributions continue to grow between now and 2020, so that we shoulder our share of the responsibility. We must take a leading role in international climate finance.
> We are also making sure that our funds are used specifically for initiatives with a lot of potential for mitigation. We need to decouple economic growth from increases in missions.[2]

The independent state of *Samoa*—a Small Island Developing State (SIDS) and as such, particularly vulnerable to climate change threats—presents a quite different discourse. It starts by contrasting the "decisiveness and unanimity" of the collective response regarding Ebola to the way that "some member states" have been responding to the climate change threat. The language is vague and elusive throughout the entire statement when it comes to ascribing responsibilities for the failure to achieve consensus and take actions. This discursive strategy of being deliberately vague and elusive is self-protective since no names are specified. It is stated that "some among our global community" remain unconvinced about the climate change threat and that "many more" did not follow up on their promises. In general, the message of this statement is that of a complaint about the behavior of "some" states and a certain distrust at the possible impact of this summit (for instance, when it is said that "Even if the impact of our efforts is negligible, we are committed to do everything possible for the benefit of our people"). However, at the same time, the statement stresses the importance of an international action grounded on the notion of a "global community," as we can see in the extract below.

> Our Pacific countries have advocated and continue to make the case that climate change has significant security implications. Sadly, some among our global

community had been dismissive and remain unconvinced. Others through their actions had been indifferent and unsympathetic. And many more had made promises that were not followed through with firm commitments and concrete action.[3]

These critiques to some countries' unresponsiveness to climate change are followed by an affirmation of the importance of the summit and the participation and commitment of all stakeholders. Subsequently, there is a statement regarding the negative discursive strategies that are often seen in climate change negotiations and a critique to those. It is said that: "Often at times we blame others for our misfortunes and the current status of our development, including telling others what they should do, by when and how, but rarely on what we can contribute to make a change." The "we" here is again ambiguous since it is not clear whether it refers to a "global community" or to "Our Pacific countries" and to SIDS. The reference to blaming others for "the current status of our development" points to poor and "developing" nations, while telling others what to do, how and when, points to a level of power presumably linked to richer, "developed" nations. Anyway, this argument appears linked to an ethical critique, associated with the idea that is wrong to blame others for our misfortunes and tell others what to do. Instead, negotiations should be focused on what "we" (all) can contribute.

Then the idea that climate change has peace and security implications is again reinforced, perhaps in a warning to developed countries that they too may suffer the consequences of this insecurity risk. There is also a strong critique and deconstruction of the ambiguous and manipulative discourse of some unnamed countries in climate change governance.

> Those suggesting that they are implementing bold actions for the sake of our vulnerable Small Island Developing States should instead take time to inform their constituents and voters, especially those that deny climate change that, in the final analysis, the actions being recommended will benefit their economies, and ultimately the very survival of their countries. With the support of genuine partners, SIDS are challenging the world to follow their lead despite their vulnerabilities.[4]

In sum, what I wanted to show with these examples is that the international negotiations at UN Climate Summits are imbued from the start with mistrust and power issues, as well as with different concepts of development, sustainability, and justice. Discursively, one finds that the issues of "North-South" appear in these statements although framed differently and through the use of different categories, but under a common denominator: *distrust*.

We also find the predominance of an ethics discourse, used both by both rich and poor countries, as well as "emerging economies." These discursive features deserve a further historical and political analysis. On the one hand, the history of climate change diplomacy has always been cut by North-South conflicts, which have made older questions of development re-emerge in this context. Historical relations marked by colonialism and imperialism, which have not ended with the twenty-first century, contributed to this mistrust, although rational self-interest, particularly interpreted through game theory and the "prisoner's dilemma" framework (see Helm, 2012), is also a factor in explaining the lack of cooperation between countries and the concern with the "free riders."

Already in the negotiations that led to the Kyoto protocol these suspicions and mistrust were much present, which had as a consequence the withdrawal of the United States of America. Mark Mwandosya, in reporting his experience from chairing the Group 77 in 1997, mentions the need for the developed and developing countries to "work together to remove the intense suspicion on the part of developing countries that flexible mechanisms are ways of allowing developed countries to buy their way out domestic action" and to "dispel the fear that the continued urging by developed countries for common action is orchestrated so that industrialized countries can continue to pollute, freely" (Mwandosya, 2000: 150–151). These suspicions on the part of the "developing" countries are related to the argument of "carbon colonialism," that is, the fact that poor countries' resources (land and forests) become subject to an international trade in emissions reduction. Thus, "early battles about the need to differentiate between the 'survival' emissions of the South and the 'luxury' emissions of the North have been compounded by claims of carbon colonialism and climate injustice" (Bulkeley & Newell 2010: 29). These claims are not without reason as economist criteria have been driving industrialized countries policies in the arc of climate change.

> Rather than prioritize fundamental changes in production and consumption of energy, the world's most industrialized countries are seeking to locate the lowest-cost ways of reducing emissions by identifying emissions reduction projects in the global south to make more money by trading their way out of trouble through the buying and selling of emissions permits. (Bulkeley & Newell 2010:110)

Thus, the North-South dimension is relevant to both the issues of responsibility and of vulnerability to climate change and to procedural and distributive aspects of climate justice.

The question of power in climate negotiation is a complex one, as there are also several concepts, levels, and dimensions of power. As Bulkeley and Newell (2010) argue, we need a broader understanding of power in climate change governance, one which takes into account more subtle ways of power exertion beyond "power over" and include analysis of how power operates through the presentation of knowledge, the inclusion/exclusion, the emphasis on some aspects of climate science and economics and not others and the language of ethics and moral responsibility. Climate governance is also shaped by and shapes the broader political and economic context and therefore, analyzing climate governance power issues entails analyzing the politics of who governs and on whose behalf.

At the international negotiations, power issues also get more complicated as the governments have been organizing themselves into blocs and negotiating coalitions in order to enhance their influence. At the one end of the spectrum there is the Organization of Petroleum Exporting Countries (OPEC) as the most hostile states to action on climate change. At the other end of the spectrum, there is the Alliance of Small Island States (AOSIS), a coalition of islands most vulnerable to the effects of sea-level rise that has been demanding for far-reaching reductions in CO2 emissions. This coalition has been supported by FIELD, an environmental legal NGO that works to bolster AOSIS negotiating capacity. In between these polarities lay the less developed countries (G77) plus China coalition. Beyond the arena of climate diplomacy, the diversity of social actors, partnerships, and instruments relevant to climate change governance further complicates the question of knowing who governs and on whose behalf as well as what is being achieved overall (Bulkeley & Newell 2010).

Finally, UN Summits can also be understood as moments of "political theater," as "performative enactments of legitimacy and authority and sites for the communication of particular examples of responsible conduct" (Death, 2011). In this perspective, it is not the achievement of results but the management of impressions that is important, including the management of legitimacy, authority, and moral responsibility to a global audience. This "political theater" was particularly visible at Copenhagen and Durban conferences as is clearly expressed by Helm (2012):

> This reached a farcical climax at the Copenhagen conference in late 2010. Imagine the scene. The runway is full of jets from all the campaigners and world leaders. Europe offers a 30 percent cut in its emissions if others follow. A huge media circus envelops the city, with proclamations and statements from green NGOs and interested parties. And what happens? At the last moment, the United States and China cut a deal outside the framework of the talks, promise to try to limit warming to 2° C, and promptly leave. Thus was born the Copenhagen Accord—to sink almost unnoticed in the months to come. (p. 5)

The UN Climate Summits, with all its problems, represent a hegemonic framing of environmental issues that silences alternative voices and perspectives. I argue that postcolonial and decolonial approaches invite us to critically examine this framework and ask the questions: "Who has the right to speak about development and how?" "Whose voices and alternatives are being suppressed?" and most important: "How can we give visibility to these 'subaltern'/alternative voices?" and "How can we construct alternative ways of thinking about development and of promoting environmental justice?" These questions will be explored in the following sections.

WHOSE VOICES AND ALTERNATIVES ARE BEING SUPPRESSED?

The unequal relationship between "North" and "South" and also among the different countries in the "North" and in the "South" affects all aspects of climate change governance. Indeed, "Who gets to define issues of responsibility, equity and justice is a function of who participates and who is represented" (Bulkeley & Newell 2010: 52). And although climate change has been framed as a global problem, deal-brokering tends to focus on a small number of actors, who traditionally have been the United States, the European Union, and Japan. Rising economies like China, India, Brazil, and South Africa also gain voice in climate change governance. On the other hand, scientists from smaller developing countries, those most vulnerable to the impacts of climate change, are poorly represented in the expert bodies of the UN Climate Change summits and thus have less capacity to influence the negotiating processes. Moreover, some smaller developing countries have limited representation, while more powerful developing countries also act in other fora, outside international negotiations.

Also, the rules and the goals of the conference are set from the beginning. In spite of the claims that climate governance is a plural and multifaceted process, at the end it is still up to the national governments to take specific actions in order to tackle the issue of climate change. Civil society and experts have only a consulting role, while the citizens in general appear to have no voice in the process. The international negotiations also misrepresent the importance of the operation of market actors and the international institutions as the World Bank (WB) and the World Trade Organization (WTO). These actors exert much more influence than it is recognized, although some civil society organizations have been calling attention to this issue. The WB, for example, exerts an enormous influence over the overall developing strategies of many developing countries and has funded several large projects for coal fuel power stations. On the other hand, some trade agreements may entail goods being transported over large distances.

The approach to address the problem of climate change is essentially through carbon emissions reductions and vague calls to investment in renewable energy sources. This approach effectively silences other alternatives, as focusing, for example, on energy consumption reduction (Helm 2012), not to mention more radical alternatives to "development" that question the principles of growth and market economy and are based on different representations of nature. As Helm argues,

> The practical question is whether these Kyoto-based summits are ultimately even positive. By carrying on a largely fruitless process for years, the need to explore alternatives is not given the priority it deserves. A credible plan B struggles to get off the ground, whilst world leaders continue to chase the deeply flawed plan A. Indeed, the negotiating process itself becomes a barrier—and an excuse—for not taking other options seriously. That is the real tragedy of Copenhagen and Durban. (pp. 170–171)

Furthermore, a market-based approach to climate change has gained widespread acceptance among hegemonic environmental and economic policy makers. This approach can actually exacerbate global inequalities by avoiding addressing issues of historical and institutional power imbalances (Dorsey, 2007).

The Kyoto pact is technocratic. It tends to see global warming's causes mainly in physical terms: the production of excessive amounts of greenhouse gases. On the whole, it declines to address institutions and power imbalances which have resulted in both the overuse and the unequal use of the atmosphere. Avoiding historical analysis, it averts its gaze from the politics of industry, the explosion in trade-related transport, subsidies for fossil fuel exploitation, the creation of consumer demand, and so on (Lohmann cited in Dorsey 2007: 9).

There is also the question of the language used in these international negotiations, this being a critical one, as speech and knowledge, as well as power, are the main tools of negotiation processes. The language of climate change has been permeated by vague and confusing market terminologies as the notions of "flexibility mechanisms," as well as by different concepts of risk, security, rights, and justice. The vagueness, imprecision, and lack of consensus on these concepts may contribute to an increase in confusion, misunderstanding, and manipulation. Indeed, vulnerability, adaptability, coping, risk, and environmental justice represent some of the most conspicuous cases (O' Brien et al. 2004). The language used in talking about climate change, not only in climate diplomacy but also in the academic sphere is predominantly linked to an ethical discourse. This type of discourse has become hegemonic in climate change academic discussion, entailing a "critical reflection on moral intuitions and conventional moral beliefs" (Kamminga 2008: 675). However, it emphasizes "the consistent, coherent, and disciplined argumentation as found in deontological and consequentialist (notably utilitarian) theories of obligation, and clarity and precision in the use of concepts such as rights, obligations, and justice" (ibid.). Thus, although the increase of ethical discourse has been framed as a positive change regarding more technocratic discourse, this discourse too represents one possible alternative among other moral discourses and raises serious concerns. For example, it can be argued that its focus on global principles of climate justice demands an improbable sense of world community and that the technical, rationalist, and abstract language of ethical discourse is not capable of any real motivating capacity toward action directed at combating climate change. From another perspective, ethical discourse fails to challenge the dominant view of environment as a natural resource for human use and may even legitimate this view by granting the inhabitants of developing countries their right to development and growth. Thus, the predominance of an ethical discourse contributes to silence the alternatives that defend radical changes in our attitude toward nature, as well as in society and global politics.

Another issue that has been largely absent of these international negotiations is the issue of procedural justice, related to the ways that mitigation and adaptation policies are designed and implemented, often creating more injustice related to local land and water conflicts.

IN SEARCH OF ALTERNATIVES

How can we give visibility to these "subaltern" voices and alternative perspectives? How can we construct alternative ways of thinking about climate change governance in order to promote greater environmental justice? Postcolonial studies comprise a heterogeneous set of critical interdisciplinary approaches that in general aim at the contestation of colonial domination, as well as the legacies of colonialism and new forms of colonial and imperial domination. The decolonial project suggests that postcolonial studies themselves need to be decolonized since they are still grounded on a Western epistemology and thus remain "a Eurocentric critique to eurocentrism" (Mignolo 2003: 665). The concept of "subaltern knowledge", core to this approach, implies transcultural and hybrid forms of knowledge linked to "forms of resistance that resignify and transform dominant forms of knowledge from the point of view of the non-Eurocentric rationality" (Grosfoguel, 2008). These forms of resistance constitute at the same time critiques to modernity/coloniality and a space from which new utopias can be imagined (Mignolo, 2003). This double potentiality of subaltern knowledge can be related to the double work of the "sociology of absences" and the "sociology of emergences" proposed by Boaventura de Sousa Santos (Santos, 2002) which aims at giving visibility to these subaltern voices and transcend the "coloniality of power, knowledge and being" (Maldonado-Torres 2007) embedded in mainstream approaches.

The "sociology of absences" (Santos, 2002) allows us to understand the present as an 'incomplete past' by making visible the experiences that were silenced or excluded from history. This entails analyzing the legacies of the "modern matrix of coloniality of power, knowledge and being" (Maldonado-Torres, 2007) and the manner in which this matrix still influences the way we speak, for example, about development, environment, and inequality. In climate change governance this is a highly relevant issue, one that is related to the language and the categories used in contemporary discourses and to talk about the "other" and their climate change policies. Thus, the "other" is "carbon colonialism." The sociology of emergences allows us to understand in which way the present we live in is an "unfulfilled present" and thus to "take care of the future", that is, to widen the horizon of possibilities and alternatives (Santos, 2002; 2011–2012).

Next I will present two interrelated dimensions that I suggest are particularly important for constructing alternative ways of thinking about climate change governance and environmental justice and discuss these in terms of the sociology of absences and the sociology of emergences: a) the dimension of the language and discourse and b) the dimension of the entities recognized as our interlocutors and ascribed with agency and rights. These are related to what can be called "The conceptual grammar of climate change, sustainability and inequality".

THE CONCEPTUAL GRAMMAR OF CLIMATE CHANGE, SUSTAINABILITY, AND INEQUALITY

As we have seen, the question of the language and discourse is fundamental to analyzing processes of negotiation and communication about environmental issues. In climate change governance we observe the re-emergence, contestation, and re-appropriation of previous categories linked to development by the different actors involved, as well as the critique and reformulation of Western concepts of nature, space and humanity by emergent alternatives from the global South. This proliferation of concepts of development, sustainability, and justice, as well as the strategic use of those in international negotiations contributes to ambiguity, miscommunication and lack of agreement. From the perspective of the sociology of absences it is important to understand how these concepts are linked to specific discourses and institutions and grounded in historical processes of domination that have operated through the exclusion of other forms of knowledge and agency. Thus, imperialism can be considered also as "an ecological project in which humans, plants and other species were shifted around the earth in schemes for colonization/conservation" (Sidaway et al. 2014: 5). Moreover, the concept of the present as the *Anthropocene* "acknowledges human activity as the dominant, universal category and agent of planetary change. As such, the concept internalizes an apprehension of the globe and nature that is measured and dated in science whose origins are in, and which expresses the power of, a Western *weltanschauung* (world-outlook)" (ibid: 5).

The sociology of absences shows the unsuitability of present conceptual grammars to adequately address the diversity of the world and its ecological demands. Through the sociology of emergences it is possible to widen our present understanding of climate change justice by including other voices and other grammars that have been previously suppressed.

One specific aspect of climate change discourse is its representation as a global problem with differing regional and local impacts. These geographies of environmental governance "tend to take space and scale for granted as pre-given, contained, natural, entities." An alternative spatial grammar of environmental should include an analysis of both the politics of scale and the politics of networks (Bulkeley 2005).

Furthermore, the concept of "global" has been criticized for being linked with a modern and colonial construction grounded on scientific representations of latitudes and longitudes and suggesting processes of imposition and dissemination. In this sense Spivak (2003) suggests substituting the concept of "global" with the concept of "planetary" as a richer and more inclusive category. As Sidaway et al. (2014) suggest, "Spivak's observation encourages us (again) to step back from the taken-for grantedness of the global and engage in its genealogy, one in which colonialism has played such a central, configuring role" (p. 5). This concept of "planetary consciousness" is inspired by indigenous texts that have been excluded from the mainstream framework of climate change governance, which is dominated by the language of modern science.

Related to this idea of planetary consciousness is the concept of *transmodernity* by the liberation philosopher Enrique Dussel. Transmodernity, as interpreted by Ghisi (apud Ateljevic 2013) entails a planetary vision of interconnected and interdependence among humans, plants, and animals, in which all beings are responsible for the Earth community. This is not a uniforming approach since "it claims that each community or region needs to be free to develop in ways that are uniquely suited to its culture, ecology, climate and other characteristics," focusing on a dialogue between world cultures (ibid.).

Indigenous texts of eco-protest build on a critique of existing socioeconomic conditions while simultaneously construct a model of the subaltern as a "knowing subaltern": "one who demonstrates historical consciousness, political awareness, advocacy and self-reflexivity" (Nayar 2014: 291). Nayar calls these discourses "eco-tropics" (playing on both "tropics" and "tropes"), arguing that these include four rhetorical modes: suffering, fear and loss, labor and community, and propose a form of 'moral economy' related with both land use and conservation and to fairness, justice, egalitarianism, and goodness.

The knowing subaltern seeks an ethical approach to land, labor and community, even as she positions all rights as communitarian. In the postcolonial context of development, this genre is therefore an indispensable tool to incite public debates about the ethics of development and the question of human rights for all classes of people (ibid.: 301).

As the case of the indigenous eco-tropics, a new conceptual grammar should mean new discourses, new approaches and not just the same approach dressed in new clothes, as it has often happened in the terrain of development and environmental governance. These indigenous approaches have not only inspired new conceptual grammars, but also new approaches to human-nature relationship by ascribing non-human entities with agency and rights.

NON-HUMAN ENTITIES AND MOTHER LAND IN CLIMATE CHANGE GOVERNANCE

The modern matrix of "coloniality of power, knowledge and being" has excluded other agencies and representations of nature and humanity-nature relationships. Postcolonial and decolonial critique has been challenged to address this issue of the non-human agency and has attempted to do so through a dialogue with the indigenous texts and by incorporating some of these into concepts like "planetary consciousness" and "transmodernity."

Relevant to this matter are the novel political articulations that have emerged out of indigenous movements. These articulations constitute hybrid alternatives to mainstream climate change governance and to the dominant paradigm of modernity grounded on the antithetical and hierarchical separation of "Humanity" and "Nature." Examples of these are State adaptions of indigenous articulations granting rights to "nature" and to "Mother Earth," namely by Ecuador in 2008 and by Bolivia in 2011. These are not without problems since there is the risk of indigenous articulations being reabsorbed into a new political hegemony, especially when these political projects do not question growth and capital accumulation as imperatives of a market economy.

In these countries—as revolutionary and well-intentioned as they initially appeared to be—the *plurinationality* and *Buen Vivir/Vivir Bien* theoretical projects did not adequately question capitalism and therefore ended up being diluted, transformed and even instrumentalized in order to meet the demands of primarily transnational capital (Ramos, Mancheno & Lopez 2014).

Some caution is thus necessary in analyzing the emancipatory potential of these proposals. Even if indigenous ways of being may instill the hope for a "new planetary consciousness," it is important to ask "what kinds of opportunities and threats does it pose for indigenous struggles to have their rights recognized with respect to country, culture and economic well-being?" (Sidaway et al. 2014). This entails a double work of the sociology of absences and the sociology of emergences, that is, a critical historical analysis that helps us understand how the modern matrix has excluded other representations of nature and human-nature relations and an analysis of the emancipatory potential of contemporary emergent alternatives to modernity and coloniality. As Casas (2014) puts it, to transcend the "coloniality of development" we have to understand how it came to be through the exclusion of other agencies.

It follows, therefore, that we cannot simply epistemologically incorporate the non-human world into our modern social, economic, and political systems without recognizing how these systems were shaped historically through coloniality, thereby uncovering the coloniality embedded in the hierarchical ontological assumptions that have shaped modern world history. This has affected *who* can express agency or rather who or what is valued as a political agent, *what* constitutes the political, and *how* this is articulated (p. 32).

The expansion of postcolonialism and progressive politics to these planetary imperatives is a key challenge with implications to the way we approach climate change governance. However, this has been a problematic task for postcolonial theory and Jackson (2014) suggests that "postcolonial and related assertions that depend on renewing forms of epistemological critique as planetary, namely by Spivak and Chakrabarty, are far less radical or transformative than is assumed" and even "reiterate ontologies grounded in unquestioned Eurocentric nature-culture distinctions" (ibid).

Moreover, postcolonialism has been the target of a lot of relevant criticisms, namely its overemphasis on colonialism and on coloniality as "an overall force determining all current sociological, economic, political and cultural scenarios in previously colonized nation-states," as well as its focus on ideological critique, instead of on imagining and creating new utopias (Ribeiro 2011: 294). And even if the decolonial project has stressed the importance of the locus of enunciation, as Ribeiro argues, "it is impossible not to recognize a strong Andean (and secondarily Mexican) accent in the decoloniality of power cosmopolitics" (ibid.: 289). In spite of these limitations, postcolonial ecocriticism and postcolonial geographies represent important alternatives to mainstream thought on environmental governance.

Today's concerns for postcolonial geographies are matters of concern for the commons, emerging social movements, biodiversity, material property rights, resource depletion, migration, cultural erasure, energy scarcity, inequality and the destructive imperatives of growth. We need to attend to these concerns in radical ways, as diverse, often contradictory and sometimes problematic as indigenous perspectives have been doing for millennia. Composing such efforts in a fundamental opening up of what indigeneity does and could mean for all living relations is surely one of the more important tasks for advancing postcolonial geographies (Jackson 2014: 85).

CONCLUSION: CLIMATE CHANGE AS A CIVILIZATIONAL WAKE-UP CALL?

In this chapter I argued for the relevance of postcolonial and decolonial studies to critically examine the processes of international negotiations and specifically, North-South (mis)communication regarding climate change, inequality, and sustainable development. I proposed that these critical approaches incite us to ask the questions of "Who has the right to speak about development and how?"; "Whose voices and alternatives are being suppressed?" and most important: 'How can we give visibility to these 'subaltern'/alternative voices?" and "How can we construct alternative ways of thinking about development and of promoting environmental justice?" These interrogations illuminate important aspects of the present mainstream approach to climate change governance, related, for example, to questions of discourse and power, performative power (linked to the idea of the summits as political theaters), power and ideology (related to the prevalence of market interests and neoliberal ideology), "cognitive power" (as linked to the power to legitimate some forms of knowledge as valid while delegitimate other forms as non-valid and also the power to dictate the "rules of the game"). But climate change governance is being enacted beyond the arena of international negotiations by several actors, for example, the climate justice movement and NGOs like the "Sinks Watch," cities, municipalities and communities among others. Even going beyond the international negotiations settings, as Bulkeley & Newell (2010) suggest, the mainstreaming of climate change can be ultimately considered a question of power:

The mainstreaming of climate change—"its integration in other policy domains and its increasing uptaking by a range of organizations (corporate, donors, civil society) beyond the realm of what was traditionally considered climate change governance," is ultimately a question of power. "The power of key actors with interests at stake will be brought to bear in determining what counts as climate governance" (Bulkeley & Newell 2010).

But as the critical approaches of postcolonial and decolonial studies illuminate questions of power as linked to exclusion and dominance in climate change governance, these approaches also highlight questions of resistance and the emergence of alternatives to the contemporary mainstream model of environmental governance and social change. Some of these critiques and alternatives entail a radical approach which not only interrogates climate change governance but also the market economy imperative of growth, the Western model of science and technology based on a dichotomy between humanity and nature and Western democracy unresolved and persistent inequalities. In spite of their limitations, postcolonial and decolonial studies may inspire further ideological as well as "utopian struggles" (Ribeiro 2011) aimed at promoting environmental and social justice. The engaged academic and the media have an important role and responsibility in giving visibility to these subaltern and alternative voices and to critically reflect on what is already happening on the ground and learning from these experiences. Can these emergent alternatives complete the "unfinished business of liberation," as it is hoped by Naomi Klein (Klein, 2014)? Can climate change constitute a civilizational wake-up call to social change? The path is made by walking.

NOTES

1. Accessed at https://papersmart.unmeetings.org/secretariat/eosg/un-climate-summit-2014/statements/
2. See footnote 1.
3. See footnote 1.
4. See footnote 1.

REFERENCES

Ateljevic, Irena (2013). "Visions of Transmodernity: A New Renaissance of Our Human History?" *Integral Review,* 9 (2): 200–219.

Bulkeley, H. (2005). "Reconfiguring environmental governance: towards a politics of scales and networks." *Political Geography*, 24 (8): 875–902.

Bulkeley, H. and Newell, P. (2010). *Governing Climate Change*. New York: Routledge.

Casas, Tanya (2014). "Transcending the coloniality of development: Moving beyond human/nature hierarchies." *American Behavioral Scientist*, 58(1): 30–52.

Death, Carl (2011). "Summit theatre: exemplary governmentality and environmental diplomacy in Johannesburg and Copenhagen." *Environmental Politics*, 20(1): 1–19.

Dorsey, Michael K. (2007). "Climate Knowledge and Power: Tales of Skeptic Tanks, Weather Gods, and Sagas for Climate (In)justice." *Capitalism, Nature, Socialism*, 18(2): 7–21.

Gosfroguel, (2008). "Para descolonizar os estudos de economia política e os estudos pós-coloniais: Transmodernidade, pensamento de fronteira e colonialidade global." *Revista Crítica de Ciências Sociais*, 80, Março 2008: 115–147.

Helm, D. (2012). *The Carbon Crunch. How we're getting climate change wrong and how to fix it*. New Haven and London: Yale University Press.

Jackson, Mark (2014). "Composing postcolonial geographies: Postconstructivism, ecology and overcoming ontologies of critique." *Singapore Journal of Tropical Geography 35*: 72–87.

Kamminga, Menno R. (2008). "The ethics of climate politics: four modes of moral discourse." *Environmental Politics*, 17 (4): 673–692.

Klein, Naomi (2014). *This changes everything: Capitalism vs. the Climate*. New York: Simon & Schuster.

Maldonado-Torres, Nelson (2007), "ON THE COLONIALITY OF BEING." *Cultural Studies*, 21(2–3): 240–270.

Mignolo, Walter D. (2003). "Os esplendores e as misérias da 'ciência': colonialidade, geopolítica do conhecimento e pluriversalidade epistémica." In *Conhecimento Prudente para uma Vida Decente, organized by* Boaventura de Sousa Santos, 631–672. Porto: Edições Afrontamento.

Mwandosya, Mark J. (2000). *Survival Emissions: A perspective from the South on Global Climate Change Negotiations*. CEEST.

Nayar, Pramod K. (2014). "Indigenous cultures and the ecology of protest: moral economy and 'knowing subalternity' in Dalit and Tribal writing from India." *Journal of Postcolonial Writing*, 50 (3): 291–303.

O'Brien, Karen, Eriksen, Siri, Schjolden, Ane and Nygaard, Lynn (2004). "What's in a word? Conflicting interpretations of vulnerability in climate change research," Oslo: CICER—Center for International Climate and Environmental Research.

Ramos, Gian Carlo Delgado, Tania Mancheno and Juan Miguel Rodríguez Lopez. (2014). "New Latin American Perspectives on Sustainable and Low Carbon Societies." In *Global transformations towards a low carbon society working paper series*, edited by Prof. Dr. Anita Engels, University of Hamburg/KlimaCampus.

Ribeiro, Gustavo Lins (2011). "Why (post)colonialism and (de)coloniality are not enough: a post-imperialist perspective." *Postcolonial Studies*, 14(3): 285–297.

Santos, Boaventura de Sousa (2002). "Para uma sociologia das ausências e uma sociologia das emergências." *Revista Crítica de Ciências Sociais*, 62: 237–280.

Santos, Boaventura de Sousa (2011–2012). "Introducción: las epistemologías del Sur" in CIDOB (org.), Formas-Otras. Saber, nombrar, narrar, hacer. Barcelona: CIDOB Ediciones, 9–22.

Servaes, Jan (ed.) (2013). *Sustainable Development and Green Communication. African and Asian Perspectives*. London: Palgrave/MacMillan.

Sidaway, James D., Woon, Chih Yuan and Jacobs, Jane M. (2014). "Planetary postcolonialism." *Singapore Journal of Tropical Geography* 35: 4–21.

Spivak, Gayatri Chakravorty (2003). *Death of a Discipline*. Columbia University Press, New York.

Tlostanova, Madina V. (2011). "How can the decolonial project become the ground for the decolonial humanities? A few reflections from the "vanished" second world," XXX1–15.

Chapter Four

Postcolonial Critical Discourse Analysis

Ruth Sanz Sabido

This chapter proposes the use of *Postcolonial Critical Discourse Analysis* (PCDA), a theoretical and methodological framework that draws upon Postcolonial Theory (PT) and Critical Discourse Analysis (CDA), in order to argue that media representations should be analyzed by taking postcolonial power relations into account. The combination of both fields stems from the observation that both CDA and PT have certain aims in common. Although they are completely independent from each other, both theories are concerned with the concept of "power" and, in their own particular ways, both seek to expose oppression and power inequalities (Bhabha 1985; Hall 1997; Prakash 1995; van Dijk 1993). While CDA deconstructs discursive strategies to uncover the ways in which power is reproduced in media discourse (Fairclough 1995; Wodak 2009: 578), PT focuses on the power imbalances derived from (post)colonial conditions, practices, and structures, which are perpetuated in contemporary societies (Krishna 2009; Young 2001). Thus, PT provides a useful theory of meaning to contextualize the application of CDA, whenever the objective is to examine discourses produced in postcolonial milieus.

This perspective has some precedents. For example, Brunt and Cere (2011) argue that Britain's role as the colonial "center" is strongly intertwined with British contemporary media cultures, so these should be explored through the lens of PT. In this chapter, I argue that PT can offer useful insights and tools for the analysis of media representations. However, PT is a broad field of knowledge, and different theories of postcoloniality developed as the result of a wide variety of (post)colonial experiences. Hence, an understanding of the historical particularities of each postcolonial context is required in order to develop an appropriate theoretical perspective that can be applied to distinct case studies. The main purpose of this study is, however, to provide an overview of the theoretical connections that exist between CDA and PT.

My argument begins with a discussion of some of the central theoretical challenges that must be considered when defining the postcolonial, with the intention of suggesting a working definition of this term that will, in turn, allow us to analyze samples of media content. This is followed by an overview of CDA, the purpose of which is to prepare the ground for the theoretical framework of PCDA itself. In this chapter, I argue that PCDA provides a useful approach to the analysis of media content insofar as it focuses predominantly on the postcolonial relations of power that underpin the production of that content. My contention is that a focus on the postcolonial helps to concentrate attention on the historical background, and therefore also on the responsibility the postcolonial has to its former colonies, a connection and an obligation which is increasingly neglected and which must be restored to its proper place.

DEFINING THE "POSTCOLONIAL"

Definitions of the term "postcolonial" are widely contested, as a result of the complex nature of PT itself. The many contradictory perspectives produced by academics become even more difficult to negotiate due to the fact that the postcolonial is deeply interrelated with ethical, political, economic, religious, and cultural issues (Eagleton 1998; Young 2001). The seemingly endless "redefinition" of the postcolonial is a recurring feature within the literature, and must therefore be addressed here. In addition, the difficulty of establishing a clear definition of the terms "colonial" and "postcolonial" arise from disagreements about whether, in fact, the postcolonial actually exists. The juxtaposition of "post" to "colonialism" implies, in simple terms, that postcolonialism began after colonialism ended. However, the notion of there being a colonial aftermath has been contested by several authors on the basis that colonial domination still continues today in one shape or another (Gandhi 1998; Harper 2001). For example, Harper (2001: 241) claims that the term "postcolonial" is usually based on the belief that the "colonial" has already passed, or that the shift away from the colonial reality and toward a postcolonial one is at an advanced stage.

Ultimately, Harper (2001: 241) argues that this is not really the case, as the "colonial" is still too close to contemporary times, so the prefix "post" can only be understood by way of alteration rather than advancement, "not because of actuality but only [. . .] because of a widening commitment to the desire to see such things left in the past". Similarly, Leela Gandhi (1998) observes that colonialism does not terminate with the end of colonial occupation and the subsequent independence of the colony. In her view, the notion of a "colonial aftermath" must not only include the history of the colonial encounter, but also the subsequent nature of its development. She also cites David Lloyd (1993: 11) when he states that colonial history must take into account those fragments of history which are still "in process," which means that what is known as postcolonialism is, in fact, still a form of colonialism.

A strictly "temporal" understanding of postcolonialism as *the time that came after colonialism* would therefore mean that the postcolonial is a new era, one that is simply defined by its chronology. In other words, such a position would suggest that the end of colonialism is simply followed by postcolonialism. This view involves accepting the oversimplified idea that the postcolonial is marked by the moment when a colony has achieved its independence from the metropolitan center, ignoring the continued influence that the former metropolis may have over the new nation after its independence. A more subtle temporal approach appears in Young (2001), who argues that many of the problems arising from the theorization of the postcolonial would be resolved by defining it as "coming after colonialism and imperialism, in their original meaning of direct-rule domination, but still positioned within imperialism[1] in its later sense of the global system of hegemonic economic power" (Young 2001: 57).

Prakash (1995: 5), following the theme of time and development, refers to postcoloniality as "a new beginning, one in which certain old modes of domination may persist and acquire new forms of sustenance but one that marks the end of an era." She argues that the postcolonial question is not whether the colonies are now totally free from domination, but whether the existing postcolonial relations (those inherited from colonial times) "can be shaken loose from the domination of categories and ideas" produced by colonialism (1995: 5). She particularly refers to the construction of categories based on binary opposites such as "coloniser" and "colonised," "white" and "black," "civilised" and "uncivilised," "modern" and "archaic," or "tribe" and "nation." Her concern is about the legacy of colonialism, that is, the effects of the previous colonial phase and the perpetuation of similar dividing categories which continue to shape the development of (postcolonial) world affairs today.

Loomba (1998) also acknowledges the definitional problem posed by the field of postcolonialism. She states that the prefix "post" implies that there is an "aftermath," and she makes a distinction between two types of aftermaths: on the one hand, the aftermath is temporal, as in "coming after"; on the other hand, the aftermath is ideological, as in "supplanting." While the temporal perspective accepts that the postcolonial begins from the date of independence, the ongoing definitional problem arises from the second implication, as it is the existence of an ideological aftermath that has been contested by critics. The notion of postcolonialism as an ideological aftermath understands postcolonial rule as a *developed* form of rule, as it has evolved from the ways in which it was implemented in colonial times. However, Loomba believes that, as long as the "inequities of colonial rule have not been erased, it is perhaps premature to proclaim the demise of colonialism" (1998: 7). From this viewpoint, the "colonial" will only end when the inherited residues of colonial times have completely disappeared from all political, economic, cultural, and social practices, giving way to a totally different form of relationship between all the inhabitants of the world. This is the ultimate objective of PT: to defend the formerly colonized people, to denounce the unequal divisions of power to which they are exposed, and to defend the existence of a truly colonial-free world in sociopolitical, economic, and cultural terms. The question remains whether it is possible to reach an advanced point in history that does not, in ideological terms, make references to, or draw its strength from colonialism.

In attempting to resolve this question, at least with regards to definition, this chapter takes the view that postcolonialism refers to the processes of decolonization by which former colonies achieved their independence, while new imperialistic contexts of economic and sometimes political domination emerged (Young 2001: 57). This perspective does not deny the fact that there are renewed forms of control in the postcolonial era. If we agree that the subsequent postcolonial forms of control and domination present distinct characteristics from those found under colonial jurisdiction, we can consider that colonialism and postcolonialism are two distinct periods with transforming features which are *specific to each phase*, even though domination and inequality still persist on various levels, depending on the particularities of the specific context.

Consequently, if we agree that there is a postcolonial era, the question then is how to establish when it begins. In order to advance the discussion and enable the formulation of an empirical approach, here the postcolonial is defined in temporal or chronological terms, that is, the postcolonial begins with the official date of independence. As discussed above, by adopting this definition I am not denying the existence of continued forms of control, nor am I suggesting that the experience of becoming "postcolonial" takes place at the exact time that independence is granted. This approach, however, allows us to establish a defined temporal marker that facilitates the research design.

CRITICAL DISCOURSE ANALYSIS

Critical Discourse Analysis (CDA) involves the study of the "relations between discourse, power, dominance, social inequality and the position of the discourse analyst in such social relations" (van Dijk 1993: 249). The field originally built upon critical linguists such as Fowler et al. (1979) and Hodge and Kress (1993), who in turn based their work on Halliday's functional grammar (1973). Initially, these studies were mainly exclusively concerned with linguistics, although they already recognised that there was a need to study linguistic elements along with "the relations between language and society and between language and mind, in a single integrated enterprise" (Hodge and Kress 1993: 2–3). The study of linguistics consequently became concerned with the ways in which language is used both to represent unequal relations of power, and to perpetuate them.

The asymmetrical distribution of power and social functions between social classes or different national or racial groups is reflected, and sustained, in language. Therefore, interest has focused more recently on the connections between the use of language and the sociopolitical practices and contexts that surround it, by placing discourse analysis within critical social theory and understanding that media discourse both constitutes, and is constituted by, social formation (Fairclough 1995). CDA explores the connections between the use of language and its context in order to draw conclusions not only about the transmission of meaning, but also about the role that this use of language plays in maintaining the conditions and relationships of power which are at the center of those meanings.

In this respect, Fowler et al. (1979: 2) argue that language embodies the inequalities of power that exists in society and that it is used to ensure that those inequalities persist. This is achieved by explicitly manipulating and creating "an apparent 'natural world' in which inequitable relations and processes are presented as given and inevitable." This type of linguistic manipulation is based on the premise that, if specific choices of words lead to contrasting views of reality, then those linguistic choices may be motivated by a will to offer a particular perspective or view of reality (1979: 1). If the use of language is determined by the will to perpetuate certain power relations, then we can argue that the production of discourse depends upon the circumstances and relationships that determine the ways in which social meanings are formed in any given context. The roles of the "more powerful" and the "less powerful" are consequently reaffirmed, reinforcing the division between those who have the power to control others, and those who are controlled (Fowler et al. 1979: 1–2).

One of the processes involved in the promotion of certain discourses (and the obscuration of others) is the naturalization of linguistic categories, "whereby elements and categories of media discourse, and its overall forms, become embedded in everyday practice and so become self-reproducing simply by being taken-for-granted as 'natural'" (Couldry 2008: 78). This apparently "natural" use of language is the focus of CDA research. CDA understands that this naturalization plays a role in obscuring certain aspects of reality, especially those related to social practices and power relations (Carvalho 2008: 162; Fairclough 1995: 54). However, it is not language itself that obscures the reality of sociopolitical structures, but the processes that surround the use of language and the production of discourse, including its naturalization and the development of communicative needs that must be served at each moment in time (Fowler et al. 1979). These communicative needs are served by institutional and media structures which work in the interest of the powerful. The role of CDA is to deconstruct the resulting discourses and the inequalities that they reproduce.

According to van Dijk (1993: 255), one of the social resources on which power is based is "the privileged access to discourse and communication." By "privileged access" van Dijk refers to the fact that different language users have varying degrees of "freedom in the use of special discourse genres or styles, or in the participation in specific communicative events and contexts," which include control over the conditions and consequences of discourse (1993: 256). In other words, there is a parallel between access to discourse, which, in journalism, involves the use of sources in the news, and social power (Bell 1991; Manning 2001). The power that social groups, institutions, or elites hold is directly proportional to the number of discourse genres, contexts, participants, audience, scope, and text characteristics that they (may) actively control or influence (van Dijk 1993: 256). There are, therefore, "hierarchies of definitional power" (Allan 1995: 131), as the reverse is also true: lack of power can be measured based on the lack of active access to discourse.

An important part of access to discourse involves access to the news media. This access is defined in terms of the news sources that provide the material that appears in the news. Overall, we can argue that there is a strong relationship of dependency between the news media and official sources, such as the government (Gans 1979). The consequence is that the media tend to reflect the interests of those in power by reproducing the categories and representations that they promote (Manning 2001), and by drawing attention to particular social issues, while other issues are not covered or receive less attention (Spector and Kitsuse 1977). The journalistic process of news gathering ensures that the powerful maintain their access to the media, perpetuating the imbalance of access to discourse and, subsequently, the power imbalance in the existing social order. Official views are privileged by the "hierarchy of credibility" that journalists rely upon and which reflects "the structures of power in society" (Manning 2001: 138). In this respect, Trew (1979: 115) argues that alternative versions can only happen if the news reports are committed to transforming the existing social order. Otherwise, the British media only allows for alternative voices to be heard marginally, as the media generally tend to reproduce official views.

Against this backdrop, CDA is concerned with exploring the ways in which reliance on certain sources determines the content of the news media, and with exposing the underlying power relations in relation to these practices. Carvalho (2008: 164) argues that "discourse" has two levels: on the one hand, the sources or social actors whose information is quoted, either directly or indirectly, in news reports; and, on the other hand, the journalists' own narrative when writing articles. While available literature on CDA considers these two levels to different extents, and most authors do not consider both at the same time, Carvalho argues that CDA analysts should pay attention to both levels of discourse.

POSTCOLONIAL CRITICAL DISCOURSE ANALYSIS

In the previous section, I have explained that Critical Discourse Analysis (CDA) seeks to critique the social relations of power which constitute, and are constituted by discourse, in order to denounce the dehumanizing and restrictive meanings and social inequalities which, as we have seen, are embedded in "dominant" discourses (Fairclough 1995; Fowler and Kress 1979: 196). These meanings must be analyzed by considering the historical context and the sociopolitical processes that shaped their formation and reproduction in media discourse. If we understand this historical context and sociopolitical processes in relation to the (post)colonial, it is worth exploring the ways in which postcolonial power relations are embedded in discursive practices. This is the objective of Postcolonial Critical Discourse Analysis (PCDA).

Martin and Rose (2003: 29) argue that the most effective way to understand the wider economic-historical context of a text and to gain a "clear view of social, cultural and economic changes at the macro level" is to explore both the text and the context that surrounds it from a discourse-historical perspective. These authors argue that feudalism, mercantilism, capitalism, and corporatism are historical developments in Western economic systems which have "tended towards an increasing reliance on abstract discursive rather than brute-physical coercion in the maintenance of inequalities" (2003: 29). While I argue against Martin and Rose's position, with respect to their separation between discursive and brute-physical coercion (since they both take place at the same time), I suggest that colonialism and postcolonialism should figure among the historical developments that they enumerate, since these two practices have played a crucial role in shaping contemporary power relations and structures around the world.

In a similar vein and as discussed earlier, Brunt and Cere (2011) argue that Postcolonial Theory (PT) is relevant to the interpretation of contemporary media cultures in order to demonstrate how these media cultures relate to the "metropolitan centre" of Britain. Developing this argument, Cere (2011: 3–12) introduces a cognitive map of concepts drawn from PT to indicate how the British media are transformed by postcolonial perspectives. These concepts include the relationship between the "coloniser" and the "colonised," "hybridity" and "mimicry," "orientalism" and "subalternity." The underlying rationale proposed by Cere is that contemporary Britain and its media production (including news production) should not be studied from the present, but should take into account how British political, social, and media discourses are shaped by the postcolonial. If the British media are infused with the historical, postcolonial connections between Britain and its former colonies, then a postcolonial theoretical framework should be considered for the analysis of discourse produced in postcolonial times. In keeping with the general premise argued by CDA, the discourses and representations derived from postcolonial times are representative of, and can be explained by, the postcolonial contexts in which they occurred.

Before exploring the tenets of PCDA, one more clarification regarding what I mean by postcolonial discourse would be useful. Bearing in mind that the postcolonial affects both the former coloniser and the former colony (Memmi 2003), the study of postcolonial discourse must explore discourses produced by any of the particular postcolonial entities. In other words, Postcolonial studies have indicated that both the colony and the metropolis are deeply affected by colonialism. Hall (1997: 246) argues that the postcolonial was "never simply external to the societies of the imperial metropolis" but was "always inscribed deeply within them." In this respect, we must acknowledge that "the West and the third world are seen as mutually constitutive entities that have emerged with their distinct characteristics due to their interaction" (Krishna 2009: 29–30). Therefore, although postcoloniality should not be understood in the same way in the metropolis as in the colony (since the roles of the metropolis and the colony were radically different in the colonial relationship, and the effects of this relationship were also profoundly dissimilar), we must acknowledge that the political, economic, social, cultural and historical effects of postcolonialism did not only impact the colony, but were also existent in the metropolis (Loomba 1998: 19). According to this view, Britain has a "postcolonial" relationship to its former colonies just as they are in a "postcolonial" position with regard to Britain, even though the consequences of the connection are considerably different. The objective of PCDA is, consequently, to explore postcolonial discourses produced within a postcolonial relationship, which means that the discourses analyzed may have been produced by any one of the postcolonial entities about the other.

THE MULTIDISCIPLINARY NATURE OF CRITICAL DISCOURSE ANALYSIS AND THE POSTCOLONIAL RUBRIC

As a method of analysis, CDA is inevitably multidisciplinary in nature, as it seeks to provide a comprehensive analysis of the relationships between text, social cognition, and social structures of power, always paying attention to "problems of oppression, injustice and inequality" (van Dijk 1993: 253). This multidisciplinary and issue-oriented approach calls for the combination of CDA with other theories and methods that can provide a critical approach to the understanding of social inequality and injustice (1993: 279). The inherent flexibility of CDA allows for a variety of "linkages among other well-established theoretical and methodological approaches" (Scollon 2001: 1), which means that CDA should draw openly from other theories of meaning in order to inform its research. In this respect, CDA benefits from PT because, through combination, PT provides CDA with theoretical insights for the development of a specific framework for discourse analysis. This framework, which is one of the existing "spin-off approaches" to CDA (Schrøeder 2012: 114), is based on (post)colonial encounters, both historical and contemporary.

Much work has already been done in applying linguistic analyses to postcolonial texts and literature (Krupat 1996; Thiong'o 1981; Tiffin 1987). Although there are some exceptions (Macdonald 2011), most available analyses focus on ethnicity and inequality. These approaches, however, do not make specific links with the postcolonial perspective, and as a result cannot be used to support the idea that understanding the specifically *postcolonial* nature of existing relations of power would help to advance the more established study of media production and representations (Brunt and Cere 2011). In order to make an advance of this kind, the causes and origins of some of the inequalities that CDA is concerned with, must be linked with the objectives of Postcolonial Critical Discourse Analysis (PCDA). This connection between the two positions would help to contextualize these inequalities, both historically and theoretically. The postcolonial approach should, therefore, be recognized as an essential tool and applied to a variety of media formats and case studies, so that the analyst can move beyond the study of literature.

Documenting PCDA as a recognized collection of studies would contribute to the strengthening of the field and its objectives in relation to the power inequalities with which both CDA and PT are concerned. Thus, the Postcolonial rubric within CDA helps to identify studies that examine discourse in relation to the power relations inherited from postcolonial backgrounds. It is also useful to acknowledge the wide range of contexts and experiences which are included within the Postcolonial heading, at the same time as we bring those postcolonial experiences together in order to define the boundaries of what constitutes this specific branch of CDA. A similar argument was made by Lazar (2007; 2008) in relation to Feminist Critical Discourse Analysis, based on the post-structuralist "view of discourse as a site of struggle, where forces of social (re)production and contestation are played out" (Lazar 2007: 4).

CLASSIFICATIONS AND SOCIAL INEQUALITY

We have seen that CDA is concerned with exposing the ways in which imbalances of power are reproduced in the discourse, while PT deals with imbalances of power which derive from (post)colonial encounters. Although they are separate theories, we may argue that they both share similar goals from their own particular perspectives. The main commonality of purpose within these theories is the impulse to denounce social inequality and injustice. While CDA takes a broader view of social inequalities, PT focuses specifically on the inequalities that relate to (post)colonial legacies. In this respect, the broad scope of CDA, which includes gender, race, and class inequalities, means that any unequal power relations that are visible in the discourse must be analyzed critically. According to Carvalho (2008: 162), the CDA researcher wants to "expose the causes and consequences of specific discourses and to denounce the social, cultural or political wrongs which they sustain." From the perspective of PT, the wrongs that are sustained result from previous colonial relations. Therefore, PCDA is a productive approach because it helps to expose some of these causes and consequences by recognizing that postcolonial legacies are at the center of some of the existing power imbalances in the world.

Earlier in this chapter, I have mentioned some of the ways in which people are classified into binary opposites (Hall 1997; Prakash 1995; Said 1978). One of the key aspects in this discussion is precisely the concept of "classification," by which different agents are defined according to certain categories. Classifications are a concern of both PT and CDA and, therefore, PCDA focuses on the discursive uses of classifications, which signify the difference between various agents, and contextualizes these uses in relation to the (post) colonial in order to shed light on the ways in which unequal relations are perpetuated within this context.

For example, the use of Orientalist classifications (Said 1978) as expressions of power becomes "both an instrument for exercising that power and containing perceived threats to that power" (Sardar 1999: 110). Orientalist discourse justified British rule thanks to the careful "enunciation of culturally nuanced knowledge," which inferiorized, exoticized and reified aspects of Oriental culture through the use of "seemingly benign and innocuous language" (Ghandour 2010: 3). For example, with regard to the emergence of Orientalist binary opposites in the Palestinian conflict, Ghandour (2010) argues that

> The introduction of conceptual basics such as 'Jews' and 'non-Jews', 'Moslems' and 'migrants', 'communities' and 'development', 'National Home' and 'Nation State', 'self-determination' and 'autonomy', 'extremists' and 'moderates', 'private' and 'public', 'religious' and 'secular', is one which has been taken for granted by historians as simply grasping and reflecting cultural realities but which, on the contrary, is deeply suggestive, fundamentally flawed, irrecuperably partial, and has contributed to the creation of novel/foreign binary oppositions and ditto cultural realities (Ghandour 2010: 3–4).

Although identifying how some of these categories are in fact a product of Orientalism may not be a straightforward task, the fact is that these categories classify and describe entities in relation to binary opposites, and they are driven by power divides and efforts to subjugate the Other.

THE "CRITICAL" PERSPECTIVE OF POSTCOLONIAL CRITICAL DISCOURSE ANALYSIS

I have stated that the aim of PCDA is to examine postcolonial discourses by placing them within the sociopolitical conditions in which they were produced, seeking a critical engagement with postcolonial relations of power, rather than providing a descriptive overview of cultural issues. One of the key elements of PCDA is, therefore, its "critical" perspective. According to Fowler and Kress (1979: 196), the "critical" nature of any linguistic interpretation is explained by the fact that so much of social meaning is implicit or hidden in texts, so we require an "activity of demystification" to unveil those meanings. In order to achieve this, critical linguists need to resist "the social processes which make language work in communication as it does" (1979: 196), for example, with reference to the naturalization of language and to established journalistic practices, which shape the communication of those meanings.

Indeed, CDA's notion of critique is derived from Adorno and Horkheimer (1977), which "consists of a desire and an obligation to intervene in social processes characterised by unequal power relations and mystifying ideologies, which are reproduced by discursive means" (Schrøeder 2012: 116). Van Dijk (1993) argues that when CDA analysts intervene in these processes, they should be explicit about their sociopolitical stance in relation to the power imbalances they address. In practice, this usually means that analysts take the perspective of

> those who suffer the most from dominance and inequality. Their critical targets are the power elites that enact, sustain, legitimate, condone or ignore social inequality and injustice. That is, one of the criteria of their work is solidarity with those who need it most (van Dijk 1993: 252).

Thus, "critical" refers to the critique (and not the description) of discourse, as well as the critique of the agents who produce the discourse with the purpose of reproducing and maintaining the existing unequal relations of power that favor them. In other words, critical scholars seek to expose the ways in which the interests of the powerful are protected and to defend the interests of those who suffer because of them (the powerless). Similarly, Fairclough (2009: 167) argues that the "critical" intent of CDA begins with a "focus upon a social wrong" in order to demonstrate how it has been constructed discursively and to face its political implications. As discussed in the previous section, this political element is concerned with exposing inequalities of power both discursively and in material terms. As Wodak and Meyer (2009: 32) point out, CDA is committed to social critique, and thus "constantly sits on the fence between social research and political argumentation."

Although some authors argue that taking a stance within a given social problem may lead to accusations of partisanship and lack of neutrality, and they condemn mixing scholarship with politics (Tyrwhitt-Drake 1999), we can also argue that the notion of neutrality toward a social issue is problematic "because it fails to recognise that all knowledge is socially and historically constructed and valuationally based" (Lazar 2007: 6). In a similar vein, Chouliaraki and Fairclough (1999) have contended that ideological commitment is an inherent part of CDA, but this does not affect its analytical ability because "the kind of interpretive work that CDA offers is closer to explanation than subjective understanding," so the theoretical and analytical value of CDA is not actually diminished (Carvalho 2008: 162).

In addition, some authors argue that the interpretative nature of CDA is also highlighted by the lack of a fixed methodological framework (Toolan 1997; Widdowson 1995). They argue that methodological diversity is problematic because CDA does not analyze discourse, but interprets it. However, I argue that methodological pluralism is not necessarily a weakness, and it can actually be considered to be a positive characteristic. This flexibility allows for the necessary theoretical, contextual, and empirical combinations and adaptations required by each specific case study, and therefore it helps to achieve the "critical" objectives of the analyses.

In PCDA, the "critical" nature of the analysis is given by the postcolonial perspective, that is, the "critical" stance is positioned in favor of the former colonized (the powerless in this relation), and seeks to uncover the ways in which those postcolonial, unequal relations of power are reproduced discursively. The refusal to be impartial and to criticize the entities that emerge as powerful is given by the nature of PT itself. Orientalism, for example, is never neutral or objective as "by definition it is a partial and partisan subject. No one comes to the subject without a background and baggage" (Sardar 1999: vii).

THE IMPORTANCE OF CONTEXT

As mentioned throughout this chapter, a crucial part in the study of discourse is related to the context in which it is produced. Van Dijk (1993), for instance, points out that CDA takes into account the fundamental causes, conditions, and consequences of discourse in order to "make a more specific contribution and to get more insight into the crucial role of discourse in the reproduction of dominance and inequality" (Van Dijk 1993: 253). Indeed, the causes and conditions in which discourse is produced are given by its context, and therefore this context must be taken into account when attempting to understand the social conditions that surrounded the production of, and are present in, discourse.

Nunan (1993) points out that there are two types of context. The first one is the linguistic context, which is "the language that surrounds or accompanies the piece of discourse under analysis." The second type of context is the non-linguistic or experiential one. This is where the "discourse takes place," and it includes "the type of communicative events [. . .]; the topic; the purpose of the event; the setting [. . .]; the participants and the relationships between them; and the background knowledge and assumptions underlying the communicative event" (Nunan 1993: 8). This type of context refers to the extratextual circumstances that surround the production of texts, and it is the one that the various historical approaches to CDA must take into account in their analyses.

However, Carvalho (2008: 163) argues that "most forms of analysis do not express awareness of the time sequence of texts nor do they clearly explain the implications of previous discursive positions on subsequent ones." She draws upon Hyatt (2005: 515) to highlight the need for an analysis of the temporal context of a text, which includes the immediate and medium-term sociopolitical contexts, the contemporary sociopolitical individuals, organisations and structures and the more long-term temporal context which includes the various assumptions of order, structures of inclusion and exclusion, and generally how a society legitimates itself and achieves its social identity (Carvalho 2008: 163).

The relevance of context, whether historical or contemporary, is closely related to what Reisigl and Wodak (2009: 88) refer to as the socio-diagnostic critique, which draws upon contextual knowledge and relevant social theories to identify and expose ideological and manipulative discursive elements in relation to the social, political, and economic conditions that shaped them. In PCDA, PT provides CDA with a macro-context by which the postcolonial perspective provides both a historical and a theoretical context. Historically, we must look at the evolution of events and conditions within each particular context in terms of its colonial past and its subsequent postcolonial relations. Theoretically, relevant postcolonial theories must be identified according to the context or case study under analysis (in this chapter, the analysis draws upon Orientalism). While the historical contextualization provides specific details about the particular colony's transition from being colonized to being "postcolonial" and its subsequent postcolonial relations, the theoretical contextualization facilitates an appropriate theory of meaning which helps to understand the ways in which postcolonial power relations are present in the discourse.

In addition, PCDA must also deal with the ways in which past events are constructed in more contemporary discourses. For example, a contemporary news article may make references to a past event. The historical approach of PCDA allows for the comparative analysis of the ways in which the same event was covered originally and how it was covered again at a later date. Thus, the concern of PCDA with context is also manifested in the recognition that processes of re-contextualization and de-contextualization may take place when a previous event is removed from its original context and is retold from a different context, or is not told at all. Although these processes are by no means exclusive of postcolonial discourses, PCDA provides a framework to interpret how the past is re-contextualized in contexts other than its original one and what these processes tell us in terms of postcolonial relations of power.

The analysis of re-contextualized events must also consider the fact that, even though we are concerned with the postcolonial era, this does not mean that the postcolonial is a homogenous time period. As with all historical phases, we must acknowledge that, while postcolonial conditions are constant in some ways (so long as the break away from the colonial heritage does not fully take place), circumstances evolve historically to the extent that the postcolonial phase may become characterized by other parallel developments and may therefore be overridden by other elements at different points in time. In these cases, PCDA remains a relevant framework because these developments still take place within the postcolonial era, but these parallel circumstances highlight the necessity of contextualizing any case studies in relation to their own histories.

CONCLUSION

In conclusion, I have argued in favor of recognizing a Postcolonial rubric within CDA, as PCDA is particularly concerned with discourses rooted in postcolonial relations of power. We have seen that CDA is concerned with "the relations between discourse, power, dominance, social inequality, and the position of the discourse analyst in such social relations" (van Dijk 1993: 249). It is concerned with issues of unequal access to discourse and information, and with the role of discourse in the reproduction of existing power relations. When analyzing social inequalities, CDA favors the oppressed or powerless and considers the broader social processes that are involved in the production of discourse. I have argued that the insights of PT, are useful to contextualize some of these broader social processes from a theoretical perspective. I have also pointed out that this postcolonial approach not only contextualizes the analysis theoretically, but it also places it historically in terms of the particular developments and scenarios that have characterized the postcolonial era in each context.

The empirical application of PCDA helps to reveal how, and the extent to which, media production and representations are shaped by postcolonial relations, based both on the textual elements that are visible in the text and those that are absent. Specifically, I have discussed the importance of analyzing linguistic classifications that reflect, and are explained by, specific ideological standpoints and power divisions. This is only one of several aspects that PCDA can help to unpack. It also offers a framework for examining other aspects such as, for example, the use of news sources which promote the postcolonial center's perspective, while other news sources (particularly those from the periphery) tend to be neglected. In addition, the focus of PCDA on the postcolonial also helps to examine the historical contextualization of contemporary conflicts and struggles that are rooted in colonial times. In this respect, we can identify the extent to which this contextualization is developed in the news coverage of those issues. Exploring them from the postcolonial approach emphasized by PCDA restores the largely neglected historical connection of the (post)colonial center to its proper place in understanding the significance of media representations.

NOTE

1. Magdoff (1978) argues that we must be clear about the difference between "colonialism" and "imperialism," as "the customary identification of imperialism with colonialism is an obstacle to the proper study of the subject, since colonialism existed before the modern form of imperialism and the latter has outlived colonialism." There

are pre-modern forms of imperialism (e.g., the Roman Empire) and the modern form which, from a historical viewpoint, follows "the colonialism of the last five centuries," which is "closely associated with the birth and maturation of the capitalist socioeconomic system" (Magdoff 1978: 117).

REFERENCES

Adorno, Theodor W., and Max Horkheimer (1977). "The Culture Industry: Enlightenment as Mass Deception." In *Mass Communication and Society*, edited by James Curran, Michael Gurevitch, and Janet Woollacott, 349–83. London: Arnold.

Allan, Stuart (1995). "News, truth and postmodernity: unravelling the will to facticity." In *Theorizing Culture: An Interdisciplinary Critique After Postmodernism*, edited by Barbara Adam and Stuart Allan, 129–144. London: Routledge.

Ashcroft, Bill, Gareth Griffiths, and Helen Tiffin (eds.) (2006). *The Post-colonial Studies Reader*. London: Routledge.

Bell, Allan (1991). *The Language of News Media*. Oxford: Blackwell.

Bhabha, Homi K. (1985). "Signs taken for wonders." In *The Post-colonial Studies Reader*, edited by Bill Ashcroft, Gareth Griffiths, and Helen Tiffin (2006), 38–43. London: Routledge.

Brunt, Rosalind, and Rinella Cere (eds.) (2011). *Postcolonial Media Culture in Britain*. Hampshire: Palgrave Macmillan.

Carvalho, Anabela (2008). "Media(ted) discourse and society: Rethinking the framework of Critical Discourse Analysis." *Journalism Studies* 9(2):161–77.

Cere, Rinella (2011). "Postcolonial and media studies: A cognitive map." In *Postcolonial Media Culture in Britain*, edited by Rosalind Brunt and Rinella Cere, 1–13. Hampshire: Palgrave Macmillan.

Chouliaraki, Lilie, and Norman Fairclough (1999). *Discourse in Late Modernity: Rethinking Critical Discourse Analysis*. Edinburgh: Edinburgh University Press.

Couldry, Nick (2008). "Media discourse and the naturalisation of categories." In *Handbook of Communication in the Public Sphere*, edited by Ruth Wodak and Veronika Koller, 67–88. Berlin, New York: Mouton de Gruyter.

Eagleton, Terry (1998). "Postcolonialism: The case of Ireland." In *Multicultural States: Rethinking Difference and Identity*, edited by David Bennett, 125–134. London: Routledge

Fairclough, Norman (1995). *Media Discourse*. London: Edward Arnold.

Fairclough, Norman (2009). "A dialectical-relational approach to critical discourse analysis in social research." In *Methods for Critical Discourse Analysis*, edited by Ruth Wodak and Michael Meyer, 162–86. London: Sage.

Fowler, Roger, and Gunther Kress (1979). "Critical linguistics." In *Language and control*, edited by Roger Fowler and Bob Hodge, 185–213. London: Routledge & Kegan Paul.

Fowler, Roger, and Bob Hodge (1979). *Language and control*. London: Routledge & Kegan Paul.

Gandhi, Leela (1998). *Postcolonial Theory: A Critical Introduction*. Edinburgh: Edinburgh University Press.

Gans, Herbert J. (1979). *Deciding What's News: A Study of CBS Evening News, NBC Nightly News, Newsweek, and Time*. New York: Pantheon Books.

Ghandour, Zeina B. (2010). *A Discourse on Domination in Mandate Palestine. Imperialism, Property and Insurgency*. Abingdon: Routledge.

Hall, Stuart (ed.) (1997). *Representations: Cultural Representations and Signifying Practices*. London: Sage.

Hyatt, David (2005). "Time for a change: a critical discoursal analysis of synchronic context with diachronic relevance." *Discourse & Society* 16(4): 515–34.

Harper, Graeme (ed.) (2001). *Colonial and Post-Colonial Incarceration*. London: Continuum.

Hodge, Robert, and Gunther Kress (1993). *Language as Ideology*. London: Routledge.

Krishna, Sankaran (2009). *Globalization and Postcolonialism: Hegemony and Resistance in the Twenty-first Century*. Plymouth: Rowman & Littlefield.

Krupat, Arnold (1996). "Postcolonialism, ideology, and native American literature." In *The Post-colonial Studies Reader*, edited by Bill Ashcroft, Gareth Griffiths, and Helen Tiffin (2006), 176–79. London: Routledge.

Lazar, Michelle M. (ed.) (2007). *Feminist Critical Discourse Analysis*. Basingstoke: Palgrave Macmillan.

Lazar, Michelle M. (ed.) (2008). "Language, communication and the public sphere: A perspective from feminist critical discourse analysis." In *Handbook of Communication in the Public Sphere*, edited by Ruth Wodak and and Veronika Koller, 89–110. Berlin, New York: Mouton de Gruyter.

Lloyd, David (1993). *Anomalous States: Irish Writing and the Post-Colonial Moment*. Durham: Duke University Press.

Loomba, Ania (1998). *Colonialism/Postcolonialism*. London: Routledge.

Macdonald, Myra (2011). "Discourses of separation: News and documentary representations of Muslims in Britain." In *Postcolonial Media Culture in Britain*, edited by Rosalind Brunt and Rinella Cere, 127–41. Hampshire: Palgrave Macmillan.

Magdoff, Harry (1978). *Imperialism: From the Colonial Age to the Present Essays*. New York: Monthly Review Press.

Manning, Paul (2001). *News and News Sources: A Critical Introduction*. London: Sage.

Martin, J.R. and David Rose (2003). *Working with Discourse. Meaning Beyond the Clause*. London: Continuum.

Memmi, Albert (2003). *The Colonizer and the Colonized*. London: Earthscan.

Nunan, David (1993). *Introducing Discourse Analysis*. London: Penguin.

Prakash, Gyan (1995). "After Colonialism." In *After Colonialism: Imperial Histories and Postcolonial Displacements*, edited by Gyan Prakash, 3–17. Princeton: Princeton University Press.

Reisigl, Michael, and Ruth Wodak (2009). "The Discourse-Historical Approach (DHA)." In *Methods for Critical Discourse Analysis*, edited by Ruth Wodak and Michael Meyer, 87–121. London: Sage.

Said, Edward W. (1978). *Orientalism*. London: Routledge and Kegan Paul.

Sardar, Ziauddin (1999). *Orientalism*. Buckingham: Open University Press.

Schrøder, Klaus C. (2012). "Discursive Realities." In *A Handbook of Media and Communication Research: Qualitative and Quantitative Methodologies*, edited by Klaus B. Jensen, 106–130. Abingdon: Routledge.

Scollon, Ron (2001). *Mediated Discourse: The Nexus of Practice*. London: Routledge.
Spector, Malcolm, and John I. Kitsuse (1977). *Constructing Social Problems*. New York: Aldine de Gruyter.
Thiong'o, Ngugi W. (1981). "The language of African literature." In *The Post-colonial Studies Reader*, edited by Bill Ashcroft, Gareth Griffiths, and Helen Tiffin (2006), 263–65. London: Routledge.
Tiffin, Helen. (1987). "Post-colonial literatures and counter-discourse." In *The Post-colonial Studies Reader*, edited by Bill Ashcroft, Gareth Griffiths, and Helen Tiffin (2006), 99–101. London: Routledge.
Toolan, Michael (1997). "What is critical discourse analysis and why are people saying such terrible things about it?" *Language and Literature* 6(2): 83–103.
Trew, Tony (1979). "Theory and ideology at work." In *Language and control*, edited by Roger Fowler and Bob Hodge, 94–116. London: Routledge & Kegan Paul.
Tyrwhitt-Drake, Hugh (1999). "Resisting the discourse of critical discourse analysis: reopening a Hong Kong case study." *Journal of Pragmatics* 31: 1081–1088.
van Dijk, Teun A. (1993). "Principles of Critical Discourse Analysis." *Discourse & Society* 4(2): 249–283.
Widdowson, Henry G. (1995). "Discourse analysis: a critical view." *Language and Literature* 4(3): 157–172.
Wodak, Ruth (2009). "Language and politics." In *English Language. Description, Variation and Context*, edited by Jonathan Culpeper, Francis Katamba, and Paul Kerswill, 576–93. Basingstoke: Palgrave Macmillan.
Wodak, Ruth, and Michael Meyer (eds.) (2009). *Methods for Critical Discourse Analysis*. London: Sage.
Young, Robert (2001). *Postcolonialism: An Historical Introduction*. Oxford: Blackwell.

Part II

CLASS ANALYSIS OF MEDIA AND CULTURE

Chapter Five

Class and Gender Inequalities in the Process of Political Communication

Canadian Illustrations[1]

Debra M. Clarke

This chapter illustrates the extent and significance of class and gender inequalities within political communication generally and, in particular, with respect to television journalism, which continues to be a primary vehicle of political communication. It calls upon original longitudinal data regarding the case of Canadian society as well as research conducted by communication scholars elsewhere. A central concern is to trace how these social inequalities are manifest in the dynamics of news production and news reception, and in such a way that television journalism, and political communication more generally, effectively contribute to the political exclusion of major social groups such as women and the working class.

Class inequalities are examined along a range of different dimensions, including the remarkable degree of homogeneity in the class origins of professional journalists and news producers generally, journalistic assumptions about the class characteristics of news publics, the capacity of journalism to construct the notion of a singular and classless "public," how social class is visible and invisible within news stories, as well as how, and how importantly, class figures within the reception of news. In the discussion of gender that follows, it is demonstrated further that reception needs to be understood principally in conjunction with production and, to a lesser extent, in conjunction with the nature of the news text that results from what continues to be a highly gendered news production process. The analysis proceeds from a brief review of the literature regarding gender inequalities within professional journalism to the presentation of original multi-modal research regarding gendered patterns of news reception in the Canadian case. Highlights of household interviews, results derived from a NVivo analysis of interview transcripts, observations regarding gender dynamics operative in reception, and pertinent material derived from news diaries and questionnaires are reported. This material is considered alongside the existent research evidence regarding gendered viewership practices.

The results suggest that the constraints of professional journalism contribute to the persistence of class differences in political participation as well as to women's limited engagement with both offline and online news sources—a limited level of engagement which in turn contributes to women's low levels of political engagement. Overall, the chapter seeks to shed light upon classical and contemporary debates regarding the relationship between journalism and political participation as well as less empirically informed debates regarding gendered conditions of news production and reception (see the entire analysis in Clarke 2014).[2]

First and foremost, the audiences to political communication need to be understood as socially structured and stratified, as Morley (1980) demonstrates powerfully in his highly influential study of the BBC program *Nationwide*'s audiences. It is very much a reflection of the circuitous trajectory of reception studies that, many years later, Kim (2004) was compelled to resurrect that long-neglected lesson in a re-analysis of Morley's data which retraces and quantifies the empirical connections between social class and news reception. Additionally, progress toward the refinement of the concept of intersectionality has redirected attention to class, together with other social traits seen to delimit a multiplicity of interpretatively significant clusters within audiences. While these are useful conceptual directions, the analytical danger is that too much emphasis can be placed upon what some perceive to be highly situated reception experiences. This can occur to the extent that some communication scholars conclude their studies of reception with exasperation regarding its multiple complexities or, faithful to the contemporary social psychology turn, with a needless insistence upon attention to extremely individuated processes of identity constitution that are seen to pivotally shape reception outcomes. More problematic are those analyses inclined to abandon, dismiss, or neglect the use of class, gender, ethnicity, and other social boundary markers to the point at which macro-social and even micro-social insights can be lost. This raises the difficult questions to be addressed in this chapter regarding how class, gender, and other social divisions among audiences figure within the news reception process.

At the micro-level of individual reception experiences, families and households must be acknowledged as important phenomena that contextualize and that can either facilitate or constrain the ways in which a particular individual responds to news stories, whether the news is received inside or outside a household setting. Whether the familial impact is inclined to constrain or facilitate a critical interpretation of news is undoubtedly a fascinating question, although even the most extensive ethnographic fieldwork cannot expect to trace and document the precise nature and extent of that familial influence, nor can individual research participants be expected to appreciate it fully and report it accurately to researchers. Nevertheless, household interviews do present the opportunity to witness directly some of the impacts of familial interactions during news reception. While familial influences extend to all other reception settings as well, with or without the actual physical presence of family members, it is within the household that such influences become most evident, rendered explicit through social interactions around the television set.

Concurrent with these significant impacts are the visible operations of the impacts of macro-level class and gender inequalities at the micro-level of the households in which news is regularly received. Clement (2002: 3) situates households together with labor markets and state practices as sites that are each "infused with particular class and gender relations." Furthermore, he clarifies a crucial point regarding how class and gender need to be perceived in relation to everyday practices and experiences within households. He makes it clear that class and gender "are not 'outcomes' so much as *organizers* of practices and experiences" (5–6, emphasis added). This is precisely how the actions of class and gender in news reception need to be understood—not as "outcomes" that somehow predispose some social groups toward inevitable and immutable interpretations and responses but, rather, as existent, powerful social conditions and sources of social division whose power resides, at least in part, in their capacity to structure and organize the different experiences of different social groups. Those different experiences can, at least to some extent, be expected to shape specific experiences of news reception and thereby differentiated and unequal experiences of the process of political communication.

Clement (2002: 18) also makes the point that "households can be complex sites for class." What has added further complexity to analyses of the operation of class within households generally, and within household news reception particularly, is the contemporary preoccupation with "identities," or "perceived interests," of *individual* social subjects, frequently understood to be tied to a multi-textured negotiation of multiple intersecting social conditions, among which class is sometimes included although no longer necessarily deemed primary. Other conditions extend, for example, to gender, ethnicity, age, nationality, and citizenship, all of which are similarly understood to contribute to how social subjects are constituted, come to perceive their social location, and identify their self-interests. Clement (e.g., 2002, 2004), Mosco (2009), and others suggest that the time has come to revive a relational conceptualization of class—one that can connect it to gender, ethnicity, and to the "*social movements* that organize the energies of resistance to class (and other forms of) power" (Mosco 2009: 191, emphasis in original). This conceptualization understands class as much more than merely a particular attribute of institutions or individuals (see also Clement 2004: 43). Above all, as Mosco (2009: 191) suggests, there is a need to connect class more tightly to hegemony.

With shared concerns, Golding (1994: 461) insisted more than two decades ago that communication research "must reconnect with wider questions of social inequality, power, and process." During the same period, Garnham (1992: 362), like many others, observed "the creation of a two-tier market divided between the information-rich (provided with high-cost specialized information and cultural services) and the information-poor (provided with increasingly homogenized entertainment services on a mass scale)." Have either of these disconnections been overcome in the twenty-first century? On the contrary, neoliberalism has effectively erased class issues, as such, from the political agenda as well as the research agenda of many scholars, while digital divides, contrary to popular mythology and the vast propaganda of ICT marketers, have become established as a new and largely impermeable dimension of social stratification, such that entire segments of the population remain without the full benefits of access to online communication. This continuing digital exclusion results in direct detrimental impacts upon various social groups (see DiMaggio et al. 2004; Mesch and Talmud 2010; Robinson 2012; van Dijk 2005; Witte and Mannon 2010), although class differences remain "the strongest predictor of digital inequality" (Robinson 2012: 91). *The extent to which digital exclusion is tied to broader forms of political and social exclusion is a very serious research question that still needs to be explored thoroughly.*

Levitas (2006, 2008) is among those stalwart researchers who challenge the observed disappearance of class politics and other such neoliberal arguments which insist that class has lost its political and even its general social significance. As she points out, one of the important distinctions missed by these arguments is

> the distinction between class politics as a form of resistance and struggle by the working classes, and class politics as a form of attack on the working classes, broadly defined as those who must sell their labour to survive. I argue that class is not dead. Class remains the key structuring principle of people's life chances … the *apparent* absence of class politics—that is a class-based politics of resistance from below—is actually the product of the *presence* of class politics: three decades of class war from above that has been successful both economically and hegemonically. (Levitas 2008: 1, emphases added)

Nevertheless, she grants that class appears to be less significant "as an organising identification for a politics of resistance and transformation" (p. 2). She explains it with reference to the particular economic and political dynamics operative under Thatcherite and New Labour neoliberalism in the UK—a set of dynamics by no means unique to that society. The rhetoric of neoliberalism there and elsewhere promotes the notion that complex identities and affiliations are associated with ethnic origin and religion. These are not, however, "intrinsically antithetical to class-based politics," although, as Levitas points out, notions of complex identities that somehow supersede class can serve to marginalize class "as the basis of collective self-understandings" (p. 3). As she concludes, "the hegemonic representation of reference to class as divisive works very well to prevent the development of class consciousness, and to conceal this still fundamental division between the super-rich and the bulk of the population" (ibid., emphasis in original).

In order to examine the significance of class and other social inequalities in the process of political communication broadly and, specifically, in the relationship between news reception and political engagement, the current project called upon a targeted sample of adults, resident in a central Canadian city, who are active in a variety of community organizations. Altogether, there were three overlapping groups of research participants who completed semi-structured questionnaires and/or agreed to unstructured household interviews and/or completed semi-structured one-week news diaries (see the complete methodological details in Clarke 2014: 135–42, 275–81). Interviews were conducted and the other data were gathered over the course of a seven-year fieldwork period that extended from 2001 to 2007. In all three samples, participants represented a wide range of diverse social characteristics. While the term "social class" may not be at the forefront of their discussions of their social locations or their motivations as activists and volunteers (nor should that be expected, in view of the discursive patterns of hegemonic neoliberalism), it is nevertheless clear that there is, among the working-class participants, a fundamental awareness of social inequalities and many of their concrete, everyday repercussions. There are certainly various levels of such awareness among many middle-class participants as well. What is also evident, particularly among the working-class participants, is a common disenchantment with the comparative invisibility of their class in news, a common dissatisfaction with the manner in which the infrequent appearances of working-class people are framed in news, and a common sense of disconnection from the middle-class manner in which news is presented. These class-based reception experiences are illustrated in the interview, news diary, and questionnaire material cited later.

Middle-class journalists and other news producers have the opportunity to fashion, or at least to participate in the creation of, their own representations, whereas their working-class audiences can only reconcile themselves to a representation of their own class that is externally imposed. This, in turn, becomes a primary source of their alienation from all class representations that appear, tacitly and otherwise, in the political discourse of news.

The discussion of class here is undoubtedly briefer than it needs to be, and it can only call upon what has been remarkably scant attention to class in the otherwise extensive scholarly and non-scholarly literature regarding journalism. It is at least possible to draw attention to questions such as how and why class is visible and in other ways invisible in news, and to the inescapable implications for the different, class-based ways in which news is received.

THE (IN)VISIBILITY OF CLASS IN NEWS

Based upon her analysis of news sources in the case of British newspapers, Karen Ross (2011: 11) sets forth a strong argument that concisely captures the essence of who continues to be heard and visible, and who remains largely unheard and invisible, in news:

> Who is invited to speak as a commentator on and in the news says vitally important things about who "counts" in society, and whose voices have legitimacy and status. The hierarchy of news values identified by Gans thirty years ago, which made clear that some sources were more equal than others, is alive and well in the twenty-first century journalist's toolbox: citizens are simply not as equal as government spokespeople, and women are almost never as equal as men. The infatuation which journalists have with the authoritative male source means there is little room for other kinds of voices, namely those of women, minorities, the general public or challengers to the status quo.

With regard to the American case, Ehrenreich (2007: 1) presents a yet more broadly sweeping picture of the class blindness that is ubiquitous throughout American news media, which she sees as "an entirely local phenomenon: the disappearance of the American working class—from the media, from intellectual concern, or more generally, from the mind of the American middle class." Her definition of working class is also comparatively sweeping, to the extent that it is seen to comprise 60 to 70 percent of the US population.[3] As she describes it, a limited and by no means unproblematic attention to the working class in the 1970s, principally in a number of noteworthy mass market films such as *Blue Collar*, *The Deer Hunter*, and *Saturday Night Fever*, eventually culminated, following the acceleration of neoliberalism in the 1980s, in the more or less complete disappearance of the working class from mainstream American media.[4] At the same time, the working class largely disappeared from academic discourse, and "discourse" itself, as a newly fashionable object of analysis, supplanted scholarly interest in class, which was largely dismissed as a pertinent social category (2007: 2). In the news, "working class people are likely to cross the screen only as witnesses to crimes or sports events, never as commentators or—even when their own lives are under discussion—as 'experts'" (ibid.).

If we ask why the working class is largely unheard and unseen in news, it is useful to consider the class backgrounds of journalists and other professionals who produce news. Their current social locations are solidly within the middle class, and there is considerable international evidence that most have spent their entire lives in that class location. It can be seen as consequential in the sense that professional journalists, while bound in many ways by the structures of the journalistic field (in Bourdieu's sense, including the news values which dictate, for example, that stories must be substantiated by official and other "authoritative" sources who are almost invariably middle-class spokespersons), can nevertheless exercise degrees of agency vis-à-vis those structures—for example, in their selection of stories and of other interviewees. In other words, while their professional need to justify a story with suitably "credible" sources frequently directs them away from the working class, particularly in view of the time constraints, there are also moments of agency in which some freedom of choice can be exercised and, during such moments, the proclivity towards middle-class stories and middle-class spokespersons is evident in the news texts that result. Hence, while we cannot call upon class monogamy exclusively to explain the class-blind character of news, it needs to be at least entertained within our accounts of that class blindness.[5]

The limits to a strictly demographic explanation of class blindness are suggested by Pritchard and Sauvageau's (1999: 288) finding that more than two-thirds of Canadian journalists declared "letting ordinary people express their views" to be a very important function of journalism. Clearly, there are structural constraints as well as specific organizational constraints that effectively prohibit the fulfillment of that perceived function, including the dictates of the journalistic field which confine the voices of "ordinary people" to brief "vox pop" or "voice of the people" segments within newscasts. As Pritchard and Sauvageau conclude, "the content of news stories is determined principally by organizational needs, not individual journalists' personal opinions" (p. 301).

To what extent can we call upon the predominantly middle-class composition of the news production workforce in order to explain working-class exclusion from news, or what may actually be a tacit or implicit classism in news content which arises from that demographic composition? Heider and Fuse (2004), in their analysis of local American broadcast news, address this question in their direct examination of newsroom decisions regarding class (On the peculiarities of news production constraints at the local level, see, for example also, Poindexter, Heider, and McCombs 2006, and Ross 2011). While their inclination is to emphasize the individuals in the newsroom and their social characteristics, there is a need to emphasize the underlying political economy of decisions that routinely exclude the working class. Their own observations reveal that only two classes exist within newsroom discourse: a privileged class of people who are in the target market and all those who are not. Rather than attribute a class bias to news producers based upon their class locations and class backgrounds, it is more useful to see this demography as a factor that reinforces what is a major structural force—namely, the fundamental economic need to attract wealthy and middle-class audiences. That those who produce news content are inclined to be middle class themselves merely helps to ensure that working-class news is absent. Heider and Fuse conclude definitively that "news was constructed as a product aimed primarily at those who had disposable income, lived in the suburbs, and had significant purchasing power" (p. 105). A news producer in their study expressed it rather bluntly: "A lot of us don't come from poor backgrounds. A lot of us don't understand that and don't think those people watch. You know, we do homeless stories when the weather gets cold and so forth because it is something we can feel compassion for. But on a day-to-day basis we aren't going to do a lot of those stories" (cited in Heider and Fuse 2004: 104). To that explanation, Kurpius (2004: 333–4) adds that there are also other factors, intrinsic to the structure of the everyday news production process, that act in conjunction with market forces to limit the working-class presence in news:

> Market forces are not the only reason for limited coverage of class. The complexity of the issue does not lend itself to television coverage. Journalists need an educational background and experience in lower and working class communities to more fully develop an understanding of class issues. This makes reporting in that area difficult at best for many reporters. Time and resource constraints also limit the possibilities for developing coverage on such a complex topic … These are not neighborhoods that journalists can simply parachute into, get a story, and get out with good contextual information that accurately portrays issues of class.

What may exacerbate the difficulties described by Kurpius is the long-standing cultural insularity of the professional middle class, a cultural insularity that some suggest has intensified with the rise of neoliberalism and the class polarizing tendencies that became evident during the 1980s. Ehrenreich (2007: 2), for example, speaks of the "natural solipsism of the professional middle class" and suggests that "classes are less likely to mix in college (with the decline of financial aid), in residential neighborhoods (with the gluttonous rise in real estate prices), or even in the malls (with the now almost universal segmentation of the retail industry into upscale and downscale components). Only the homeless disturb the middle class's contemplation of itself and its self-images."

In her comments cited earlier, Ross made reference to Gans's seminal *Deciding What's News*, which, as long ago as 1979, demonstrated that "the news especially values the order of the upper-class and middle-class sectors of society" (Gans 1979: 61). Gans demonstrated further that, because journalists are positioned within these sectors themselves and many have never experienced life outside of these classes, it is the wealthy and middle classes who are best represented in news. Almost a quarter-century later, in his *Democracy and the News*, Gans (2003: 104) expresses his regrets that "the newsroom class makeup, and therefore the racial one, remain sadly deficient. Good intentions are clearly not working and in the academy as in the newsrooms, new recruitment methods and criteria of merit must be invented to end discrimination against people of working class origin and varied skin colors."

As Hindman's (2009) seminal research in *The Myth of Digital Democracy* demonstrates, the news dominance of white middle-class men extends from print and broadcast newsrooms to online news sites and the entire blogosphere of political communication. A great paradox of the Internet is that, despite the claims of marketers and scholars who have insisted upon its "democratizing" potential, the empirical reality is that the same exclusivity characteristic of so-called old media has been replicated throughout cyberspace (see also McChesney 2013). Hindman's documentation clearly establishes that online political discourse is dominated by a remarkably small group of men who are exceptionally well equipped with the resources needed to establish a strong presence and voice. The economic power of the few corporations that control digital information flows, in conjunction with related technological factors that intrinsically favor a hierarchical rather than a collective egalitarian Internet exchange, ensures that existent structures of social inequality and political exclusion are perpetuated and reinforced. In Hindman's words, "ultimately, blogs have given a small group of educational, professional, and technical elites new influence in US politics. Blogs have done far less to amplify the political voice of average citizens" (p. 103). (See especially his summary of class, gender, and ethnicity data in Hindman 2009: 122–5). Moreover, Schradie's (2012: 569) analysis of social inequalities in the blogosphere concludes: "Instead of a trend toward more egalitarian findings, blogging shows a consistent gap … [I]t is socio-economic class inequality that is most persistent." Some of the ways in which these class-based exclusions figure within news reception are considered in the following section.

THE SIGNIFICANCE OF CLASS IN NEWS RECEPTION

The extensive history of class bias in scholarly and non-scholarly visions of audiences has been traced by the historical sociologist Richard Butsch (see especially Butsch 2000, 2001, and 2008). Sociologists Paul Lazarsfeld and Robert Merton first used the term "narcotizing dysfunction" in 1948 to describe media effects, with the implication that working-class people in particular were especially vulnerable to the perceived "narcotic" effects that—so it was believed but never demonstrated—would literally immobilize them and thereby necessarily preclude their participation in civic life (Lazarsfeld and Merton 1948). Quantitative survey research supported by commercial sources, including American networks such as CBS and NBC as well as advertising agencies, and reported to general readers in books such as *The Age of Television* (Bogart 1956), *The Effects of Mass Communication* (Klapper 1960), *Living with Television* (Glick and Levy 1962), and *The People Look at Television* (Steiner 1963), led to the creation of the concept of the heavy viewer, defined by the sheer quantity of viewing. The concept of the heavy viewer, and the distinction between light and heavy viewers, clearly suited the interests and needs of the advertisers and broadcasters who financed such research. The quantitatively measured heavy viewing later came to be associated with indiscriminate viewing as well as with a parental failure to supervise children's viewing, all of which were attributed to working-class viewers and became known as a syndrome called "passive viewing" (Butsch 2008: 131, 174–5). Significantly less research attention was directed at "active" viewers who presumably used television selectively (or at least used it less, because other leisure pursuits are affordable to middle-class viewers) and who presumably restricted children's viewership.

As Butsch (2008: 131) found in his historical analysis, one of the worst outcomes of this early television research was "the construction of the image of the inert, slovenly, working class male television viewer." For example, in *Living with Television* (1962), two market researchers, Ira Glick and Sidney Levy, focus upon class differences and literally equate working-class viewers with children who sought "immediate gratification" from television and who cultivated no other interests. In contrast, wealthier viewers were perceived to be selective and tasteful in their television spectatorship, displaying high levels of cultural capital. Butsch (2008: 131) points out that "such descriptions contributed to the larger discourse that used television use as an indicator of status." Arguably, it also contributed to the disconnection between, on the one hand, scholarly researchers, who are commonly without any direct personal experience of working-class life and, on the other hand, the television medium as well as television research in general and television reception research in particular.

Unfortunately, the class biases of predominantly middle-class scholars also crept into research regarding children's television use. A pivotal early study was carried out by Wilbur Schramm and his graduate students at Stanford, Jack Lyle and Edwin Parker, who reported their results in *Television in the Lives of Our Children* (Schramm, Lyle, and Parker 1961). Their work established a path that has been well-traveled by many publications about children and television and that also influenced the direction of the oft-cited US Surgeon-General's reports in 1972. That path began, directly and explicitly, with class bias. Schramm and his students literally introduced their argument with a claim that television effects were contingent upon a family's social norms, "by which they meant social class differences. Particularly striking is the negative language they used to characterize the working class and to summarize their findings about them" (Butsch 2008: 131).

It was argued that the middle class pursued a "work ethic" that resulted in less television viewing and in viewing that was principally directed at documentary and self-improvement programs. In contrast, what was perceived as the working-class "pleasure ethic" was presumed to increase both the overall amount of television viewing and the volume of entertainment and fantasy programs viewed. That entire viewership group was labeled the "fantasy group," which ostensibly contrasted sharply with the middle-class "reality group" (Schramm, Lyle, and Parker 1961, cited in Butsch 2008: 132). Furthermore, "fantasy" was associated with passivity, surrender, emotion, and pleasure, while "reality" was connected to activity, alertness, cognition, and enlightenment. It was concluded that working-class men—a gender bias was also operative—were overwhelmed by their personal troubles and therefore pursued escape and relaxation, while middle-class men courageously confronted their own challenges and resolved their own problems. These sharply divergent class-based visions nurtured their ultimate argument that middle-class children are socialized in households distinguished by a "mature" television usage pattern of deferred gratification, whereas working-class children are victimized by their "immature" parents in accordance with what was termed the "Principle of Maturation" (Butsch 2008: 132). Buckingham (2001) also makes the all too frequently missed point that "the debate about children and media . . . is really a debate about other things, many of which have very little to do with the media. It is a debate that invokes deep-seated moral and political convictions" (cited in Press 2011: 107).

All of the traits that were associated with the middle-class "reality group" are linked with good citizenship, while the opposite was the case for the working-class "fantasy group." Most important, as Butsch points out, Schramm and his students acknowledged the stereotypes in their analysis, claimed that their use of the term "social class" was not intended to be pejorative, and yet their analysis effectively awarded legitimacy to the class-based stereotypes as it granted them the seal of "scientific" approval. This is particularly consequential if we remember that their work and other early works about television were not restricted to the confines of scholarly discourse but, rather, were widely distributed beyond the scientific community, addressed to and marketed to the population at large. Finally, as Butsch (2001: 113) carefully clarifies, there are no grounds to contest either the rigor of the research that was conducted or the overall findings or the motives of the researchers. In fact, the strengths of the methods utilized, and what some might interpret as the "sympathetic outlook" of the authors with regard to the working class, rendered the class bias all the more persuasive, and even led it to appear entirely appropriate.

As Butsch is concerned to do, we must always examine the assumptions underlying the interpretations of those early research findings. These assumptions came to pervade both academic and popular perceptions of working-class reception experiences. That pathway of thought regarding class-distinctive media effects, established not long after the medium of television was first introduced, is paralleled by, and in many ways supported by, the class-biased imagery featured in the medium of television itself (and in other media as well).

The class bias spans decades of argumentation regarding "media effects" and it extended to all subordinate groups, including children, women, and various ethnic minorities, all of whom were seen as somehow susceptible, vulnerable, and intellectually incapable of defense against the declared dangers of television and other media usage. Alongside that trajectory, visual images and other non-visual representations unfavorable to the working class were extended to all subordinate social groups and the intersections between them, such that, for example, working-class children were more readily identified as "juvenile delinquents," who were judged in courts that were distinct from adult courts. However, those scholars who actually observed working-class people and their use of television, first in the 1950s and later in the 1970s and beyond, found that working-class men were actually resistant to televisual content that contradicted their own values. During the 1970s, for example, working-class viewers of *All in the Family* were found to object strongly to its class-biased content. Likewise, working-class women interviewed about daytime serials in the 1980s expressed nothing that could be interpreted as a "vulnerability" to the ideological output of the programs.

Casey (2010: 226) argues that "there remains a tendency within sociology to categorize the working classes according to three camps; namely, as 'romantic rebels,' as vulnerable desperate victims and/or as dangerous and deviant . . . [W]hat is absent from much class-based sociology is a fair and realistic picture of the everyday processes and practices of 'being' working class." Also absent from news is news about the working class and, particularly, news about those everyday processes and practices of "being" working class, including, as Casey describes them, the "pains and pleasures" of working-class life (p. 228). This also tends to render the working class invisible in many respects and to situate it outside of the sight lines of communication scholars.

Another outcome is that there are persistent, daily disparities between how news represents the social order and the everyday realities of the class experiences of audiences. For example, among her sample of young Canadian students, Madeley (2005) found that middle-classness was associated with normality, despite the presence of working-class students, who, in this respect, were largely uncritical of the dominance of middle-class subjects and related visions of classless publics. Perhaps less surprisingly, however, the working-class students at the same time demonstrated a much clearer and well-developed understanding of the class structure, to a much greater extent than their middle-class counterparts.

Casey suggests that confusion regarding the nature of contemporary class identities, together with persistent news presentations of a "classless public" within British society, has occurred alongside a reticence to discuss class. The reticence is not exclusive to those who participate in sociological research. It has also led to what Casey perceives, together with Morley and other British scholars, as a shift away from class-based analysis within sociology (see also Skeggs 1997, among others). Yet, as Morley argues, while the working class is fragmented along lines of gender, ethnicity, geographical region, and so forth, it has by no means disappeared, and there is no reason to abandon the use of "class" as a unitary social category. Just as there are contemporary feminists who apologize about the treatment of "gender" as a unitary social category, it would be absurd to claim that gender inequalities are no longer meaningful.

Bourdieu's *Distinction* (1984) assumes a special importance in the understanding of class as a phenomenon that encompasses a complete range of experiences, including "being" working class and "being" middle class. As he articulates in his own analysis of class differences in media usage and political choices, "it is possible to draw fairly precisely the simultaneously political and cultural dividing-line between the working classes . . . and the middle classes" (1984, 446–7). This analysis led Bourdieu to assert that "political choices are much less independent of social class than is generally supposed" (p. 453).

At this juncture, it will be useful to illustrate some of the many ways in which class matters to the target audiences sampled here. A number of representative comments appear below, including two examples of questionnaire comments and a final news diary entry that are all the more compelling in view of the absence of specific questions regarding representations of class in news or working-class exclusion. Such issues arose frequently during interviews, especially those with working-class participants, and commonly at the initiative of the interviewees.

"Sometimes I feel that the little people or lower-income people are left out of a lot of news because no one wants to hear our stories. Maybe if there was more publicity about how we struggle day to day." (Working-Class Woman (WCW), age 38, Questionnaire)[6]

"It is very evident to me that, as a worker and trade unionist, our news, events, points of view, and stories are muted or excluded altogether from the media—except when we are on strike, subject to massive layoffs, or die horribly in large numbers. I would like to see the creation and growth of a mass worker-controlled media where our stories can finally be told." (Working-Class Man (WCM), age 49, Questionnaire)

And at the conclusion of his one-week news diary, the following unemployed participant wrote:

> "It's interesting that as this week ends I feel more than ever like a bystander without much to do with the world as it changes so fast and so much, day to day. It's hard to follow all the lives, economies, governments, wars, who's the "good guy," who's the "bad guy." I think as I change jobs—it's just that the economy news is a bit discouraging. I'm sure that my own desperate feeling taints my perspective." (WCM, age 44, News Diary)

Unquestionably, the predominantly middle-class character of news is a concern expressed by both working- and middle-class audiences, who perceive a more or less direct connection between the social class of journalists and the treatment of class in news. Consider, for example, the words of the following middle-class woman (MCW):

> "Let's take two journalists. One came from, you know, a very wealthy family, you know, just walked through, tuition was never a problem. They didn't have to work, they didn't have a student loan, nothing. You know, they drove their new car to class every day. And then you have the other journalist who had student loans and scholarships and, you know, bought used furniture and photocopied their books, things like that, and, you know, took the [subway] to school every day. I think they're going to look at the same story and have a different view on it. Definitely, definitely. *But that's human nature and I don't think that can be helped* . . . If they are writing a story, let's say, on a CEO of a company who is being investigated for embezzlement, you've got to look at the story one way, and report it one way, and the other is going to look at it and report it [with] a totally different slant on it. Definitely. The next day they go and they do a story on—let's see—somebody stealing a couple of steaks from a grocery store. They're going to look at these stories and report them differently. The one that, you know, never had to worry about feeding their family

is not going to understand why somebody would have to do that." (MCW, age 39, Interview, emphasis added)

GENDER INEQUALITIES IN PROFESSIONAL JOURNALISM

Sociologists of every theoretical inclination, whether feminists or not, are compelled to recognize that gender is a primary category of social organization. In the multidisciplinary study of journalism, however, gender is only infrequently the focus of research attention. The discussion here addresses the broad question of how gender figures within the process of news reception. Just as class issues are better understood if we trace the entire trajectory from production through to reception, where gender issues are concerned news reception needs to be understood in conjunction with news production as well as the nature of the news text that results from a highly gendered production process.

In the nineteen nations regarding which data were summarized by Weaver (2005: 47), the average proportion of female journalists was one-third or 33 percent. Interestingly, Robinson (2005: 183) found that male journalists are inclined to interpret the one-third participation rate of women as closer to a more equitable one-half. Fröhlich's (2007) research even suggests that the proportion of women journalists, at least in Western societies, has actually declined since the mid-1990s. The numbers alone are highly deceptive, and the greater proportion of women in television journalism adds to the deception. Their on-air appearances in television news create the false impression that women are numerically and otherwise closer to equality with their male colleagues. In reality, literally all of the international and national data demonstrate otherwise. (See also Geertsema's 2009 response to Fröhlich's results).

The vast and persistent gender inequalities within the journalism profession have been extensively documented and discussed (see, for example, Chambers, Steiner, and Fleming 2004; Franks 2013; Global Media Monitoring Project 2010; Lang 1999; Mahtani 2005; North 2009a, 2009b, 2009c; Poindexter 2008; Robinson 2005, 2008a, 2008b; Ross 2010; Torkkola and Ruoho 2011; Whitt 2008; Zelizer 2004). Robinson's (2008b: 83–4) transnational evidence regarding management-level positions demonstrates that women continue to be largely excluded from any exercise of control over the output of news production. In the United States, a tiny 0.8 percent of newspaper editors-in-chief were found to be women, while in Canada the figure was comparatively higher, although still pathetically low, at 10 percent. Furthermore, "European figures demonstrate that their 'glass ceilings' are located at the *bottom* of the managerial hierarchy in comparison to North America" (p. 83, emphasis in original), with the effect that European women find it difficult to penetrate any level of the managerial ranks. Women are somewhat better represented in television news management, where in Canada 18 percent of executive producer positions are occupied by women while in the United States the figure is 12 percent (p. 84). Robinson's comparative 1975 and 1995 survey data demonstrate that the proportion of women among Canadian print journalists increased from 21 to 28 percent during that twenty-year period. The increase in women's representation was no more than 7 percent over the course of two decades, and it remains below the international norm. Among broadcast journalists, women's representation increased by 17 percent (p. 125).

Despite these increases in their numbers during the two decades, women continued to be assigned to lesser beats, experienced slower promotion rates, and were paid less than their male colleagues (Robinson 2008a: 125–6). Beyond the limited range of social characteristics shared by journalists yet not shared with their audiences, those who have studied the everyday operations of print and broadcast newsrooms invariably observe their fundamentally masculinist character, associated with a professional work culture from which women, as well as working-class men and non-whites of both genders, are largely excluded. Those women and non-whites who do enter newsrooms experience that work environment very differently than their white male colleagues.[7]

The remarkable persistence of these extensive gender inequalities across time and place points to the fundamentally gendered nature of news production, which continues to characterize professional journalism and, within it, the journalistic field. Bourdieu's concept of the journalistic field captures those fundamental commonalities in the process whereby news is conceptualized, gathered, and subsequently disseminated to news audiences. While it is also important to appreciate cross-cultural and historical variations in journalistic practices, there is nevertheless a readily identifiable set of core practices and principles associated with news production—practices and principles that extend across national boundaries and that remain stubbornly resistant to change. In addition to the concrete everyday material practices, which require that news be pursued in accordance with established criteria of newsworthiness, there are also the "symbolic practices" that serve to sustain the predominantly masculine character of newsrooms as well as the news produced within them. Robinson (2008a: 131–2) discusses three such symbolic practices that have been widely documented by researchers in Canada, Europe, and elsewhere. These include the newsroom's communicative style, variously described as "locker room humour" (Melin-Higgins and Djerf-Pierre 1998, cited in Robinson 2008a) or "banter" focused upon team sports, and gender-biased jokes. In the Canadian case, Robinson's participants identified the centrality of football and ice hockey within informal newsroom discussions, contact sports in which women's participation is not widely legitimated and in which women are not generally encouraged to acquire strong interests. In Robinson's words, "this informal communication practice turns out to be a not too subtle mechanism for excluding female reporters from workplace interactions and making them feel like outsiders" (p. 131).

A second gendered aspect of newsroom culture is the competitiveness through which beat assignments and interview assignments become objects of internal struggle rather than cooperative arrangements. One key result is that women are routinely assigned to beats and interviews perceived to be low priority, gender-appropriate, or "soft" stories (such as those concerned with health or parenthood). Other examples of masculinist newsroom practices, and other dimensions of the gendered division of newsroom labor, have been examined by Stuart Allan (2010), Djerf-Pierre (2011), North (2009a, 2009b, 2009c), Poindexter (2008), Poindexter and Harp (2008), Ross (2011), and Ross and Carter (2011), among others.

Alongside the exclusion of women from significant journalistic, editorial, and management positions within newsrooms, there is the ongoing, persistent, and very much related exclusion of women from significant positions within the news that is produced—for example, their exclusion from the sight of audiences in roles such as "expert" news sources and op-ed writers in newspapers, as well as the exceptionally well-documented overall absence of women's voices throughout what are fittingly termed "malestream" broadcast, print, and online news media. In 2010, the Informed Opinions research organization, formerly known as Media Watch, monitored the commentary pages of six major English- and French-language daily newspapers in Canada as well as the guest lists of three well-known radio and television discussion programs, only to conclude that "women's perspectives are missing in action in some of the highest profile media vehicles most likely to influence Canadians' opinions on key public policy issues. Both English- and French-language media chronically underrepresent women's views" (Informed Opinions 2010: 1). Included in their sample were *The Globe and Mail*, the *National Post*, the *Ottawa Citizen*, *Le Devoir*, *Le Droit*, CBC Radio's *The Current*, CTV's *Power Play*, and the RDI program *Sans Frontieres*. Only 16 percent of the op-eds in these six newspapers were written by women, while women columnists comprised only 15 percent of the regular contributors in the English-language dailies and only 23 percent in the French-language dailies. The overall gender ratio, including newspaper columns, op-eds, signed editorials, and discussion program contributors, was a mere 20 percent, or no more than one woman's voice amid every five men's voices (pp. 1–2). In sum, there can be no dispute that the gender gap, both in news production and in news content, continues to be, as the Informed Opinion researchers describe it, "dramatic" (pp. 1–2). Franks, in her more recent summary of the data (2013: 49), concludes bluntly that "the content of news stories is overwhelmingly male."

GENDERED NEWS PRODUCTION AND GENDERED NEWS RECEPTION

Despite a somewhat greater numerical presence of women within newsrooms—or, as Fröhlich (2007) suggests, what has actually been a reduction in their numbers since the mid-1990s—news organizations in Canadian society and elsewhere remain both quantitatively and qualitatively dominated by men. Regarding the impact upon the long-gendered nature of news content, Robinson's comparative evidence (2005: 179, emphases in original) demonstrates: "the *assumption* that greater employment of females in the media professions will *automatically* lead to more equitable portrayal[s] of women and their concerns is definitely mistaken." Freeman (2001: 18), as a well-experienced female journalist and journalism historian, regards it as "naïve" to believe "that an increase in the number of women in the newsroom would necessarily translate into better coverage of women and their issues."

One reason why it cannot be assumed that more women in journalism will mean more women in news stories, or better representations of women, or more women's news is the extent of both horizontal and vertical gender segregation (Robinson 2005: 166). Horizontal gender segregation is persistently evident in the differentiation between beats, interviews, and types of stories assigned to women and men, while vertical gender segregation continues to be evident in men's dominance of the managerial hierarchy within news production. Not surprisingly, both forms of gender segregation become manifest in news content, a relationship that has been extensively documented.

A very extensive current source of comparative data is the Global Media Monitoring Project (GMMP), which documents the representation of women and men in news. GMMP research has been conducted by literally hundreds of researchers around the globe in a coordinated project that has produced data in five-year cycles since 1995. The most recent report, issued in 2010, examines the news produced by a total of 1,365 newspapers, radio stations, and television stations in a total of 108 countries representing 82 percent of the world's population. Online news was also monitored, including seventy-six national news websites in sixteen countries and eight international news websites. The four GMMP studies produced to date—in 1995, 2000, 2005, and 2010—have all demonstrated clearly that:

> Women are grossly under-represented in news coverage in contrast to men. The outcome of under-representation is an imbalanced picture of the world, one in which women are largely absent. The studies equally showed a paucity of women's voices in news media content in contrast to men's perspectives, resulting in news that presents a male-centred view of the world. (GMMP 2010: 1)

While at least half of the world's population is composed of women, in 1995 only 17 percent of the people discussed in news were women, a figure that increased slowly to what was still no more than 24 percent in 2010. Of those who were interviewed or whose voices were otherwise heard in news, women remain confined to the "vox pop" or "ordinary people" categories, in which their representation increased from 34 percent in 2005 to 44 percent in 2010. Regardless of these minimal gains, in 2010 a full 80 percent of "experts" and 81 percent of spokespersons were men (GMMP 2010, 2). With respect to the contributions of women journalists relative to their male colleagues, the proportion of news stories reported by women across the three media of newspapers, radio, and television increased from 1995 until 2005. The 37 percent figure attained in 2005 remained at that level in 2010, due to a decrease of eight percentage points in the proportion of radio news stories reported by women between 2005 and 2010. Women presented less than half (49 percent) of the total radio and television news stories in 2010, a decline of 4 percent since 2005 and lower than the 1995 level of 51 percent. Moreover, in terms of classically gendered news topics, men in 2010 reported 60 percent of stories regarding the economy, 67 percent of stories regarding "politics/government," and 65 percent of stories in the "crime/violence" category (p. 2). The most recent data demonstrate once again that stories by male journalists exceed those by female journalists throughout virtually all news topics. While most topics have seen at least minimal increases in the extent of reportage by women, the proportion of "science/health" stories reported by women has actually declined since the year 2000 (2). Significantly, therefore, increases in the presence of women in news—whether as journalists or as news subjects (i.e., individuals who appear in news stories)—cannot be seen as either consistently progressive or steady, nor is there any necessary relationship between women's greater presence in news and improved representations of women. On the contrary, as these extensive international data demonstrate, there are regular instances of decline in the presence of women. Above all, the overall extent of improvement in the quantity of women's voices compared to men's voices is astonishingly limited.

With respect to the visibility of women in prime-time evening newscasts, then, men continue to report the majority of the stories, men continue to dominate the "expert" roles in these stories, and men otherwise occupy a much more visible presence throughout the news that is offered by all media, including online news that draws extensively from offline news sources. If anything, what is sometimes observed as an increased women's presence can be seen as disadvantageous to women in that it often amounts to little more than their greater visibility in so-called man-on-the-street interviews. (See, for example, the misinterpretations of women's increased presence in the profession by Erin Research 1993, cited in Robinson 2005: 166). Clearly, that classic journalistic term is in itself telling with respect to the hegemony of masculinism in news. In accordance with journalistic field traditions, the practice is to randomly catch members of "the (classless, ungendered, singular) public" off-guard and query them about their "feelings" regarding a current news event. Again, it is too easy to *assume* that structured gender inequalities in professional journalism have lessened and that women's presence in news has increased, based upon nothing more than sheer impressions that women appear more frequently in television news, whether as journalists, "expert" sources, or perhaps as "*woman*-on-the-street" vox pop interviewees. Even in the case of the latter, however, there are empirical data such as those gathered by Cross (2010), who found in her analysis of television election coverage that twice as many men as women appear in vox pop interviews. In her words, "the 'man on the street' is, on average, still literally true" (p. 419).[8] Also excluded from these segments, and indeed from all news content, is the entire working class—who, like women, comprise a majority of the population. Moreover, the intersectionalities of reception operate in such a way that working-class women experience a twofold exclusion by virtue of their class as well as their gender.

What gender-differentiated reception patterns have been documented? There are a number of insightful discussions regarding gender differences in media consumption generally (e.g., Ang and Hermes 1991; Baehr and Gray 1995; Beale 2008; Schwichtenberg 1994; Wood 1994) and the gendered use of particular media such as television (e.g., Hermans and van Snippenburg 1996; Kaid and Holtz-Bacha 2000; Montiel 2006; Press 1991, 1989; van Zoonen 1993; Wood 2009) and the Internet (e.g., Bimber 2000; Helsper 2010; Kennedy, Wellman, and Klement 2003; Menzies 1999; Shade 2002). At the general level, Bird (2003), for example, points to frequent findings of basic gender differences in communication styles, whereby women are inclined to be collaborative and inclusive while men are inclined to be more confrontational and concerned to make decisive points that "win" an argument (see also Maltz and Borker 1982; Tannen 1993). Internet scholars suggest that the argumentative male style is the dominant mode of communication in that medium (e.g., Coates 1998, cited in Bird 2003: 66). The confrontational style of television news—notably, where political pundits form a panel to debate news topics—can be off-putting to many women viewers. Another recurrent finding, one that makes good sense to sociologists familiar with the still-gendered division of household labor, is the pattern whereby women's television spectatorship is somewhat erratic and intermittent in view of their domestic labor, particularly in those households in which the work includes child care.[9] On the other hand, men's television spectatorship can be more focused and intense, with the opportunity to watch entire programs without interruption. The documentation of this well-established and continuing pattern, observed repeatedly through the course of the present analysis, harks back at least as far as Morley's analysis in *Family Television* (1986: 150).

In *Gendered Media*, Karen Ross (2010) summarizes a number of the documented gender differences in digital media use. For example, women tend to view relatively few websites, spend less time overall on the Internet, and are more likely than men to view the net from home (p. 127ff.). While men are much more inclined to download music, play interactive games, cruise porn sites, and seek other Internet entertainment, women are more likely to use the net as a means of personal communication with those in their social networks and in order to obtain general information (not necessarily news-related). In the words of Ross: "Women are more likely to use the Internet instrumentally rather than recreationally, seeing the computer and the Internet as tools rather than technologies" (128). She concludes that "although the hardware of technology might be gender neutral, its appropriation and use certainly is not" (p. 147).

In addition to gender differences in the choice of medium, there is a significant gender gap in terms of interests in different types of news content. Men's content priorities include sports and international news, whereas women tend to privilege local news over international news. In general, women are inclined to express least interest in business news and local sports, while men are least interested in fashion and lifestyles stories, food pages, and letters to the editor. Despite these expressed differences that appear to enjoy continuity over time, business news and sports news are invested with much higher levels of staffing resources by newspapers and other news media. Women are therefore inclined to make greater use of books and magazines as information sources, also because these serve their interests more effectively in terms of time management and their daily shifts of paid and unpaid labor. Arguably, these print media can also be seen as less inclined toward gendered information. The keyword here is "arguably," in view of the dominance of white middle-class men in newspaper and magazine bylines.

Historically, broadcasters have tended to be the least well informed of all news producers regarding the interests and needs of their women audiences, who are frequently assumed to share the interests of men and who are commonly perceived to constitute a homogeneous group undifferentiated by important social characteristics such as age, class, education level, and ethnicity. Yet beyond the apparent misinformation and mistaken assumptions about women viewers, of greater explanatory weight in the exclusion of women is the recurrent and readily observable disconnection that many women experience during news reception: stories that, as brief tidbits of news, appear unconnected to each other and unconnected to women's everyday experiences, stories that tell only what happened and not why it happened, and news content that repeatedly fails to address women's interests.

The present research was conducted with a targeted sample of community activists, which raises seemingly perennial issues such as the absence of any necessary linkage between community activism and full-scale political engagement, regardless of how the latter might be conceptualized. There was a concern to examine empirically the contribution of professional journalism to the frequently observed disjuncture between active community participation and a well-informed critique of the social order that inspires a politically driven agenda. Apart from Bourdieu, the sources of theoretical influence here include Gramsci and his classical formulations regarding the nature of hegemony, the widely granted consent that it requires, and the conditions that are prerequisite to the development of "organic intellectuals" who might inspire and/or organize challenges to that consent. While it cannot be argued that there is a direct or even a necessary relationship between journalism and political exclusion, it nevertheless appears to be at least one means to explain the extent of exclusion found among the research participants. The participants include those of different classes, genders, and those with other diverse social characteristics, all of whom commit themselves in various ways to work toward the betterment of their communities at the local, regional, national, and/or global levels. In the case of women, it was rare not to observe a disenchantment that could be traced to the inability of professional journalism, especially network television journalism, to either adequately inform them about the social world or to engage them in progressive movements to change it.

What follows are a few examples that illustrate the operation of intersectionality as well as gender-based commonalities in news reception. The first is that of a working-class woman (WCW) whose rage responses increased her blood pressure. She explained why she has essentially abandoned daily television news viewing:

> WCW: I found that, as a diabetic, my blood sugars go up when I watch the news . . . I wasn't watching it and in preparation for this [interview] I thought I should watch the news once in awhile and find out what's going on in the world and so I watched it, and I watched CPAC but CPAC was okay—the parliamentary

channel—and my blood sugar went up [laughs]. But that's because of the war, that the US will attack no matter what, you know.

And did you find that you experienced anger as you watched it?

WCW: Anger, frustration. I hate when the CBC [promotes the war in] Iraq, just like as if they're copying right from the American networks, you know. I think that's a chauvinistic [story], you know, as if they can boss another country and another religion and another culture way across the world. They have no business interfering. Mostly because I know about the suffering from the sanctions, I was just pretty upset . . . [later in the same interview] I do get angry. I think my blood pressure's going up too . . . well, it's temporary, it will go back down again. Well, Dr. Hans Selye, he's an authority on stress, advises people not to watch the news. And my mother's former doctor, he's dead now, but he told her not to watch the news. They put all the horrible tragedies of the world and all the atrocities on and that's what you get for an hour and occasionally you get a nice story here and there, something positive. It's mostly fires, earthquakes, murders, child abuse, elder abuse." (WCW, age 53, Interview)

Another case is that of a middle-class woman (MCW) in her sixties who reported that she had little interest in either news or politics until she was influenced by a new partner (identified here as "D") during her late fifties:

MCW: He is my primary source. He keeps me informed, because he might flip it [the television] on several times a day . . . [before she coupled with her partner] I didn't even watch news or pay attention to news for fifty-seven years. D's got an outward focus, a political interest. He's got a strong political interest, and my focus has been inner. Now being more with D and his exuberance about it, I'm taking more interest in politics.

Would you say that you were apolitical before?

MCW: It just wasn't my focus. It wasn't a priority. But that's changing. And I want to be aware, and I'm becoming active with D." (MCW, age 60s, Interview)[10]

The following case of a divorced working-class woman (WCW) with two adolescent sons resident in her one-parent household illustrates a more common pattern whereby those of her class and gender are without either the time or the incentive to undertake regular news viewing:

WCW: I don't get to watch news much. I listen to the radio. I don't read the papers, and I don't usually get to see the news at eleven. I usually go to bed. And at six, I'm making supper, so I don't get to see the newscast very often . . . When I sit down in the evening, I want to be entertained . . .

Sometimes I think I'm happier not knowing what's going on in the world. You don't have to think about all of that stuff that happens. It may be a naïve

> way of looking at things, but I'm an optimistic kind of person and I like to be happy as much as I can, and the news is not a happy thing. Most of it . . . the newscast, for the most part, is pretty depressing." (WCW, age 46, Interview)

Perhaps most striking is the fact that this woman was not even inclined to read one of the many newspapers delivered to her house regularly for her son's paper route, not even while she drove him along his route during snowy days. Even under those circumstances, in which newspapers were available to her at no cost and right next to her in her vehicle as she waited while her son delivered them, she was still not inclined to read the news. While it might appear to be extraordinary, her case exemplifies a recurrent pattern of disconnection from news in any form and a related disconnection from any form of political engagement, apart from volunteer labor that is not ordinarily perceived to be "political" in nature. By virtue of their social class as well as their gender, working-class women such as the one cited above are effectively twice removed—or experience "double the distance," as it were—from the middle-class masculinist culture of professional journalism. If, as Liebes and Katz (1993: x) argue, "decoding is an interaction between the culture of the viewer and the culture of the producer," then, within the limitations of the social conditions of news production and reception, there is little or no basis of interaction.

CONCLUSION

While we can draw attention to seemingly linear connections between a singular social trait and a particular interpretation that follows from it, as a social condition of news reception, we also need to dissect the points of intersectionality in which, for example, the class-gender nexus that we observe in news production connects with a parallel class-gender nexus in news reception. Of the two social conditions in that nexus, class clearly figures more importantly than gender. While it is perhaps excessively reductionist to insist, like Ebert and Zavarzadeh (2008: 139), that "all social differences, such as gender, are effects of class," it is nevertheless difficult to overlook the preeminence of class vis-à-vis other social conditions of news reception.

Similarly, it is evident that the relationship between news reception and political participation is by no means a straightforward linear relationship. There is little question, however, that levels of political knowledge are invariably found to be strongly related to levels of political participation. Scholars associated with a variety of theoretical perspectives commonly share the perception that political knowledge is a vital prerequisite to political participation. That relationship has been demonstrated repeatedly, to the extent that it is exceptionally well established. On the other hand, attention to the *structurally induced* restrictions upon active political engagement—manifest, for example, in the limitations of news production which tend to exacerbate political information inequalities—is too often largely absent from, and/or inadequately theorized within, political communication research. In particular, there might be greater attention to structural constraints such as those fundamental social inequalities that underpin inequalities in both political knowledge and political participation. The frequently veiled attention to formal education as "the principal factor" underlying participation inequalities masks their ultimate source in the class structure.

Finally, there are a number of important points to observe regarding the political activities of those in the Canadian samples. The organizations from which participants were drawn extended across the full range of "civil society organizations"—from community service organizations staffed by volunteers to trade union locals to more avowedly "political" organizations with formally articulated social justice objectives. One might expect a gradation, therefore, in their respective levels of political participation, yet in fact there was no such strongly evident linearity based upon organization type. Overall, there are differences between different types of participants—whether activists, union members, or volunteers—as one would expect, yet these differences do not extend to the common reception ambiguities, including the fundamental information inequalities, that are experienced by all and that become manifest in political participation inequalities. In essence, their experiences of political *exclusion* can be seen to derive from a number of sources, of which news reception is but one.

NOTES

1. This chapter was originally published as Clarke, Debra. "Social Conditions of Reception: Class, Gender, and Other Social Divisions." *Journalism and Political Exclusion*. Ed. 117750. Montreal: MQUP, 2014. Print.

2. I wish to acknowledge the permission of McGill-Queen's University Press, publisher of *Journalism and Political Exclusion: Social Conditions of News Production and Reception* (2014), to reproduce a number of interview quotations and other material here.

3. In her definition of working class, Ehrenreich (2007: 1) includes "not only industrial workers in hard-hats, but all those people who are not professionals, managers, or entrepreneurs; who work for wages rather than salaries; and who spend their working hours variously lifting, bending, driving, monitoring, keyboarding, cleaning, providing physical care for others, loading, unloading, cooking, serving, etc."

4. See, however, Butsch (2011) who examines the significance of the few yet recurrent "male working-class buffoons" featured in prime-time American network television family series between 1946 and 2004.

5. It is also important to consider Morley's (2009: 489) argument regarding "class essentialism" in audiences research, in which he raises the question of who is qualified to judge whether working-class people are adequately represented.

6. The following acronyms are used here to identify the class and gender of the research participants who are cited: MCM (Middle Class Man), MCW (Middle Class Woman), WCM (Working Class Man), and WCW (Working Class Woman).

7. On the experiences of women journalists in what continue to be highly gendered and strongly masculinist newsrooms, see Franks (2013), North (2009a, 2009b, and 2009c), Poindexter (2008), and Robinson (2005).

8. These very cheaply produced segments, often used to fill air time, especially in the production of local news, serve the needs of the political economy of local and other levels of news production. As Cross (2010: 419) suggests in her study of Canadian television election coverage, vox pop segments can also be seen to serve a need to convey voter populism.

9. Women are more likely than all other demographic groups to perform household labor during their time spent with television. Of course, other groups are not necessarily visually and aurally attentive to the television screen.

10. A minority of research participants preferred not to specify their exact age in the questionnaire; in these cases, only the decade appears.

REFERENCES

Allan, Stuart. 2010. *News Culture*, 3rd ed. Maidenhead, UK: Open University Press.

Ang, Ien and Joke Hermes (1991). "Gender and/in Media Consumption." In *Mass Media and Society*, ed. James Curran and Michael Gurevitch, 308–28. London: Edward Arnold.

Baehr, Helen and Ann Gray (eds.) (1995). *Turning It On: A Reader in Women and Media*. London: Oxford University Press.

Beale, Alison (2008). "The Expediency of Women." In *Feminist Interventions in International Communication*, ed. Katharine Sarikakis and Leslie Regan Shade, 59–73. Lanham, MD: Rowman & Littlefield.

Bimber, Bruce (2000). "Measuring the Gender Gap on the Internet." *Social Science Quarterly* 81 (3): 868–876.

Bird, S. Elizabeth (2003). *The Audience in Everyday Life: Living in a Media World*. New York: Routledge.

Bogart, Leo (1956). *The Age of Television: A Study of Viewing Habits and the Impact of Television on American Life*. New York: Frederick Ungar Publishing.

Bourdieu, Pierre (1984). *Distinction: A Social Critique of the Judgement of Taste*. Trans. Richard Nice. Cambridge, MA: Harvard University Press.

Buckingham, David (2001). "Electronic Child Abuse? Rethinking the Media's Effects on Children." In *Ill Effects: The Media/Violence Debate*, 2nd ed., ed. Martin Barker and Julian Petley, 63–77. New York: Routledge.

Butsch, Richard (2000). *The Making of American Audiences: From Stage to Television, 1750–1990*. Cambridge: Cambridge University Press.
Butsch, Richard (2001). "Class and Audience Effects: A History of Research on Movies, Radio, and Television." *Journal of Popular Film and Television* 29 (3): 112–20.
Butsch, Richard (2008). *The Citizen Audience: Crowds, Publics, and Individuals*. New York: Routledge.
Butsch, Richard (2011). "Ralph, Fred, Archie, Homer, and the King of Queens: Why Television Keeps Re-Creating the Male Working-Class Buffoon." In *Gender, Race, and Class in Media: A Critical Reader*, 3rd ed., ed. Gail Dines and Jean M. Humez, 101–9. Thousand Oaks, CA: Sage.
Casey, Emma (2010). "Struggle and Protest or Passivity and Control? The Formation of Class Identity in Two Contemporary Cultural Practices." *European Journal of Cultural Studies* 13 (2): 225–41.
Chambers, Deborah, Linda Steiner, and Carole Fleming (2004). *Women and Journalism*. London: Routledge.
Clarke, Debra M. (2014). *Journalism and Political Exclusion: Social Conditions of News Production and Reception*. Montréal: McGill-Queen's University Press.
Clement, Wallace (2002). "The Class-Gender Nexus in Comparative Perspective." Paper presented at the annual conference of the Canadian Sociology and Anthropology Association, Learned Societies Congress, Toronto, June.
Clement, Wallace (2004). "Revealing the Class-Gender Connection: Social Policy, Labour Markets, and Households." *Just Labour* 4 (1): 42–52.
Coates, Norma (1998). "Can't We Just Talk About Music: Rock and Gender on the Internet. In *Mapping the Beat: Popular Music and Contemporary Theory*, ed. Thomas Swiss, John M. Sloop, and Andrew Herman, 77–99. Malden, MA: Blackwell.
Cross, Kathleen Ann (2010). "Experts in the News: The Differential Use of Sources in Election Television News." *Canadian Journal of Communication* 35 (3): 413–29.
DiMaggio, Paul, Eszter Hargittai, Coral Celeste, and Steven Shafer (2004). "Digital Inequality: From Unequal Access to Differentiated Use." In *Social Inequality*, ed. Kathryn M. Neckerman, 355–400. New York: Russell Sage.
Djerf-Pierre, Monika (2011). "Gender Equality, Journalism, and the Good Society." *Feminist Media Studies* 11 (1): 43–51.
Ebert, Teresa L., and Mas'ud Zavarzadeh (2008). *Class in Culture*. Boulder, CO: Paradigm.
Ehrenreich, Barbara (2007). "The Silenced Majority." *Z Magazine*, October, http://www.zcommunications.org/the-silenced-majority-by-barbara-ehrenreich.
Franks, Suzanne (2013). *Women in Journalism*. London: I.B. Tauris.
Freeman, Barbara M. (2001). *The Satellite Sex: The Media and Women's Issues in English Canada, 1966–1971*. Waterloo, ON: Wilfrid Laurier University Press.
Fröhlich, Romy (2007). "Three Steps Forward and Two Back? Women Journalists in the Western World Between Progress, Standstill, and Retreat." In *Women in Mass Communication*, 3rd ed., ed. Pamela J. Creedon and Judith Cramer, 161–76. Thousand Oaks, CA: Sage.
Gans, Herbert J. (1979). *Deciding What's News: A Study of CBS Evening News, NBC Nightly News, Newsweek, and Time*. New York: Random House.

Gans, Herbert J. (2003). *Democracy and the News*. New York: Oxford University Press.

Garnham, Nicholas (1992). "The Media and the Public Sphere." In *Habermas and the Public Sphere*, ed. Craig Calhoun, 359–76. Cambridge, MA: MIT Press.

Geertsema, Margaretha (2009). "Women and News: Making Connections Between the Global and the Local." *Feminist Media Studies* 9 (2): 149–72.

Glick, Ira, and Sidney J. Levy. (2005 [orig. 1962]). *Living with Television*. New Brunswick, NJ: Transaction Publishers.

Global Media Monitoring Project (GMMP) (2010). *Who Makes the News? GMMP Report 2010*. See http://www.whomakesthenews.org/images/reports_2010/gmmp-global-report-en-2010.pdf.

Golding, Peter (1994). "Telling Stories: Sociology, Journalism, and the Informed Citizen." *European Journal of Communication* 9 (4): 461–84.

Heider, Don and Koji Fuse (2004). "Class and Local Television News." In *Class and News*, ed. Don Heider, 87–107. Lanham, MD: Rowman & Littlefield.

Helsper, Ellen (2010). "Gendered Internet Use Across Generations and Life Stages." *Communication Research* 37 (3): 352–74.

Hermans, Liesbeth, and Leo van Snippenburg (1996). "Women's Use of Television News." In *Media Use as Social Action: A European Approach to Audience Studies*, ed. Karsten Renckstorf, Denis McQuail, and Nicholas Jankowski, 139–50. London: John Libbey.

Hindman, Matthew (2009). *The Myth of Digital Democracy*. Princeton, NJ: Princeton University Press.

Informed Opinions (formerly Media Watch) (2010). "Women's Perspectives MIA in Influential News Media." See www.informedopinions.org/?q=node/4.

Kaid, Lynda Lee, and Christina Holtz-Bacha (2000). "Gender Reactions to Television Political Broadcasts." *Harvard International Journal of Press/Politics* 5 (1): 17–29.

Kennedy, Tracy, Barry Wellman, and Kristine Klement (2003). "Gendering the Digital Divide." *IT and Society* 1 (5): 149–72.

Kim, Sujeong (2004). "Rereading David Morley's *The 'Nationwide' Audience*." *Cultural Studies* 18 (1): 84–108.

Klapper, Joseph T. (1960). *The Effects of Mass Communication*. New York: Free Press.

Kurpius, David D. (2004). "Television Civic Journalism and the Portrayal of Class." In *Class and News*, ed. Don Heider, 325–37. Lanham, MD: Rowman & Littlefield.

Lang, Marjory (1999). *Women Who Made the News: Female Journalists in Canada, 1880–1945*. Montreal: McGill-Queen's University Press.

Lazarsfeld, Paul F., and Robert K. Merton (1948). "Mass Communication, Popular Taste, and Organized Social Action." In *The Communication of Ideas*, ed. Lyman Bryson, 95–118. New York: Harper.

Levitas, Ruth (2006). "The Concept and Measurement of Social Exclusion." In *Poverty and Social Exclusion in Britain: The Millennium Survey*, ed. Christina Pantazis, David Gordon, and Ruth Levitas, 123–60. Bristol, UK: Policy Press.

Levitas, Ruth (2008). "Whatever Happened to Class Politics?" *Soundings* Class and Culture Debate, http://www.lwbooks.co.uk/journals/soundings/class_and_culture/levitas.html.

Liebes, Tamar, and Elihu Katz (1993). *The Export of Meaning: Cross-Cultural Readings of* Dallas. Cambridge: Polity Press.

Madeley, June M. (2005). "Situations of Viewing: Class, Gender, and the Everyday Practices and Processes of Watching Television." PhD diss., McMaster University.

Mahtani, Minelle (2005). "Gendered News Practices: Examining Experiences of Women Journalists in Different National Contexts." In *Journalism: Critical Issues*, ed. Stuart Allan, 299–310. Maidenhead, UK: Open University Press.

Maltz, Daniel N., and Ruth A. Borker (1982). "A Cultural Approach to Male-Female Miscommunication." In *Language and Social Identity*, ed. John J. Gumperz, 196–216. Cambridge, UK: Cambridge University Press.

McChesney, Robert W. (2013). *Digital Disconnect: How Capitalism Is Turning the Internet Against Democracy*. New York: The New Press.

Menzies, Heather (1999). "The Bias of Space Revisited: The Internet and the Information Highway Through Women's Eyes." In *Harold Innis in the New Century: Reflections and Refractions*, ed. Charles R. Acland and William J. Buxton, 322–38. Montreal: McGill-Queen's University Press.

Mesch, Gustavo, and Ilan Talmud (2010). *The Social World of Adolescence in the Information Age*. New York: Routledge.

Montiel, Aimee Vega. (2006). "(A Long Way To) Building One's Own Citizenship: Housewives, Politics, and Television News in Mexico." *Particip@tions* 3 (2).

Morley, David (1980). *The "Nationwide" Audience: Structure and Decoding*. London: British Film Institute.

Morley, David (1986). *Family Television: Cultural Power and Domestic Leisure*. London: Comedia.

Morley, David (2009). "Mediated Classifications: Representations of Class and Culture in Contemporary British Television." *European Journal of Cultural Studies* 12 (4): 487–508.

Mosco, Vincent (2009). *The Political Economy of Communication*, 2nd ed. London: Sage.

North, Louise (2009a). "Gendered Experiences of Industry Change and the Effects of Neoliberalism." *Journalism Studies* 10 (4): 506–21.

North, Louise (2009b). "Rejecting the 'F-word': How 'Feminism' and 'Feminists' Are Understood in the Newsroom." *Journalism* 10 (6): 739–57.

North, Louise (2009c). *The Gendered Newsroom*. Cresskill, NJ: Hampton Press.

Poindexter, Paula M. (2008). "Finding Women in the Newsroom and in the News." In *Women, Men, and News: Divided and Disconnected in the News Media Landscape*, ed. Paula M. Poindexter, Sharon Meraz, and Amy Schmitz Weiss, 65–84. New York: Routledge.

Poindexter, Paula M. and Dustin Harp (2008). "The Softer Side of News." In *Women, Men, and News: Divided and Disconnected in the News Media Landscape*, ed. Paula M. Poindexter, Sharon Meraz, and Amy Schmitz Weiss, 85–96. New York: Routledge.

Poindexter, Paula M, Don Heider, and Maxwell McCombs (2006). "Watchdog or Good Neighbour? The Public's Expectations of Local News." *Harvard International Journal of Press/Politics* 11 (1): 77–88.

Press, Andrea Lee. (1989). "Class and Gender in the Hegemonic Process: Class Differences in Women's Perceptions of Television Realism and Identification with Television Characters." *Media, Culture, and Society* 11 (2): 229–51.

Press, Andrea Lee. (1991). *Women Watching Television: Gender, Class, and Generation in the American Television Experience*. Philadelphia: University of Pennsylvania Press.

Press, Andrea Lee. (2011). "Feminism and Media in the Post-Feminist Era: What to Make of the 'Feminist' in Feminist Media Studies." *Feminist Media Studies* 11 (1): 107–13.

Pritchard, David, and Florian Sauvageau (1999). "English and French and Generation X: The Professional Values of Canadian Journalists." In *Canada, The State of the Federation, 1998–99: How Canadians Connect*, ed. Harvey Lazar and Tom McIntosh, 283–306. Montreal: McGill-Queen's University Press.

Robinson, Gertrude J. (2005). *Gender, Journalism, and Equity: Canadian, U.S., and European Experiences*. Cresskill, NJ: Hampton Press.

Robinson, Gertrude J. (2008a). "Feminist Approaches to Journalism Studies: Canadian Perspectives." *Global Media Journal—Canadian Edition* 1 (1): 123–36.

Robinson, Gertrude J. (2008b). "Journalism as a Symbolic Practice: The Gender Approach in Journalism Research." In *Global Journalism Research*, ed. Martin Löffelholz and David H. Weaver, 79–89. Malden, MA: Blackwell.

Robinson, Gertrude J. and Armande Saint-Jean (1998). "Canadian Women Journalists: The 'Other Half' of the Equation." In *The Global Journalist: News People Around the World*, ed. David H. Weaver, 349–70. Cresskill, NJ: Hampton Press.

Robinson, Laura (2012). "Information-Seeking 2.0: The Effects of Informational Advantage." *Reset: Social Science Research on the Internet* 1 (1). See http://www.journal-reset.org/index.php/RESET/article/view/5.

Ross, Karen (2010). *Gendered Media: Women, Men, and Identity Politics*. Lanham, MD: Rowman & Littlefield.

Ross, Karen (2011). "Silent Witness: News Sources, the Local Press, and the Disappeared Woman." In *Gendered Transformations: Theory and Practices on Gender and Media*, ed. Tonny Krijnen, Claudia Alvares, and Sofie Van Bauwel, 9–23. Bristol, UK: Intellect.

Ross, Karen and Cynthia Carter (2011). "Women and News: A Long and Winding Road." *Media, Culture, and Society* 33 (8): 1148–65.

Schradie, Jen. (2012). "The Trend of Class, Race, and Ethnicity in Social Media Inequality: Who Still Cannot Afford to Blog?" *Information, Communication, and Society* 15 (4): 555–71.

Schramm, Wilbur, Jack Lyle, and Edwin Parker (1961). *Television in the Lives of Our Children*. Stanford, CA: Stanford University Press.

Schwichtenberg, Cathy (1994). "Reconceptualizing Gender: New Sites for Feminist Audience Research." In *Viewing, Reading, Listening: Audiences and Cul-*

tural Reception, ed. Jon Cruz and Justin Lewis, 169–80. Boulder, CO: Westview Press.

Shade, Leslie Regan (2002). *Gender and Community in the Social Construction of the Internet*. New York: Peter Lang.

Skeggs, Beverley (1997). *Formations of Class and Gender*. London: Sage.

Steiner, Gary A. (1963). *The People Look at Television*. New York: Alfred A. Knopf.

Tannen, Deborah (ed.) (1993). *Gender and Conversational Interaction*. New York: Oxford University Press.

Torkkola, Sinikka, and Iiris Ruoho. (2011). "Looking for Gender Equality in Journalism." In *Gendered Transformations: Theory and Practices on Gender and Media*, ed. Tonny Krijnen, Claudia Alvares, and Sovie Van Bauwel, 203–20. Bristol, UK: Intellect.

van Dijk, Jan A.G.M. (2005). *The Deepening Divide: Inequality in the Information Society*. Thousand Oaks, CA: Sage.

van Zoonen, Liesbet. (1994). *Feminist Media Studies*. Thousand Oaks, CA: Sage.

Weaver, David H. (2005). "Who Are Journalists?" In *Making Journalists: Diverse Models, Global Issues*, ed. Hugo de Burgh, 44–57. London: Routledge.

Whitt, Jan (2008). *Women in American Journalism: A New History*. Chicago: University of Illinois Press.

Witte, James C., and Susan E. Mannon (2010). *The Internet and Social Inequalities*. New York: Routledge.

Wood, Helen (2009). *Talking with Television: Women, Talk Shows, and Modern Self-Reflexivity*. Chicago: University of Illinois Press.

Wood, Julia T. (1994). *Gendered Lives: Communication, Gender, and Culture*. Belmont, CA: Wadsworth.

Zelizer, Barbie (2004). *Taking Journalism Seriously: News and the Academy*. Thousand Oaks, CA: Sage.

Chapter Six

Black Anglophone Oligarchy in Jamaica

An Alliance of Media and State

Nova M. Gordon-Bell

Jamaica's independence in 1962 ended over four and a half centuries of European colonial rule. The virtual genocide of indigenous peoples and the reconstitution of the island as a collective of forcibly transported and enslaved peoples, the vast majority of whom were taken from West Africa, characterized Spanish and British domination of the island and left a legacy of political, economic and social inequality. Acemoğlu, Johnson and Robinson (2001), propose a link between the type of colonization a country experiences—conquest and settlement or exploitation—and a country's growth and development trends. Sokoloff and Engerman (2000) also suggest a link between a history of inequity and the development of institutions that retard growth as they protect elite interests. Despite pockets of extreme wealth in the island, Jamaica's economy struggles. Jamaica's debt is estimated at 141.6% of GDP (World Bank, 2014). Considered one of the slowest growing developing countries in the world, Jamaica's limited gains continue to be threatened by high youth unemployment and crime. Despite the success of many Jamaicans in business, sports and the creative industries, the country has not been able to convert its considerable potential—human and material—into meaningful social and economic growth.

Analyses of nation-states in the Anglophone Caribbean post-independence call attention to elite domination (Hintzen 1997, 2001), coloniality of citizenship (Kamugisha 2007), state predation (Gray 2004) and states in crisis (Bogues 2002a; Henke 2004) having high legitimacy deficits (Henry 2000) and experiencing hegemonic dissolution (Meeks 1996). Jamaica is such a "post colony" (Bogues 2002b) and the following pages highlight the economic, political and cultural processes fueling social inequality in modern Jamaica and the role the Jamaican media play in that process.

ENVELOPMENT

Nationalist leaders who inherited governance of the island in 1962 were mainly colored (mixed-race) professionals and educated blacks who emerged from the middle stratum of the racially stratified colonial society. They articulated a nationalist ideology of self-determination and democracy for the island. West Indian philosopher, C.L.R. James rejected the notion that these new leaders, having been the beneficiaries of the best of British education, training, and culture, were the natural proponents of democracy for newly independent Caribbean nations. The West Indian experience of Britain, James suggested, had never been democratic. Instead, it had been an experience of brutal power, and this was what a middle-class-driven state would replicate in the British West Indies (James 1962: 121). Having acquired the social and economic resources to take control of the formal society, the politically ambitious members of the colored and educated black middle stratum would not be eager to share democracy or "freedom" with the wider society (James, 1962).

Sankatsing (2003), writing forty-one years after C.L.R. James, reflects on the failure of the nationalist legacy and attributes this failure to a concept he calls *envelopment*, the uncritical assimilation of perspectives from the developed world without consideration of our context, culture, evolution, internal social dynamism, and history (pp. 2–3). We continue, Sankatsing suggests, as trailer societies allowing our development strategies to be determined by the developed world's agendas and priorities. Envelopment, the antithesis of development, prevents meaningful social and economic progress and increases existing social inequities.

The cultural tropes emerging from Jamaica's history as a trailer society and a slave society serve to legitimize the island's continued subordinate position in its international relations and the pervasive internal social inequalities. The relationship with the United States of America was particularly important in the shaping of the economic ideologies to which the state committed itself post-independence. Dupuy (2001) describes how Caribbean leaders negotiated their countries' development within the terms of a global economic ideology that continued to facilitate Western economic expansionism. North America soon replaced Britain as the locus for Jamaican aspirations. With American consumerism equated with modernity and development, the dramatic change in the lifestyle and tastes, values and consumption habits of the region (Dupuy 2001; St. Rose 2007) meant that the island, having won political independence, remained firmly in a state of economic dependence. Middle stratum nationalist ideology framed this dependence as a natural process in the global economy (Hintzen 2001). Historically disadvantaged groups in the society were, and continue to be, asked to surrender their aspirations for collective survival in the face of continued economic crisis. The exploitation and inequality which had defined colonial Jamaica's internal and external relationships had not been resolved before a new rationalization for inequity evolved: the national interest.

Post-independence, opportunities to address this economic and social disadvantage were compromised by the partisan interests of the political middle stratum who tied citizens' access to opportunities and resources to party loyalty and service. *Political clientelism* became the means by which the political middle stratum manipulated the economic plight of the historically vulnerable groups in the lower stratum. The *National Report on Political Tribalism 1997* describes how political parties use their control of resources, especially housing and jobs, to control and exploit the poor lower stratum.

While access to privileged social, cultural, political, and economic resources under colonial rule facilitated the rise of this brown and black middle stratum elite, it is the electoral process that plays a critical role in legitimizing this middle-stratum oligarchy and creates the illusion of a free and democratic society. The state, the formal extension of the party in power, is sovereign and acts autonomously. The ability to coerce the electorate and manipulate the electoral process became a critical requirement as the nationalist leaders remain unable to generate economic growth.

The Articulation of Jamaican "Classes"

Brown's (1978) redefinition of class is useful for exploring social inequality in Jamaica. In any society, Brown posits, there can only be three classes: a conservative class, a destructive class, and a transformative class (pp. 8–9). A class is a group involved in converting human consciousness into historical action to preserve, destroy, or transform society. Status groups exist in all societies (Brown 1978) and in Jamaica status groups cohere around variables such as race, ethnicity and socioeconomic status. Using Brown's construct of class, however, a group only presents as a "class" when it is consciously engaged in action to maintain, destroy, or transform society.

In Jamaica, conservative class action presents in systems that frame envelopment as development, producing policies that ignore context, culture, evolution, internal social dynamism, and history (Sankatsing 2003). The dialectical relationship between conservative class action and destructive class action is implicit. Destructive class action, locked in violent binary opposition to conservative class action, seeks to destroy the status quo without proffering meaningful alternatives. Transformative class action demystifies the hegemonic and interrogates its own terms of engagement with others in the collective. Halpern (1996) from whose theory of transformation Brown constructs his redefinition of class, defines transformation as "the conscious and creative breaking and refashioning" of previous modes of encounter and interaction among people. This rendition of transformation harmonizes with Sankatsing's emphasis on creation and creativity as central to development and the need for former colonies to learn to trust their own endogenous energies.

Brown's broader framework for understanding class frees political, social, and cultural analyses from the reductive focus on the economic and the pitfall of rendering "masses" as either passive recipients of domination and exploitation or perpetrators of violent resistance. It also suggests that members of privileged groups can, as creative agents, recast new engagements with others in the collective. A class acting to preserve, destroy, or transform society may comprise members of different socioeconomic groups, races, ethnicities, creeds, or gender. This conceptual framework foregrounds the possibility of freeing the present and the future from the overwhelming influence of the past through human agency and creativity.

Confronting reified truth criteria that legitimize and validate inequality and exploitation in the epistemic and cultural common ground of a collective (Van Dijk 1998: 2004) is central to transformative class action. As meanings gain ascendancy, as they become hegemonic, they lose their group specificity and pervade the common ground of knowledge. They become culture. As culture, ideas that were once group specific now present as belonging to people across different groups in the collective. Denuding culture of its apparent innocuousness refocuses us on the extremely high stakes in the process of class contestations.

Hegemonic forces maintain ascendancy through ongoing negotiation in the face of social changes and challenges. Their objective is always the preservation of those core ideas that preserve power. To maintain the central idea of essential white superiority, for example, these forces ceded privilege to the mixed race, the "coloreds" by virtue of that group's association with "whiteness." While they originally suffered legal and social disabilities, the coloreds/browns were accepted into positions that dark-skinned Afro-Jamaicans were denied (Bryan 1991; Johnson 2004) allowing them social and economic mobility. The layered economic and caste structure of nineteenth-century Jamaica (Johnson 2004) is arguably evident in twenty-first-century Jamaica. Social tensions in modern day Jamaica are still defined consistently in terms of "brown-Jamaica" and "black-Jamaica." Acting as part of a conservative class, "brown Jamaica" were slow to use their power to help the black community (Johnson 2004). Then as now, the racial divide remains a serious area of friction in the island (Brown 1978: 45).

The negation of the "personhood" of the Afro-Jamaican was not merely discursive but a critical part of the ideological mechanism for legitimizing a system of economic exploitation. Consequently, black aspirants to the middle stratum of the Jamaican collective, have now, as they did then, a more compelling need than their brown counterparts to separate themselves from the poor black lower stratum. This need became reified in the institutional cultures where educated black groups had power and influence: education, religion, civil and social services (Bryan 1991; Moore and Johnson 2004). Colonial education systems and professional training taught this group the lessons in self-negation, dependence on Britain, and emanation of British colonial values and norms (Bryan 1991). Embedded in this acculturation would be a natural predisposition toward and acceptance of authoritarianism and many of the essential terms of conservative colonial ideology.

Burdened with skin color that still signified inferiority, many among the educated black middle stratum shared the pejorative understandings of "blackness" and "Africanness." As the condition of poor blacks in the island worsened with a struggling agricultural sector and burgeoning urban ghettos, the association of blackness with crime and urban squalor (Moore and Johnson 2004: 10–11) fueled the black middle stratum need to separate itself from the black lower stratum. The need to emanate "whiteness" through social and cultural accoutrement became more desperate. Mastery of the "Queen's English" marked their superiority over Creole-speaking black laborers (Moore and Johnson 2004). Membership in the Church of England, and other European-based denominations, countered the lower stratum's seeming affinity for indigenous forms of religious expression that evinced African retentions or continuities (Patterson 2000). The formation of class identities among the groups who would form the new leaders of an independent Jamaica was the very definition of envelopment. Jamaican-born Stuart Hall (2001) describes how Caribbean people understand and "know" ourselves to be subordinate to a foreign "self" not as something imposed on us but through our own "inner compulsion" and willingness to conform to the norms of our colonial masters (pp. 394–5). This was especially true for the person of black African descent seeking personhood and identity within the context of a conservative class ideology in Jamaica.

Today, members of the black middle stratum often present as the most passionate members of a conservative class, using their positions as educators, civil servants, ministers of religion, et. cetera, to preserve a society of colonial values through their control of the symbolic instruments of their professions (Austin 1984; Bryan 1991; Moore and Johnson 2004; Patterson 2000). As a conservative class, they construct and prescribe *a self* that situates other Afro-Jamaicans "outside" of society. This construct serves as legitimization of the dispossession evident among the lower stratum who, the discourse suggests, are poor as a result of their own essential inferiority.

The rise of an educated or skilled black middle stratum therefore held very little real opportunity for the evolution of a transformative consciousness in the Jamaican collective, certainly not one that would result in reducing inequalities. "Otherness" now was not just a position imposed on blacks by whites or "browns," but by blacks on other blacks. The naturalness of educated colored and black middle stratum leadership post-independence was constructed as self-evident.

The colored and black middle stratum used the plight of the black laboring classes as the platform to further establish their power through leadership of trade unions and political parties aligned with the trade unions. While reifying the notion of the black lower stratum as "laborers, the coloured and black middle stratum represented the employer/employee relationship as mutually beneficial" (Richards 2002: 349) for nationalist ideology, distracting black laborers from the continued devaluation of their personhood as people of African descent. Consistent with conservative British colonial ideology, nationalist leaders saw any call to African pride as a threat to nation-building. The colored and black middle stratum, through trade unionism—the seedbed of the modern political movement—silenced the "race" issue in the largest black working-class population in the British West Indies (Richards 2002: 351).

An Oligarchic System of Exploitation and Domination

Offering the laboring classes a "Jamaican" identity would provide probably the only common ground the new leaders wished to share. With "all of us" being "Jamaican," nationalist ideologues could construct their power and privilege without seeming to run afoul of the concept of self-determination, equality, and a free society where these were understood in limited terms as the removal of white British colonial masters. Working with ideological terms of colonial authoritarianism, privilege, and state autonomy that were culturally familiar to the collective (Gray 2004) the nationalist elite would not expect any resistance. The Afro-Jamaican underclasses should "know" and understand the naturalness of his/her betters to rule and appreciate his/her own place in the social order without anything having to be said about race or color.

Oligarchy is not antithetical to democracy where an understanding of democracy is limited to an electoral process. While the electoral form of democracy is a necessary condition for a just society, it is not a guarantee of democracy or the sharing of power (Hadenius and Teorell 2005). Where the electorate lacks the economic and cultural resources to participate as citizens, then democracy becomes meaningless and the existence of minority rule is not only facilitated; it is endorsed and legitimized by the "appearance" of majority consent. Oligarchy as the politics of wealth defense (Winters 2011) and specifically the defense of concentrated wealth includes, in the Jamaican context, the middle stratum's defense of privilege and status. The relatively peaceful transition of control from the colonial oligarchs to the new leadership evinces an insignificant alteration in ideology in regard to social inequalities experienced by the Afro-Jamaican lower stratum majority. The *oligarchic system of exploitation and domination,* constructed by the British to defend its wealth in the island, was never dismantled by the new breed of local leaders who were shaping their own control of the collective.

That there were alternative perspectives and other potential leaders for an independent Jamaica is obfuscated by a conservative reading of Jamaican history. Such a reading implies that oppressed Afro-Jamaicans lacked the facility for contemplative response to exploitation and were only capable of sporadic violent uprisings and atavistic rage (Beckles 2000). Centuries of enslavement and systemic inequality did not remove the Afro-Jamaican sense that s/he was being exploited and unjustly treated. Evidence of agency, of efforts to respond to context and environment with a view to self-actualization is evident in the history of the Afro-Jamaican community (Dunkley 2013). The examples of marronage are evident. The history of domination and exploitation in Jamaica pre- and post-Independence is therefore not simply about the passive compliance of the powerless to structures of first colonial then middle stratum state domination.

The antagonism colonial leaders and then nationalist leaders had to groups espousing alternative articulations of nationhood and identity, especially those that sought to revalue African identity, robbed the Jamaican collective of potential for transformation. The articulations of identity and ethnicity proposed by Jamaica's Marcus Garvey were denounced by nationalist leaders at independence (Martin 1976). Bogues (2002b) bravely explores the attempts of an Afro-Jamaican revolutionary and religious leader, the "infamous" Claudius Henry, to organize Afro-Jamaicans at home and abroad to prepare first for repatriation to Africa and later for rebellion against the state. Bogues (2002b) identifies the Henry movement as an "explicit moment of subaltern intervention" (p. 26) and attributes the crisis that now faces the nationalist state elite to their lack of consideration of the lived experiences of the Afro-Caribbean person.

The hegemony of conservative class ideologies makes it difficult to evolve consensus about what would have constituted transformational ideologies and class action in Jamaican society. Many of the groups proposing alternative approaches to society were represented as illegitimate and criminal, first by the colonial government and then the ruling middle class nationalist elite. The role of the media was, and is today, critical in representing these alterative ideologies as dangerous. Lewis (2001) suggests that political analysis consider the role of the British Colonial Office in the positioning of an elite from the middle stratum as leaders of an independent Jamaica while leaders with alternative perspectives and ideologies were crushed.

In light of the political, social, and cultural context outlined, the absence of appropriate policies to address the colonial legacy of asset inequality among the mass of the people (Richards Elliott and Palmer 2008) present as major retardants to development in Jamaica and facilitates the continued plight of disadvantaged groups. Fifty-two years after independence, no fundamental institutional adjustments to address the problem of limited land tenure exist. The state is still predisposed to support the plantation legacies of asset and wealth inequity (Richards Elliott and Palmer 2008). Richards Elliott and Palmer point to a number of these policies: policies that privilege those who produce for export (usually large land-owners and corporations) ignoring the need of local farmers who produce for domestic consumption; the state's pursuit of foreign investment through devaluation ignoring the steady decline of the Jamaican exchange rate despite high interest rates; the creation of a burgeoning distributive sector with a large low-wage labor force which has served to increase gaps in income distribution; institutional rigidity which prevents the state from countering historical trends of inequality and low growth (p. 193). In a context where the vast majority have no property or material interests, the system works, inevitably in the service of an elite few.

For many in the black majority, the political party system remains their only available access to influence the system (Stone 1973: 20). Obika Gray's description of a Jamaican state locked in a pernicious negotiation with the most vulnerable among the urban poor (Gray 2004) graphically illustrates this domination of which Hintzen (1997) writes and the role of the political parties in securing state domination. The state which Gray describes (2004) has the dubious flexibility of formal and informal power. Through legislation it can restrict and contend with resistance and implement the terms of its ideologies through the courts and law enforcement. Informally, it deploys—often with plausible deniability—armed criminal thugs to discourage resistance across the society.

Richards Elliot and Palmer (2008) point to Jamaica's maintenance of a parliamentarian majoritarian model when all evidence suggests that a proportional system would be more representative of a truly democratic system. The current system relies on the parliamentarian majoritarian model to consolidate party control of state resources despite the deleterious effect this has on the quality of governance in the collective. What Gray says of this type of parasitic rule is important for a proper understanding of elite domination in Jamaican collective and Black Anglophone oligarchy. Gray describes this parasitic rule as being in the interest of the specific group that controls the state; it is not *for* the rich upper stratum or *against* the poor; it is for the elite political middle stratum who do what they have to do to defend their privileged position. It will both defend and subvert its own policies if needed (p. 8). Gray (2004) refers to the Jamaican state having to expunge rebellious challenges from below (p. 8). Lewis (2001) defines the Jamaican state as, "the site of middle class elite mobilization of the people" and talks about Jamaica's, "necessary preoccupation with the state" (p. 127).

The apparent impotence of other status groups within the middle stratum to confront the oligarchy in their midst is a complicating factor. While there is clear marginalization of the Creole-speaking Afro-Jamaican from the lower stratum, it is important to an overall understanding of the nature of Anglophone oligarchy in the island that one appreciates the extent to which the political middle stratum intimidates others in the middle stratum. Fear of the political middle stratum and what is perceived as their ability to deploy thugs from the dangerous lower stratum or, alternatively, the state's armed forces, against opposing groups is typical in Jamaica. Alternatively, through a system of corruption endemic to the political party system, potentially productive members of the middle stratum are prevented from accessing legitimate state benefits if they fail to demonstrate loyalty to the party in power (Robotham 2007). The ostracism these black businesspeople also experience from the non-black commercial classes and traditional economic power brokers completes their exclusion from mainstream influence.

THE "EMERGENCE" OF A JAMAICAN "IDENTITY"

The cultural stranglehold the oligarch's maintain on formal society marginalizes emerging Creole-speaking Afro-Jamaican entrepreneurs and potential leaders. Composition of the middle stratum in the Jamaican collective continued to evolve post-independence with a group who originated in the black lower strata and who, through work-related migration, trade or the acquisition of non-traditional but marketable technical skills, gained affluence without the cultural trappings valued by the society's middle stratum elite (Stone 1973 and Lewis 2001). Many of these new arrivants would find, however, that the existing oligarchs needed a guarantee of personal and political loyalty if they were to enjoy the benefits of access to the resources of formal society.

The paucity of attention paid to language rights (Devonish 2002) evinces this coloniality of citizenship and further handicaps the island's Creole-speaking majority. Creole-speaking citizens, despite affluence and influence, are assigned "lower stratum status." Though given the "vote," these Jamaicans are generally alienated from the processes of formal power (Lewis 2001) and this alienation is legitimized in dominant discourse. Formal society treats language *rights* as unimportant, even irrelevant and resists efforts to amend formal systems to better facilitate the Creole speaker.

As an alternative, the state offers state-funded institutions and festivals as an approved space for folk and popular culture. In the context of cultural rituals for song and dance, cultural expressions from the lower stratum are relegated to the artistic and the ornamental while the naturalness of middle stratum language, manners and acculturation for the important affairs of state and for personal and professional development are endorsed and legitimized.

Beyond the issue of language, middle stratum domination of formal society contextualizes education strategically as a benefit tied to "ability." Students with "ability" must be identified and given opportunities. Invariably, the disadvantages faced by socioeconomically disadvantaged groups are unaccounted for and state-funded "free places," ostensibly in the service of the poor, evolved over time to serve the children of the middle stratum who, with access to better resources, have a competitive advantage in vying for these positions. Assignment to a valorized high school, schools with a history of association with middle and upper stratum groups and European-based churches, presents successful youngsters with access to better teachers, learning resources and social associations for navigating a collective dominated by the middle stratum.

Government secondary schools set up by the state and traditionally seen as the schools for the lower strata, continue to be the schools for those who "do not do as well" as those assigned to elite schools. Although some of these institutions have been showing tremendous achievements in their output of successful students, their continued association as a category of schools for the black lower stratum makes them unattractive to the more affluent in the collective. Jamaica's education system is easily the most poignant illustration of inequality and Anglophone middle stratum oligarchy in the collective.

The relevance of language rights and an equitable education system to confronting inequality in Jamaica is important. Without these resources, disadvantaged groups face another kind of social dependence. Accompanying middle stratum elite domination of the state is the middle stratum domination of various bodies and agencies claiming to "speak" for the dispossessed. Not-for-profits and nongovernmental agencies constitute another space where advocates from the middle stratum claim to represent the lower stratum which "obviously" has neither the language nor the competencies to represent its own interests and needs middle stratum agents. The Jamaican middle stratum elite are, as a consequence, able to expand their social and cultural capital, consolidate and defend their power and influence. Through a nationalist ideology, this group can actively pursue common interests with owners of economic power locally and internationally without disturbing the façade of "nationalism" and "sovereignty" (Hintzen 1997).

These relations of affinity (Hinztin 1997) between Jamaican elite groups and international agencies and organizations deepen unquestioning adaptation of formulae from the north. In the pursuit of "funding" we surrender the creative consideration of our own realities and exacerbate our current dilemma (Richards Elliott and Palmer 2008). The symbiotic relationship between the political middle stratum and the local technocracy complete the triadic collaboration with multinational interests. Richards Elliott and Palmer (2008) suggest that the mere fact of having colored and black home-grown leaders does not guarantee successful development where these leaders continue to operate using old technologies of governance.

The critical role of media in conservative class action in Jamaica must be part of any analysis. As a cultural industry, media draws its truth criteria from cultural common ground of knowledge. Through its significatory practices and choices, media acts to preserve, destroy or transform society. As significant contributors to the epistemic and cultural common ground, their products are social texts (Fiske and Hartley 1994; Goldman and Rajagopal 1991) and these texts are important ideological artifacts in ongoing class contestations.

The Role of Media Professionals

Before independence, information and communication technology evolved for colonial control of the empire (Dunn 2014). The development of the media industry in Jamaica post-independence provided new professional spaces for aspiring brown/black middle stratum professionals who either emerged from or became part of the middle stratum through access to education or social associations. The most successful and influential local media houses today are owned and operated by groups from the upper stratum who employ middle stratum professionals to run their organizations. It is in the complex reality of middle stratum domination of the state and the marginalization of the non-Anglophone lower stratum that media professionals play out their role as social mediators and ideological arbiters. Daily decision making as regards operations and framing of content clearly reflects the conservative ideology that maintains status quo even as the media interacts with counter-hegemonic groups. It is in the tropes and rituals of media operations that we see Black Anglophone nationalism's finest ideological work.

In Jamaica, one need not be a "professional" journalist or "trained" media practitioner where the appropriate acculturation is evident in language, dress deportment, and social association. The radio call in programs, for example, have come to characterize Jamaican radio. The host invariably oscillates between roles as counselor and censor. Many from marginalized groups find assistance in getting state or private sector attention for their concerns through these programs. The middle stratum mediator for the Creole-speaking underclass is now not only a feature of politics, trade unionism, and advocacy groups but of media as well.

Television in Jamaica has been accused of facilitating North American cultural invasion of the island and undermining nationalist efforts to build a strong local culture. Until 1994, the state had the monopoly on television broadcasting which it started in 1963. Originally, nationalist leaders looked to television to assist in the project of development and modernization. They anticipated that exposure to foreign worlds through television would move the populace out of its essential backwardness. It appeared that at the outset of the venture, nationalist leaders feared the essential backwardness of the underclasses more than they feared foreign influence.

Television came to Jamaica through a foreign consortium made up of Thomson Television International, the National Broadcasting Corporation of America, and Television International. The Jamaican Government "owned" the company, but financial and other direction came through the consortium. Members of the consortium were owners of commercial television stations in their own countries—Britain, the United States of America. The Jamaican national leadership had underestimated the baggage that would come with this expert assistance (Nettleford 1993). The introduction of television constituted little more than the retrofitting of the young nation for its role as consumer and peripheral trailer society in a larger global industry.

Nettleford speaks of North American media having "hi-jacked" the region's media, invaded the Caribbean people's intellectual space and bombarded the region "by every means possible" (Nettleford 1993: 129). Brown (1995) counters however that Caribbean citizens, and Jamaicans in particular have been eager consumers of American media content and technologies (Brown 1995: 52). That the people on the screens don't look like the majority of us would hardly deter a populace schooled for centuries in the negation of the black-African person. We could accept this new form of cultural invasion because our encounters with the British had taught us to valorize the likenesses of our "masters." Seeing these Caucasian subjects on our screens was not only aesthetically pleasing, it was culturally and ideologically appropriate for our ingrained self-hate.

Radio and newspapers in Jamaica typically carry a larger percentage of local content than does television. These media, however, continue to evince conservative class action. Jamaican Creole is virtually absent from local newspapers currently although there were isolated instances of Creole use by some columnists in the past. Radio has sporadic and limited instances in which Creole is used for formal programming, that is, news broadcasting. English is the predominant language of "serious" media in Jamaica. Creole is the language of the sound-bite, comedic advertising and entertainment programming.

News is a local product and ostensibly focuses us on our collective selves. It provides ample evidence of middle stratum control. Jamaican news is overwhelmingly about the state. That news is about politics (Gans 1980: 29) is not peculiar to Jamaica but it is nevertheless useful in maintaining the practice of politics in Jamaica and the dominance of the political middle stratum through the state. Our history makes the news a significant ideological tool for conservative class action. What Lewis describes as the Jamaican's "necessary preoccupation with the state" (Lewis 2001: 127) and Stone refers to as the Jamaican masses "only" means through which to influence the Jamaican power structure (Stone 1989: 20) has tangible expression in the form and content of local news stories.

News logic provides legitimacy to a political directorate of dubious character which has historically preyed on the populace for individual and partisan political and economic advancement. Even as it reports on state scandals and the misdeeds of its officers, news naturalizes the state. News presence is overwhelmingly distributed to the state and its agents. Other groups from the middle strata—professionals and leaders in nonpolitical contexts—typically appear in news stories where they interact with state officials or have some connection to "hard" news contexts that is, crime, violence and fatalities. Even as news content fixates on the state, it consistently situates the Afro-Jamaican Creole-speaking lower stratum as violent criminals, social malcontents, and victims.

Johnson (2008) suggests that despite the ideological frames media uses for its subjects, marginalized groups in the Jamaican collective do co-opt media coverage and use it as a platform to air their dissatisfaction with poor infrastructure and state services. Media, especially television broadcast media, craves visual spectacle for its daily offerings. The extent to which this action by underclass groups meaningfully counters dominant ideological representations of the poor and dispossessed as criminals, malcontents, or victims, is questionable. The cries of "We want justice!" that have become the standard fare of news broadcasts of citizen protests scarcely seem to disturb middle stratum state dominance and may, unfortunately, have become trivialized and even ridiculed by the more privileged in the collective.

It is undeniable that counter hegemonic voices have access to mass media, especially through entertainment programs, to "chant down" the system. These voices use these conceded spaces to effect significant challenge to hegemonic ideologies and to make themselves required fare of any broadcast medium needing to survive commercially in modern Jamaica. Through its regulatory systems, however, the state is able to buttress the defenses of conservative class interests and circumvent the commercial imperative in order to insist on what is to be considered acceptable and permissible. While regulations about content seemed to concur with the general society's codes of "decency," directives seem to target cultural expressions emerging from the Black Creole-speaking lower stratum.

In February 2009, Jamaica's state regulatory body, the Broadcasting Commission, issued a directive on the transmission of sexually explicit content. The directive prohibited broadcasting companies from airing any material that reflected the highly sexualized "daggering" dance form and any lyrics suggesting the act of "daggering." Critics insisted that the "daggering directive" reflected the state penchant for countering cultural forms coming from the lower strata's "dancehall" music while ignoring equally "indecent" cultural forms emerging from the middle and upper strata. Some members of the public called for similar restrictions to be put on the broadcasting of highly sexualized dance forms and lyrics associated with soca/calypso, a genre of Caribbean music which had become characteristic of upper and middle strata social events and festivals in Jamaica. Two weeks after the issuing of the "daggering directive," a second directive was issued which would include Soca and Calypso forms and Hip Hop.

Media in Jamaica are vital elements of the consumer economy and exist primarily to advertise goods and services in the profit environment. Information dissemination, and news, are "ancillary functions" to the profit making purpose (Brown 1995). It is in the interest of its commercial function that media negotiates a tenuous relationship with marginalized groups; it reinforces the prescribed terms of conservative middle stratum ideology and upper stratum interests while it seeks to profit from and exploit the increasingly lucrative cultural artifacts of marginalized groups in the collective. In the face of increasing competition from local and international media, Jamaican media struggles to maintain critical ideological non-negotiables on behalf of elite groups while, in the interest of its bottom line, maintaining its relevance to groups on the margin. Within the terms of dominant ideology, however, media must still represent and signify this other "Jamaica" as undesirable and aberrant. This has become a significant challenge as the cultural forms characteristic of underclass groups in the Jamaican collective continue to be in demand locally and abroad. To execute this delicate balance of maintaining ideological relevance and commercial survival, the Jamaican media relies heavily on state regulatory machinery to shield it from counter-hegemonic challenges that demand legitimacy. Media can exclude resistant ideologies and counter-hegemonic expressions on the basis of "the regulations" and preserve its image as a popular institution.

CONCLUSION

Despite having new players in the industry, media in Jamaica still has not ventured far from conservative class action. Radio broadcasting has increased exponentially over the past twenty years with non-traditional institutions coming forward as media owners: educational institutions, churches, and community groups. The ideological landscape has not altered significantly however, with the offerings—religious or secular—still remaining essentially committed to the consensus of mainstream values and norms. The reliance on private sector sponsorship and funding through advertising prevents any significant counter-hegemonic action in content or operation. As the pool of advertisers decreases, and media houses rely increasingly on a few large private companies and the state for advertisements, the possibility of significant ruptures with conservative ideology seems unlikely.

While media facilitates coverage of the state and the activities of its agents and professes a watchdog role in the society, its commercial and institutional needs keep it from raising larger questions about the legitimacy of the state and its collaboration with local and external commercial interests in restricting opportunities for growth among less privileged groups. Major departures from conservative class action in media seem to await the emergence of new sources of funding with alternative perspectives on development and social progress in Jamaica. The creativity and internal dynamism needed to become the engine of a new age in Jamaica's development are threatened less by external forces and more by the operations of black, Anglophone elite groups within the society to maintain their control of state resources, state power, and formal society. The link between inequality and essentially non-democratic political systems are evident. The connection between inadequate development of the island's human capital and the preservation of archaic authoritarian systems of governance through which an elite constructs its own power is past debate.

REFERENCES

Acemoğlu, Daron, Simon Johnson and James Robinson (2001). The colonial origins of comparative development: an empirical investigation. *American Economic Review* 91: 1369–1401.

Austin, Diane (1984). Symbols and ideologies of class in urban Jamaica. In *Culture, race and class in the Commonwealth Caribbean*, ed. Michael G. Smith, 76–85. Mona, Jamaica: Dept. of Extra-Mural Studies, University of West Indies.

Beckles, Hilary (2000). Caribbean anti-slavery: The self-liberation ethos of enslaved blacks. In *Caribbean slavery in the Atlantic world: A student reader*, eds. Verene Shepherd and Hilary Beckles, 869–878. Kingston: Ian Randle Publishers.

Bogues, Anthony (2002a). Nationalism and Jamaican political thought. In *Jamaica in slavery and freedom*, eds. Kathleen Monteith and Glen Richards, 363–387. Kingston: UWI Press.

Bogues, Anthony (2002b). Politics, nation and postcolony: Caribbean inflections. *Small Axe* 11: 1–30.

Brown, Aggrey (1995). Caribbean culture and mass communication technology: Re-examining the cultural dependency thesis. In *Globalization, communications and Caribbean identity*, ed. Hopeton Dunn, 40 -54. Kingston: Ian Randle Publishers.

Brown, Aggrey (1978). *Color, class and politics in Jamaica.* New Brunswick: Transaction Books.

Bryan, Patrick (1991). *The Jamaican people: 1880–1902.* London: MacMillan Caribbean.

Devonish, Hubert (2002). "Language rights, justice and the constitution," *The Sunday Gleaner,* January 13, 2002. http://jamaica-gleaner.com/gleaner/20020113/focus/.focus1.html.

Dunkley, Daive A. (2013). *Agency of the enslaved: Jamaica and the culture of freedom in the Atlantic world.* London: Lexington Books.

Dunn, Hopeton. S. (2014). Imperial foundations of 20th-century media systems in the Caribbean. *Critical Arts: A South-North Journal of Cultural & Media Studies* 28(6):938–957.

Dupuy, Alex (2001). The new world order, globalization and Caribbean politics. In *New Caribbean thought: A reader*, eds. Brian Meeks and Folke Lindahl, 521–536. Kingston: The University of the West Indies Press.

Fiske, John and John Hartley (1994). *Reading television.* London: Routledge.

Gans, Herbert (1980). *Deciding what's news : A study of CBS evening news, NBC nightly news, Newsweek and Time.* USA: Vintage.

Goldman, Robert and Arvind Rajagopal (1991). *Mapping hegemony: Television news coverage of industrial conflict.* London: Ablex Publishing.

Gray, Obika (2004). *Demeaned but empowered: Social power of the urban poor in Jamaica.* Kingston: University of the West Indies Press.

Hadenius, Axel and Jan Teorell (2005). Cultural and economic prerequisites of democracy: Reassessing recent evidence. *Studies in Comparative International Development* 39:87–106.

Hall, Stuart. (2001). Negotiating Caribbean identities. In *New Caribbean thought: A reader*, eds. Brian. Meeks and Folke Lindahl, 24–39. Kingston: The University of the West Indies Press.

Halpern, Manfred (1996). *The archetype of capitalism: A critical analysis in the light of a theory of transformation*. San Francisco: American Political Science Association.

Halpern, Manfred (1976). A redefinition of the revolutionary situation. *Journal of International Affairs, 23*(1): 54–75. Columbia University, School of International Affairs.

Henke, Holger (2004). Ariel's ethos: On the moral economy of Caribbean existence. *Cultural Critique* 56:33–63.

Henry, Paget (2000). *Caliban's reason: introducing Afro-Caribbean philosophy*. London: Routledge.

Hintzen, Percy C. (2001). Rethinking democracy in the postnationalist state. In *New Caribbean thought: A reader*, eds. Brian Meeks and Folke Lindahl, 104–126. Kingston: The University of the West Indies Press.

Hintzen, Percy C. (1997). Reproducing domination, identity and legitimacy constructs in the West Indies. *Social Identities: Journal for the Study of Race, Nation and Culture* 3 (1): 47–76.

James, Cyril L.R. (1962). *Party politics in the West Indies*. San Juan: Vedic Enterprises.

Johnson, Hume Nicola (2008). "Performing" protest in Jamaica: The mass media as stage. *International Journal of Media and Cultural Politics* 4(2): 163–182.

Johnson, Tekla Ali (2004). The enduring function of caste: colonial and modern Haiti, Jamaica, and Brazil: The economy of race, the social organization of caste, and the formulation of racial societies. *Comparative American Studies: An international journal* 2(1): 61–73.

Kamugisha, Aaron (2007). The coloniality of citizenship in the contemporary Anglophone Caribbean. *Race & Class* 49 (2): 20–40.

Lewis, Rupert (2001). Reconsidering the role of the middle class in Caribbean politics. In *New Caribbean thought: A reader*, eds. Brian Meeks and Folke Lindahl, 127–143. Kingston: The University of the West Indies Press.

Martin, Tony (1976). *Race first: The Ideological and Organizational Struggles of Marcus Garvey and the Universal Negro Improvement Association*. Mass. USA: Majority Press.

Meeks, Brian (1996). *Radical Caribbean: From black power to Abu Bakr*. Barbados: The University of the West Indies Press.

Moore, Brian L. and Johnson, Michele. A. (2004). *Neither led nor driven: Contesting British cultural imperialism in Jamaica*, 1865–1920. Kingston, Jamaica: University of the West Indies Press.

Nettleford, Ralston (1993). *Inward stretch outward reach: A voice from the Caribbean*. London: MacMillan.

Patterson, Orlando (2000). The constituent elements of slavery. In *Caribbean slavery in the Atlantic world: A student reader*, eds. Verene Shepherd and Hilary Beckles, 32–41. Kingston: Ian Randle Publishers.

Richards Elliott, Dawn, and Ransford W. Palmer (2008). Institutions and Caribbean economic performance: Insights from Jamaica. *Studies in Comparative International Development 43:181*–205.

Richards, Glen (2002). Race, class and labor politics in colonial Jamaica: 1900–1934. In *Jamaica in slavery and freedom: History, heritage and culture*, eds. Kathleen Monteith and Glen Richards, 340–362. Kingston: University of the West Indies Press.

Robotham, D. (2007) "Corruption and the Black Bourgeoisie," *The Sunday Gleaner*, October 28, 2007. http://jamaica-gleaner.com/gleaner/20071028/cleisure/.cleisure2.html.

Sankatsing, Glenn (2003). "The Caribbean Between Envelopment and Development." http://www.crscenter.com/The%20Caribbean%20between%20Envelopment.%20and%20Development.pdf.

Sokoloff, Kenneth L., and Stanley L. Engerman (2000). History lessons: institutions, factor endowments, and paths of development in the new world. *Journal of Economic Perspectives* 14:217–32.

Stone, Carl (1989). Power, policy and politics in independent Jamaica. In *Jamaica in independence: Essays on the early years,* ed. Ralston Nettleford, 20–29. Kingston: Heinemann.

Stone, Carl (1973). *Class, race and political behavior in urban Jamaica.* Kingston: Institute of Social and Economic Research, University of the West Indies.

St. Rose, Marius (2007). Culture and economics: Is socialization a constraint on our development? In *Economic theory and development options for the Caribbean: The Sir Arthur Lewis memorial lectures 1996–2005,* 107–123. Jamaica: Ian Randle.

Van Dijk, Teun A. (2004). Discourse, knowledge and ideology: Reformulating old questions and proposing some new solutions. In *Communicating ideologies: Multidisciplinary perspectives on language, discourse, and social practice,* eds. Martin Pütz , JoAnne Neff-van Aertslaer, and Teun A. van Dijk, 5–38. Frankfurt am Main: Peter Lang—Europäischer Verlag der Wissenschaften.

Van Dijk, Teun A. (1998). *Ideology: a multidisciplinary approach*. London: Sage.

Winters, Jeffrey A. (2011).Democracy and oligarchy. *American Interest* 7, (2): 18–27.

World Bank (2014). "Jamaica Overview." http://www.worldbank.org/en/country/jamaica/overview

Chapter Seven

Media Representation of Class Issues in Turkey

A Review on Media Coverage of Work-Related Rights

A. Fulya Sen and Y. Furkan Sen

INTRODUCTION

Neoliberal policies were implemented in the UK and United States under both the Thatcher and Reagan administrations in the 1980s and have since been adapted around the world. These policies include privatization, de-regulation of financial sectors, increased openess to foreign trade and investment, and cuts to public welfare spending. Since the 1980s, the labor conditions have changed considerably in comparison with prior periods in most so-called welfare states. A broad definition of a welfare state could be a system whereby the state undertakes to protect the health and well-being of its citizens, especially those in financial or social need, by means of grants, pensions, and other benefits. In other words, a system of social protection, family sustaining wages, strong labor unions, and good quality public social services. However, the working class has gradually lost these (and other) social security guarantees in Turkey.

Wessels (2014: 106) has defined the character of work as a driver of social change. For instance, during the industrial period, while a collective factory-based workforce could organize to lobby for improved working conditions through the trade union movement, in the current global economy this is no longer the case. Workplace deregulation has undermined the organized working class. Winlow and Hall (2013: 14, 70) have pointed out the reduction of employment opportunities and wages, and the restriction of the legal entitlements of low-wage earners during the neoliberal period.

On the other hand, the question of why so many working and non-working poor people voted for neoliberal political parties that created policies directly antagonistic to their class interests needs to be addressed as well. The fundamental issue at stake is that the working class is no longer represented in the political arena.

It is clear to us that the world is unfair, unequal and full of inequality. Social inequalities can be differences in income, resources, power, and status within and between societies (Warwick-Booth 2013: 2). According to the OECD *Report on Inequality and Poverty* (2013: 3), Nordic and Central European countries have the lowest inequality of disposable income, while inequality is high in Chile, Mexico, Turkey, the United States, and Israel. In Turkey, there is relatively little media coverage of working-class and class inequalities as a general public issue. Curran's arguments being related to the US media can also apply to Turkey. Curran (2011: 37) argues that poverty tends to be depicted in terms of "poor people." Accordingly, news reports about poverty are more likely to focus on instances of poor people rather than the causes of poverty or public policies related to this. The American media have long encouraged the view that poverty arises from personal deficiencies with complete disregard to the causes of poverty.

The media rarely consider the macro-level causes of impoverishment, such as inequality of opportunites in education and healthcare, underemployment due to economic shifts and fatal accidents at work as well as issues of subcontracting. Media representations are increasingly determined by different social contexts on a global scale. Power relations are encoded in media representations, and media representations in turn produce and reproduce power relations by constructing knowledge, values, conceptions, and beliefs (Orgad 2012: 25).

The problematic issue of this study is the loss of the relevence of the working-class in the process of global capitalism and, consequently, neglected class issues and work-related rights by the mainstream media. The goal of this study is to debate the *invisibility of class identity* in the mainstream news media and to examine the media representations of class, labor issues, and work-related rights as a part of social welfare rights. This will be attempted examining news texts concerning the deaths of mine workers, subcontracting systems, precarious working conditions, flexible working systems, and the unfair distribution of income in the mainstream and social-democrat media. In order to analyze this landscape of representations and the relationship between capitalism and the mass media, this chapter is based on the political economic approach which emphasizes the economic/material dimensions of the mass media.

This study focuses on the ways in which the media discusses labor rights, work-related rights, and how the political economy of the media industries influences media content on social inequalities. This chapter argues that media contents have often reproduced the inequalities that exist in a society based on class. That is to say that the dominant class has control over the media industry, and media content has typically reflected their perspectives of the world. This chapter starts with a summary of the social-welfare rights and the process of neoliberalism. The next two sections move from a literature review on representation of the working class in media and a quantitative analysis of the newspapers' coverage of the work-related rights to a qualitative analysis.

SOCIAL-WELFARE RIGHTS AND THE CHANGING WORKING CLASS IN THE PROCESS OF NEOLIBERALISM

The twentieth century has seen a radical transformation of both the idea and the institutions of social welfare. The most significant catalysts for public social welfare policy changes have been the century's major economic and political developments, such as the First World War, the 1930s economic depression, the Second World War, the postwar economic boom, and the economic recessions and re-structuring of the 1970s and 1980s. The first three postwar decades constituted a period of continued economic growth and prosperity, and can be defined as the *golden years of the welfare state*. Public social welfare programs were expanded to include a variety of population groups (Dixon and Scheurell 2002: 233). Welfare states have mostly been trying to reduce economic inequality through welfare benefits and services, as well as through educational and health systems. It tried to reduce significant economic inequalities by means of often interconnected policies regarding social protection, labor participation, education, working and living conditions, and health care (Oorschot and Finsveen 2009: 190).

The period between 1945 and the early 1970s was a long period of economic stability and prosperity for most of the Western nations. Often referred to as the Long Boom, this Keynesian/Fordist settlement between capital and labor, of mass production and mass consumption was reinforced and supported by the welfare state. The emergence of economic liberalism, increasing globalization, the reconstruction of the welfare state and the move toward a more market-driven approach to social provision has radically reshaped policies in all these fields, calling for new perspectives and new tools of analysis. With the "winding back" of the welfare state, the emergence of a new conservatism and attacks on established social and civil rights, it is important that policy makers and policy analysts who are concerned about protecting and advancing rights seek to critically appraise these basic concepts and categories. Neo-liberal policies have radically altered the public domain through privatization, downsizing, the contracting out and rationing of services and an emphasis on local and individual autonomy (Barns et al. 1999: 2, 11).

The welfare state has been the subject of major controversies over the past several decades. The neoliberal political revolutions of the 1980s—Reaganism in the United States, Thatcherism in the UK—got their focus and raison d'être largely by promising to dismantle the governmental formations built up during the previous half century. These reform movements promised smaller government, lower taxes, an end to entitlements, and a host of social benefits that would accrue from self-reliance rather than governmental largesse. In the West, the growth of postwar welfare states has caused concern about the proper domains of state action, the allegedly negative effects of welfare upon its recipients, and the economic costs of these social policies. Global changes in the social and institutional worlds are rapidly outdistancing our understanding of the state's capacities. The welfare-state project has often been referred to as a middle path or *third way*. This way is usually seen as threading between two equally unsavory alternatives: state-planned socialism versus laissez-faire capitalism. As a result, the welfare state is widely regarded as a redistributive and regulatory mechanism, one that acts as a counterweight to the capitalist economy (Olson 2006).

Esping-Andersen (1990: 1–3) notes that the welfare state has been approached both narrowly and broadly. Those who take the narrower view see it in terms of the traditional terrain of social improvements, such as the transfer of income and social services. The broader view contains issues of employment, wages, and the overall components of the welfare state-complex. The extension of social rights has been the salient characteristic of welfare states. Social rights are also associated with people's living standards independent of pure market forces. *Equality* has always been what welfare states were supposed to produce, yet the image of balance has always remained rather vague. The issues of de-commodification, social stratification, and employment are keys to a welfare state's identity. According to Esping-Andersen (1990: 22), de-commodified rights develop differentially in contemporary welfare states. In a social-assistance dominated welfare program, rights are not so much attached to work performance as to a demonstrable need. A second dominant model espouses compulsory state social insurance with fairly strong entitlements. The third dominant model of welfare, namely the Beveridge-type-citizens' benefit, may appear the most de-commodifying. It offers a basic, equal benefit to all, irrespective of prior earnings, contributions, or performance.

In the 2000s, social assistance practices were transformed and led to an explosion in de-facto government programs carried out by an extraordinary swarm of NGOs, voluntary organizations, and private foundations. "Neoliberalism" has become the name for a set of highly interested public policies that have vastly enriched the holders of capital, while leading to increasing inequality, insecurity, loss of public services, and a general deterioration of a quality of life for the poor and working classes (Ferguson 2009). Neoliberalism has returned to the laissez-faire economy of the nineteenth century, where capital had relatively few social obligations imposed on it. The politics of social consensus and social democracy emerged in the 1930s after the laissez-faire economy crashed worldwide, and the welfare state has become the symbol of a compromise between the demands of labor and capitalist imperatives (Wayne and O'Neill 2013: 490).

Bauman (2005: 71) separates the poor classes into different categories. Accordingly, "*working class*" evokes an image of a class of people who have a role to play in the life of a society, who make a useful contribution to that society as a whole. "*Lower class*" evokes an image of a class of people who stand or are cast at the bottom of a ladder which they may yet climb, and so exit from their present inferiority. The term "*underclass*" belongs to the imagery of a society which is not all-embracing and comprehensive, which is smaller than the sum of its parts. Underclass evokes an image of a class of people who are beyond classes and outside hierarchy, with neither chance nor need of re-admission; people without role, making no useful contribution to the lives of the rest, and in principle are beyond redemption.

Marxist theory has made important contributions highlighting some still relevant points for consideration in relation to the existence of social stratification. Notably, the deliberations about capitalism and inequality have focused on the differences in social and economic resources. According to a Marxist perspective, the wealth of the ruling class is based not on land ownership, rather, it is related to production. Inequality within society brought many social problems, such as the increasing drive for profit, called the constant crisis of profit, the accumulation of wealth and the alienation of workers who are simply part of a machine of mass production (quoted in Warwick-Booth 2013: 16). According to Öngen (2012: 14), Marx's most notable contribution to the theory of history is not the discovery of the existence of classes or the class struggle, rather the *causal relationship* between the existence of classes and the developments in production. Marx (2004: 772) splits these into the sources of revenue respectively as wages, profit, and land-rent. In other words, the wage-laborers, the capitalists, and landowners are a modern society's three major class forms in the capitalist mode of production. Curran (2006: 142) points out that a traditional Marxist view of conflict between social classes defined by their relationship to the system of production was increasingly rejected, mainly because it failed to take account of the more complexly stratified and differentiated nature of contemporary society.

As Warwick-Booth (2013) indicates, a relationship also exists between social class and social inequality. Inequality associated with class position arises in all places across the globe. Social class is defined as social stratification resulting from the *unequal distribution* of wealth, power, and prestige. Along with the neoliberal globalization process it has been claimed that class divisions are dying and are no longer significant. Consumers have more power within contemporary society; thus class is marked by the ability to purchase consumer goods, rather than by social class or status. The dominant contemporary form of stratification is based on economic differences, with people being categorized into social classes according to their occupation. Newman and Lennon (2004: 116) highlight that Americans do not talk about class at all, and the structure of work has undergone a change from the welfare poor to the working poor in the United States. Many people grow up in homes with the disadvantages of living in a working poor family. Even for those members of the second generation, whose parents arrive with the credentials, skills, and human capital to avoid the low-wage labor market, the threat of *downward mobility* into the working poor is all too real.

Global neoliberalism leads to the *social exclusion* defined as a multidimensional concept, including not only income, but also other indicators that describe the conditions of the lifestyle. Social exclusion is a process associated with the lack of jobs, income, and education and training opportunities, as well as social and community networks and activities. The people exposed to the social exclusion have little access to power and decision-making bodies and thus often feel powerless and unable to take control over decisions that affect their day-to-day life (Adaman and Keyder 2005). The problem of social exclusion reflects a broader problem of the society during periods characterized by the restoration of liberal capitalism and the marketization of the social structure with an almost total absence of political, economic, or ideological alternatives. Neoliberal culture sees the poor and unemployed as unfortunate victims of circumstance in need of state assistance. They are being viewed with distrust, as lazy and prone, for reasons of faulty genetics and sub-cultural values, to criminality and violence.

In addition, the political representation issue of the working class has also emerged in this neoliberal era. It should be questioned why many working and non-working poor people vote for neoliberal political parties that create policies directly antagonistic to their class interests. The fundamental issue at stake here is that in many respects voters from traditional working-class areas are no longer politically represented. Since the 1980s, the workplace and work practices have been transformed. Job competition is no longer simply an internal matter for national governments and domestic employers; it has become global in its reach. Trade union membership and its influence has declined significantly, wages are down in real terms, and there now exists a culture of precariousness and a general sense that jobs can be immediately extinguished despite low wages, high productivity and sustained profitability (Winlow and Hall 2013).

In the context of the socioeconomic and political inequalities of capitalist class relations, the acquisition of rights of the working class depends on the struggles against neoliberalism, austerity, and authoritarian governments. As

İnal and Akkaymak (2012) explain, the economic system of Turkey was based on a planned development model and the import-substitution industrialization of the pre-1970 era. However, in line with the neoliberalization efforts in many other countries in the late 1970s, Turkey liberalized the market mechanism to converge the national economy with global capitalism. This structural change came with the 24th of January 1980 measures, which were reinforced by the September 12, 1980, military coup. In 1983 the liberal Özal government came to power and obtained the support of the International Monetary Fund (IMF) and the United States. Kaya (2008: 161–163) argues that the Turkish social class structure has changed significantly since 1980. This economic globalization and industrialization has brought about a *dual process of proletarianization and polarization.* Proletarianization occurred through a transition from Turkey's agrarian tradition, a relative decline of the public sector, and an expansion of classes who sell their labor without workplace authority. Polarization entailed the growth of private-sector entrepreneurial, professional, and managerial classes, and a simultaneous expansion of the informal sector. The share of manufacturing employment and the low-skilled labor classes expanded at rates much higher among women than among men, contributing to rapid proletarianization. Proletarianization is defined as the entrance of the masses into private-sector paid employment without a workplace authority. Especially representative of proletarianization are those who work in manufacturing, services, and those who were previously employed in agriculture, the public sector, or were out of the labor market (especially women). Overall proletarianization occurs in the lower and middle of the occupational and class distribution in the form of private-sector employment. Buğra and Keyder (2006: 213) have argued that the transformation under the constraints of globalization and neoliberalism involved a change from an egalitarian corporatism, where both the rural population and urban informal sector employees were excluded from the formal social security system in Turkey. The present government's (AKP) approach to these problems reflects a liberal heritage, combined with social conservative values, which are premised on the centrality of the family and the significance of communal solidarity. This conservative liberalism with an Islamic touch dominates the reform process without a serious countervailing opposition from advocates of a rights-based approach to social policy.

In particular, Turkey's social security system is the primary indicator of the neoliberal policies of the ruling party, the Justice and Development Party (AKP). The new social security law (*Law on Social Security and General Health Insurance*) represents a significant step in the ongoing process of the commodification of social security and public health in Turkey. The current ruling party is the most decisive implementer of the neoliberal paradigm in all spheres from the legal to sociocultural. Neoliberal ideology considers social security spending to be an injurious intervention into the functioning of the market. In a market setting, every good has a price and social security is no exception. In this respect, there is nothing social about it. Pursuing the neoliberal path, the legislation demonstrates that every commodity has a certain price in the market, and human life is itself a commodity (Cosar and Yegenoglu 2009). Neoliberal policies, which form the basis of the globalization process, have created a new model of accumulation and led to many problems, such as unemployment, impoverishment, exclusion of public services all over the world. The main characteristics of this period are the liberalization of capital movements, flexible manufacturing and flexible working, privatization, and subcontracting. Labor relations depending on trade unions in the period of welfare state were reshaped by this neoliberal mentality.

THEORETICAL BACKGROUND ON MEDIA REPRESENTATIONS OF SOCIAL INEQUALITIES AND WORKING CLASS

The representation of the condition of the working class in the media and political discourse is fundamentally linked to this changing socioeconomic condition of the working class. Since the neoliberal project took the place of the post-1945 Welfare State, the socioeconomic situation has worsened considerably. The right to good housing, education, and health care has been eroded as social stratification has deepened. Full employment has been abandoned as a policy goal and replaced with unemployment, underemployment, casualized labor, and zero-hour contracts (Wayne and O'Neill 2013: 489). "Why are media representations of the social world different from the external (real) world?" is an important question in order to understand the structures and functions of media in society. Representations reproduce the dominant discourses again and again. Media promote the dominant ideology. Mass media texts include contradictory messages, both expressing the dominant ideology and partial and least challenging worldviews. In other words, different ideological perspectives, representing various interests with unequal power, engage in a struggle in the media. While some ideas have the advantage, others are barely visible or difficult to communicate in certain forms because they are unfamiliar. Moreover, economic forces determine the nature of media products. The economic dimension of the media industry is a critical component for further analysis (Croteau and Hoynes 2014).

For Marx and Engels consisted the economic base of a society of the forces and relations of production in which culture and ideology are constructed to help secure the dominance of ruling social groups. This influential "*base/ superstructure*" model considers the economy the base of society. Cultural, legal, political, and other forms of life are conceived as "superstructure" which grows out of and serves to reproduce the economic base.

> "The ideas of a ruling class are in every epoch the ruling ideas. The class which is the ruling material force of society is at the same time its ruling intellectual force. The class which has the means of material production at its disposal, consequently also controls the means of mental production, so that the ideas of those who lack the means of mental production are on the whole subject to it" (Marx and Engels [1976], 2012: 31).

The political economy approach of the mass media shows how media represent unequal power relationships in the social world. Media content is socially constructed and does not reflect the inequalities and truths of the social world. This gap between the real world and media representations of the social world is associated with the media ownership structure. The political economy of communication focuses on the economic sides of the corporatization, media and political power relationships, and consumption.

According to Wasko et al. (2011: 1–5), capitalism has become a generalized phenomenon with the globalization of markets now a central theme. Along with these developments, the tension between private interests and public good has been significantly exacerbated. While public policy efforts are strained, privatization moves forward, and the abuse of private power is blatant and commonplace. A critical political economy is more important than ever to understand these developments. A political economy represents a critical orientation to the study of the media and challenges unjust and inequitable systems of power. Garnham (2012: 171–174) highlights that the production and dissemination of mass culture are rooted in the material dimension. He offers a new perspective on the relationship between the economic and ideological dimensions of media against reductionist explanations that favor either a simple economic determinism or an ideological autonomy. Mass media are ideological tools of ruling-class domination either through direct ownership or, as in the case of broadcasting, via ruling-class control of the State. One of the key features of the mass media within monopoly capitalism has been an exercise of political and ideological domination through the economic.

Several cultural studies have focused on how dominant (capitalist) ideology permeates mass media. A good deal of cultural studies are centered on questions of representation; that is, on how the world is socially constructed and is represented in meaningful ways. Cultural studies has argued that language is not a neutral medium for the formation of meanings and knowledge about an independent object world existing outside of language. Cultural studies has been concerned with modern industrialized economies and media cultures organized along capitalist lines. The representations are produced by corporations driven by the profit motive. Cultural studies analyzes who owns and controls cultural production; the distribution mechanisms for cultural products; the consequences of patterns of ownership and control for contours of the cultural landscape (Barker 2013: 7–9). In this context, media are part of the superstructure as an ideological and hegemonic tool.

Lull (2014: 39–40) defines the hegemony as a power or dominance that one social group holds over others and argues that social class differences in today's world are not determined solely by economic factors. Accordingly, ideological influence is crucial in the exercise of social power. Owners and managers of media industries can produce and reproduce the content favorable to them far easier than other social groups because they manage socializing institutions, and make sure that the public arena is dominated by the dominant ideology. Hall et al. (2013: 14) define the concept of representation as the *production of meaning through language*. Languages can use signs to symbolize, reference objects, people and events in the so-called real world. Meaning is produced by the practice. The concepts which are formed in the mind function as a system of mental representations which classify and organize the world into meaningful categories.

Class underlies the media industry in a distinctive way. Class considerations connect advertisers, producers, content, and audiences. For instance, newspapers receive about two-thirds of their revenue from advertisers, not readers, so they are more sensitive to advertisers' expectations in the business relationship. In addition, newspaper publishers are not the only ones who recognize that affluent people are more important for the media industry than poor or working-class people. Whereas there are predominantly working or lower middle-classes in the real world, the media portray the social world as a place heavily populated by the middle class. In general, news media tend to highlight issues of concern to middle- and upper-class readers and viewers. For example, stock market reports are the primary issues of economic news. In the United States, the vast majority of the public is unlikely to be interested in reports on the stock market. On the other hand, media coverage of labor is almost an extinct breed. News represents regular people as consumers, but it hardly ever addresses them as workers. Hard news usually features people in positions of power, such as politicians, professionals, and corporate executives (Croteau and Hoynes 2014: 209–216).

In the industrial era, the generalized belief was that capital accumulation came from fixed investments and economies of scale. The logic of stable, fixed capital accumulation had social and political consequences as the working class tended to toil together in large factories, mines, and docks, leading to a physical and cognitive/cultural proximity which allowed workers to share experiences and build solidarity. In the twenty-first century, class is seen as a *transforming object* characterized by the expanding sphere and changing nature of capitalist exploitation under a neoliberal ethos. The neoliberal working class is both expanding into new parts of the population that fall under the capitalist logic, as well as fragmenting the urban service-sector working class which becomes more isolated than the industrial proletariat. Given their atomized and isolated societal positioning, the neoliberal working class faces a more challenging prospect of generating relations and thus a different and arguably more complex process of constructing a class identity (Wolfson and Funke 2013: 5).

Education, occupation, and income are generally used as criteria to define the working class. Educational levels tend to shape a worker's economic and life trajectory in profound ways. An educational level is a proxy for skill level or human capital which, in turn, is a central determinant of not only the job a worker holds today, but also the kind of job that worker can expect to hold in the future. Using occupation data to define the working class has the advantage of tapping directly into a traditional definition. A manual worker clearly belongs to the working class. A third way to define the working class is to use income data. By that measure, the working class is simply those who do not have much money (Teixeira & Abramowitz 2008: 3).

On the level of production, the move from Fordism to *post-Fordism* involves a shift from mass production of homogeneous goods to small batch customization from uniformity and standardization of flexible, variable production for niche markets. The new configuration of production, politics, consumption, lifestyles, identities, and aspects of everyday private life constituted a condition that has been dubbed "new times." The "new times" approach explores a wide-ranging set of cultural, social, and economic issues and the connections between them. These include flexible manufacturing systems, consumer lifestyles, globalization, new social and political movements, state deregulation and privatization of welfare, the reconfiguration of class structures. In this context, it has been argued that what is being witnessed is a terminal decline in the manual working class, a rise in service and white-collar work, and an increase in part-time and flexible labor. This is leading to new social divisions. Two-thirds of the population is relatively well off, while one-third is either engaged in non-skilled, part-time work or variations of a new underclass of the unemployed and unemployable (Barker 2013: 147–149). In the process of global neoliberalism, the flexible employment, precarious and low-wage labor has become widespread, resulting in a steady decline of economic and social rights. As a result of neoliberal state policies, the problem of poverty and unemployment has increased. It has become the dominant understanding of wage flexibility and the precariousness of the labor force working conditions. Historically, these changes have corresponded to the period after the 1980s and have gained new dimensions in the 1990s and 2000s.

As Kendall notes (2005), the media rarely discuss class explicitly, but their portrayals of the classes generate perceptions that influence behavior. Media represent the upper class more positively than the poor and working classes. The poor and working classes are largely ignored in the media. In addition, the poor and homeless are often discussed in terms of statistics concerning the demographics of the poor. Welfare recipients and the homeless are frequently depicted as violating middle-class values. In contrast, when the media deal with the issues of poverty, the discussion tends to revolve around children, the elderly, and the ill. The media rarely consider macro-level causes of impoverishment, such as educational opportunity or underemployment due to economic shifts. Media images reproduce the idea that clothing, manners, and speech patterns of the working class are not as good as those of the middle or upper classes. The media depictions of the classes ignore societal and structural determinants of class positions, causes that are heavily emphasized in the sociological literature.

Gillborn (2010) argues that the "working class" is positioned in popular and political discourse as an undifferentiated mass of non-elite people. Accordingly, contrasting discourses focused on the white working class by turning them into victims or deviants in the British media. For instance, the white working class has been portrayed as such in popular and political discourse during late 2008. The essential values of neoliberalism have been reasserted as natural, moral and efficient through two apparently contrasting discourses. First, a victim discourse has been presented of white working people, and their children in particular, as suffering educationally because of minority racial groups and their advocates. Second, the discourse of degeneracy has been presented as an immoral and barbaric underclass as a threat to social and economic order.

Lawler (2012: 410–414) researched the relationship between whiteness and working class and has argued that whiteness has come to be a signifier of white working-class existence using press discussions of the BBC's "White Season" as a framing device. The BBC has launched a series of television programs (five documentaries and one drama) under the heading "The White Season." In these programs it has been questioned that the working class is becoming invisible in Britain. A major theme that emerged from the press commentary of the series was a defense of the white working-class existence. Whereas right-of-center newspapers (such as *The Times*, *The Telegraph* and

The Mail) tried to cast this defense in terms of the "damage" done by immigration and multiculturalism, representing the white working class as at the sharp end of government policies, the left-of-center titles (*The Guardian, The Independent* and their Sunday editions) framed the narrative in terms of the deleterious effects of globalization, the decline in Britain's manufacturing base and the impacts of the neoliberal reforms of the 1980s and beyond.

Golding (1999: 151) has demonstrated that coverage of social security is at low levels in the media. According to his research covering all national UK news media from October 1996 to September 1997, there were just twenty-four stories primarily about social security on the BBC's main evening television bulletin, eleven on ITN, and in broadsheet newspapers not many more (twenty-six in *The Guardian*, twelve in *The Times*). Social security is not big news, even compared with other social policy areas like education, housing, or health. Social security, like other areas of social policy, is first and foremost about politics. Poverty, benefits, and welfare, are refracted through the legislative cycle in the media. It has diminished attention for issues of social policy, social security, and poverty in the major media.

In Western capitalist societies, elite media fulfill the function as everyday watchdogs on behalf of the upper middle class and middle class and its particular interests (Berglez 2006: 55). The political economy of traditional mass media in Western societies has evolved significantly. The trends of privatization, conglomeration, trans-nationalization, and deregulation have amplified and broadened the mercantile logic of media operations (Dahlgren 1991: 9–10). Curran (1991: 47–52) has argued that an autonomous media from both state and market forces represents the divergent interests in the public domain. One of the major defects of the market system is that it tends to lead to a narrowing of the ideological and cultural diversity of the media. The free-market approach excludes broad social interests from participating in the control of the main media. It leads to concentration of media ownership, and it promotes cultural uniformity. An adequate media system should enable the full range of political and economic interests to be represented in the public domain.

COVERAGE OF WORK-RELATED RIGHTS IN THE TURKISH NEWS MEDIA

Lately the increase of work-related deaths in Turkey have led to a rethink of the importance of the social citizenship concept, worker's rights and occupational safety. The welfare state means the concept of the state providing social justice based on social rights. The principal social rights include: the right to work, the right to collective bargaining, trade unions, strikes, and social security rights. The *Turkish Constitution* has preserved these social rights (Çoban 2009: 6–8). Article 2 of the 1982 Constitution describes the Turkish Republic, inter alia, as a welfare state. Article 5 of the Constitution explains the fundamental aims and duties of the state: "To ensure the welfare, peace, and happiness of the individual and society. To strive for the removal of political, social and economic obstacles which restrict the fundamental rights and freedoms of the individual in a manner compatible with the principles of justice and of the social state governed by the rule of law; and to provide the conditions required for the development of the individual's material and spiritual existence." Article 65 speaks about the limits of social rights in the Constitution. This article was amended in 2001. The 2001 amendment changed the title of the Article as: "The boundaries of the social and economic duties of the state." The Article goes on as follows: "The State shall fulfill its duties as laid down in the Constitution in the social and economic fields within the limits of its financial resources, taking into consideration the priorities appropriate to the aims of these duties."

Barns et al. (1999: 6) have highlighted that the social policy tradition also needs to be distinguished from public policy writing. Accordingly, this distinction operates at two levels: area and perspective. As far as the *area* is concerned, public policy texts typically deal with a broad range of policies including macro and micro economic reform, industrial relations, transport, the environment, health, education, and (less often) welfare. In contrast, social policy texts restrict themselves to areas more naturally linked to the welfare state: health, education, income security, and employment are the prime examples. In relation to *perspective*, public policy writings focus on the institutional settings of political decision making, the actual operations of power and the influence of interest groups, while social policy writings center on the normative bases and distributional consequences of particular policies.

On May 13, 2014, 301 miners lost their lives in Turkey's worst industrial disaster, in the western town of Soma, in the Manisa province. In September, Turkey was shaken by an accident at the construction site of the Torun Center residence project in the central Istanbul neighborhood of Mecidiyekoy, when a construction elevator car fell from the 32nd floor of the building, killing all ten of the workers inside. In October 2014, five months after the accident in Soma, another mining accident happened in the Ermenek district of the Karaman province. The mine flooded and killed eighteen miners who were trapped inside. According to *Sendika.org news* (as of December 2, 2014), the Turkish Statistical Institute (TUIK) concluded that in 2013 about 2 to 3 percent of the total workforce experienced some form of an accident over the last twelve months. In 2007, this percentage was 3 percent. In total numbers, this amounts to 706,000 work-related accidents per year. The mining and quarrying sector is responsible for about 10 percent of the accidents. The electricity, gas, steam, water and sewerage sector for 5.2 percent, and the construction industry for about 4.3 percent of all work-related accidents. In these sectors, no progress in worker safety was observed between 2007 and 2013. These figures are considerably higher than the official figures provided by the government's Social Security Institution. According to these numbers, the total number of work-related accidents in 2013 was 74,871. Recent events in Turkey led to the conclusion that workers' safety is an issue of growing concern. The figures at hand confirm that workers in Turkey run a considerable risk of encountering a labor-related accident, and a significant number of employees die on the job every year. While the number of accidents and labor related deaths do not seem to decrease dramatically over the years, some positive evolutions are evident regarding working conditions. More and more employers in Turkey feel that their workplaces are of no threat to their employee's health and safety. These employers also feel their employees are sufficiently informed about the safety risks. Notwithstanding these positive evolutions, there is still a large gap compared to EU averages. Work-related safety should remain on the priority list of the Turkish labor market policy makers.

Media content is, of course, a powerful source of meaning about the social world and illustrates how different groups, circles, and opinions are represented in the media setting. This study attempts to reveal the approach of the news media concerning the destructive impacts of neoliberalism and the policies of the ruling party (AKP) on the working class by examining the media coverage of social rights, in particular, the basis of work-related accidents, occupational safety, and social security rights. The first objective was to debate the point of view of the media to neoliberal policies and the structural partiality of mainstream media in favor of the government through the information published on the mining disasters in Soma and Ermenek. Secondly, to debate the concepts which are related to social citizenship and situations such as unemployment, minimum wages, social security, income distribution inequality, cancellation of labor contracts, the subcontracting system and to examine how the media contributes to the strengthening of the dominant ideology and neglect the class-based inequalities.

For that purpose, the mainstream and pro-government *Sabah* daily and *Cumhuriyet*, a secular, center-left daily newspaper, were examined. Relevant data of the news during the period of the mining disasters in May through October 2014 were analyzed by using qualitative content analysis. In addition, the keywords concerning welfare rights during the one-year period in the news texts were also analyzed.

Table 7.1. Main Themes on Soma Mine Disaster (May 13–20, 2014)

Newspaper	*Neglect of Government/ Major Criticism on Neoliberal Policies*	*Neglect of Employer/ Personalization of Issues*	*Grief and Sorrow*
Sabah	—	3	5
Cumhuriyet	4	1	2

Given that the mining sector in Turkey was once firmly under governmental control, those who have criticized the process of privatization under the AKP, felt a degree of justification after the Soma disaster. The AKP's economic governance has caused the restriction of labor rights. Throughout the past decade, Turkey's economy has grown steadily, benefiting significantly from cheap labor and low costs of production (Müller 2014). Widespread shock and outrage dominated reports in the Turkish media after the mining disaster in Soma. There is unanimous agreement that this is a "dark day" for Turkey. However, some different comments were disclosed in the liberal and left-wing press. While *Sabah* proclaims that "Turkey is crying," "Our beloved ones are underground," says the headline in the secular daily *Cumhuriyet.* These different narratives exist in *Cumhuriyet* and *Sabah* newspapers. In particular, *Cumhuriyet* highlighted that the policies of government cause the death of workers. In the news article titled "Leave tale; you murdered," *Cumhuriyet* blamed the government. The subcontractor system is also mentioned as a major reason for this disaster. Moreover, the owner of the mining company was charged with neglect of safety precautions. These dramatic aspects of the incident were also mentioned in the news. We see that *Sabah* focuses on only the dramatic aspect of the incident and disregards the central issues created by neoliberalism, such as the unfair working conditions, workplace safety, and labor exploitation. This disaster has been recognized as a spontaneous incident, and responsible political actors have been concealed. *Cumhuriyet* as a left-wing newspaper focuses not only on the grief felt in the country but also analyzes the possible reasons for the disaster and emphasizes that this is "not an accident, (but) murder." Pro-government *Sabah* also mourns the victims of the disaster.

Table 7.2. Main Themes on Ermenek Mine Disaster (October 29, November 4, 2014)

Newspaper	*Neglect of Government/ Major Criticism on Neoliberal Policies*	*Neglect of Employer/ Personalization of Issues*	*Informative Explanations About Rescue Workings*
Sabah	—	9	10
Cumhuriyet	6	4	10

The news content is important to illustrate the viewpoint of media relating to social policies in terms of workplace accidents in the Turkish mining industry. Similar to previous findings, *Cumhuriyet* criticized the ruling party for the inadequacy of legal arrangements and a chain of neglect, and reported on the rescue efforts. Moreover, the mining company was the target of criticisms due to acquisitiveness and inadequate inspections. Despite the critical news narratives, it is apparent that certain issues are not dealt with, such as: the strong relationship between the poor working conditions, exploitation, and neoliberalism. Critical news of the government is not covered in *Sabah* newspaper. In general, this disaster has been reported as a major defect of the mining company and its responsibility to the ruling party. By focusing on rescue efforts and the Energy Minister's explanations, the subcontracting system and the real reasons for the accident were not mentioned. The mainstream media displayed the hard conditions and deaths as a dramatic story and portrayed the workers in the framework of despair and poverty. While trade unions and professional organizations in the mining sector have emphasized that privatization and the use of subcontractors have severely weakened workplace safety, the mainstream media excluded these reasons and roots of the poverty, and reduced the incidents to a mistake of the mining company.

The *Worker Health and Occupational Safety Assembly* released its annual report on occupational mortalities in Turkey. According to the report, at least 1,886 workers died on the job in Turkey. Among the deceased workers, 1,754 were men, 132 were women, and 54 were children (Bianet, 2015). The Soma and Ermenek mining disasters' many deaths have symbolic value in terms of the rights of labor and the destructive impacts of neoliberal policies.

The mind-set of the news media on welfare rights over labor rights and right to work, which are the components of welfare rights and economic rights, is essential to illustrate in terms of the relationship to the dominant ideology, mainstream media and politics in general. *Sabah* depends on huge

Table 7.3. Media Coverage of Work-Related Rights through Key Concepts (June 1, December 31, 2014)

Key Concepts	*Cumhuriyet*	*Sabah*
Unemployment	224	—
Labor and worker safety	3	2
Strike	80	—
Workers' resistance movements	2	—
Income distribution inequality	3	—
Labor rights	15	—
Subcontracting system	15	28
Minimum wage	65	—

capital groups for advertising and has close ties to the government. It has built itself based upon traditional capitalist values. Concepts related to welfare rights and questioning the neoliberal policies are disregarded in its news content. In particular, it highlighted the new arrangements in employment, which do not change the nature of relations of production, in place of political economy aspects of the working-class's issues. *Sabah,* a liberal-conservative newspaper, has an insensitive approach to class relations and workers' rights. Nothing was found in any news articles when searching for the keyword of "unemployment" in *Sabah*. Although issues such as worker safety and workers in the subcontracting system are reported in *Sabah* newspaper, it should be considered how these are used in the news context. For instance, one of the headlines in *Sabah* is: "A great gospel for millions of people." In this article, while the regulations for employees are emphasized, there is no criticism on the neoliberal structure underlying it. Moreover, these laws and regulations were described positively. On the other hand, The *Cumhuriyet* newspaper, unlike the mainstream media, reported on the impacts of neoliberalism for the working class. As a result of neoliberal policies, the welfare state has declined, and income inequality has increased. During this period, strikes failed and the power of unions was broken.

CONCLUSION

The practices of class struggle are based on the relations of production. The economic structure determines the political and ideological structure. In this sense, the struggle has also continued on political and ideological levels in terms of the working class. Class identity has been pushed into the background, and class struggles have lost the power and momentum during the neoliberalism period. Working-class identity is not given coverage or recognition in the mainstream news media. Also, inequality is legitimized, and the poor are mostly excluded from news media. The media reflect the well-established dominant ideological images and position but ignore the flaws in the government structure and the defects in the current version of capitalism. Neoliberal policies mean that the majority of the population loses the gains of a welfare state. In the mainstream media, it is nearly impossible to see a news story about welfare benefits, unemployment insurance, or the legal rights of workers to form a union, or to learn about health and safety hazards in the workplace. Deep social inequalities created by neoliberal policies are normalized, and, for a public sphere, which struggles for welfare rights, is no place in the mainstream media. The media tend to marginalize dissent and allow the dominant political power and dominant private interests to prioritize their messages across to the public in ways that promote the dominant ideology and suppress oppositional or dissenting voices.

The results of the content analysis on work-related rights have demonstrated that the economic and social rights of wage-labor power are largely ignored, and the capitalist world order is legitimized by the mainstream news media. In contrast to the pro-hegemony approach of the mainstream media, the center-left media include some critical perspectives and focus on the issues of the working class.

Whereas the issue of class inequality is excluded from mainstream media, the conflicts and struggles against neoliberal policies are debated by the anti-government and social democratic media. It is important that media represent the powerless classes, all aspects of the economic and social inequalities should be discussed, and all media should provide acurate news relating to the issues of the working class in order to assist in the development of a pluralist democracy.

REFERENCES

Adaman, Fikret and Keyder, Çağlar (2005). "Poverty and Social Exclusion in the Slum Areas of Large Cities in Turkey." Accessed: December 7, 2014, http://spm.ku.edu.tr/wp-content/uploads/pdf/povertyexclusion.pdf.

Barker, Chris (2013). *Cultural Studies: Theory and Practice*. 4th Edition, London: Sage.

Barns, Ian, Dudley, Janice, Harris, Patricia and Petersen, Alan (1999). "Introduction: themes, context and perspectives." In *Poststructuralism, Citizenship and Social Policy*, edited by Petersen, Alan, Barns, Ian, Dudley, Janice and Harris, Patricia, 1–22, London: Routledge.

Bauman, Zygmunt (2005). *Work, Consumerism and the New Poor*. Berkshire: Open University Press.

Berglez, Peter (2006). "The Materiality of Media Discourse: On Capitalism and Journalistic Modes of Writing." Örebro Studies in Media and Communication 4. Accessed: August 4, 2013, http://oru.diva-portal.org/smash/get/diva2:136846/FULLTEXT01.

Bianet (2015). "1,886 Workers Die on the Job in 2014." Accessed: January 2, 2015, http://bianet.org/english/labor/161247–1–886–workers-die-on-the-job-in-2014.

Bugra, Ayse and Keyder, Çaglar (2006). "The Turkish welfare regime in transformation." *Journal of European Social Policy*, 16 (3): 211–228, doi: 10.1177/0958928706065593.

Çoban, Ali Rıza (2009). "Social Rights in Turkish Constitutional Law," *Comparing Constitutional Adjudication: A Summer School on Comparative Interpretation of European Constitutional Jurisprudence*, Accessed: December 28, 2014, http://www.jus.unitn.it/cocoa/papers/PAPERS%204TH%20PDF%5CSocial%20Turkey%20Coban.pdf.

Cosar, Simten and Yegenoglu, Metin (2009). "The Neoliberal Restructuring of Turkey's Social Security System." *Monthly Review*, Volume 60, Issue 11, Accessed: January 9, 2015, http://monthlyreview.org/2009/04/01/the-neoliberal-restructuring-of-turkeys-social-security-system/.

Croteau, David and Hoynes, William (2014). *Media/Society: Industries, Images, and Audiences*, Thousand Oaks, California: Sage.

Curran, James (2011). *Media and Democracy*. New York: Routledge.

Curran, James (2006). "Media and cultural theory in the age of market liberalism." In *Media and Cultural Theory*, edited by James Curran and David Morley, Oxon: Routledge.

Curran, James (1991). "Rethinking the media as a public sphere," In *Communication and Citizenship: Journalism and the Public Sphere*. Edited by Peter Dahlgren and Colin Sparks, 27–57. New York: Routledge.

Dahlgren, Peter (1991). "Introduction," In *Communication and Citizenship: Journalism and the Public Sphere*. Edited by Peter Dahlgren and Colin Sparks, NY: Routledge.

Dixon, John P., and Scheurell, Robert P. (2002). "Social Welfare in Transition: 1900–2000." In *State of Social Welfare: The Twentieth Century in Cross-National Review*, edited by John P. Dixon and Robert P. Scheurell, 233–245, Westport, CT: Greenwood Press.

Esping-Andersen, Gøsta (1990). *The Three Worlds of Welfare Capitalism*. Cambridge: Polity Press.

Ferguson, James (2009). "The Uses of Neoliberalism." *Antipode*, Vol. 41 No. S1, 166–184, doi: 10.1111/j.1467–8330.2009.00721.x.

Garnham, Nicholas (2012). "Contribution to a Political Economy of Mass-Communication." In *Media and Cultural Studies: Key Works*. Second Edition, Edited by Meenakshi Gigi Durham and Douglas M. Kellner, Malden: Wiley-Blackwell.

Gillborn, David (2010). "The White Working Class, Racism and Respectability: Victims, Degenerates and Interest-Convergence." *British Journal of Educational Studies*, 58:1, 3–25, doi: 10.1080/00071000903516361.

Golding, Peter (1999). "Thinking the unthinkable: Welfare reform and the media." In *Social Policy, the Media and Misrepresentation*, edited by Bob Franklin, 146–156, London: Routledge.

Hall, Stuart, Evans, Jessica and Nixon, Sean (Eds.) (2013). *Representation. Second Edition*, London: Sage.

Inal, Kemal and Akkaymak, Guliz. (Eds.) (2012). *Neoliberal Transformation of Education in Turkey*. [Online] Available at: http://www.palgraveconnect.com/pc/doifinder/10.1057/9781137097811. Accessed: November 28, 2014.

Kaya, Yunus (2008). "Proletarianization with polarization: Industrialization, globalization, and social class in Turkey, 1980–2005." *Research in Social Stratification and Mobility*, 26: 161–181.

Kendall, Diana (2005). *Framing Class: Media Representations of Wealth and Poverty in America*. Lanham: Rowman & Littlefield Publishers, Inc.

Lawler, Steph (2012). "White like them: Whiteness and anachronistic space in representations of the English white working class." *Ethnicities*, 12 (4): 409–426, doi: 10.1177/1468796812448019.

Lull, James (2014). "Hegemony." In *Gender, Race, and Class in Media: A Critical Reader*, Fourth Edition. Edited by Gail Dines and Jean M. Humez, Thousand Oaks: Sage.

Marx, Karl (2004). *Kapital, (Capital),* Üçüncü Cilt (Volume III), Yayına hazırlayan: Friedrich Engels, Eriş Yayınları.

Marx, Karl and Engels, Friedrich (2012). "The Ruling Class and the Ruling Ideas." In *Media and Cultural Studies: Key Works*. Second Edition, Edited by Meenakshi Gigi Durham and Douglas M. Kellner, Malden: Wiley-Blackwell.

Müller, Hendrik (2014). "The Dire State of Labor Rights in Turkey." Accessed: January 9, 2015, http://www.turkeyanalyst.org/publications/turkey-analyst-articles/item/346–the-dire-state-of-labor-rights-in-turkey.html.

Newman, Katherine and Lennon, Chauncy (2004). "Working Poor, Working Hard: Trajectories at the Bottom of the American Labor Market." In *Social Inequalities in Comparative Perspective*, edited by Fiona Devine and Mary C. Waters, 116–140, Malden: Blackwell Publishing Ltd.

OECD (2013). "*Crisis squeezes income and puts pressure on inequality and poverty: New Results from the OECD Income Distribution Database.*" Accessed: July 14, 2014, http://www.oecd.org/els/soc/OECD2013–Inequality-and-Poverty-8p.pdf.

Olson, Kevin (2006). *Reflexive Democracy: Political Equality and the Welfare State*. Cambridge, Massachusetts: The MIT Press.

Oorschot, Wim van and Finsveen, Ellen (2009). "The Welfare State and Social Capital Inequality, European Societies, 11:2, 189–210. Accessed date November 25, 2014, DOI: 10.1080/14616690802155346.

Orgad, Shani (2012). *Media Representation and the Global Imagination*, Cambridge: Poltiy Press.

Öngen, Tulin (2002). "Marx ve Sınıo." (Marx and Class), *Praksis* 8, 9–28.

Teixeira, Ruy and Abramowitz, Alan (2008). "The Decline of the White Working Class and the Rise of a Mass Upper Middle Class." *Brookings Working Paper*, Accessed: July 22, 2013, http://www.brookings.edu/~/media/research/files/papers/2008/4/demographics%20teixeira/04_demographics_teixeira.pdf.

Warwick-Booth, Louise (2013). *Social Inequality*, London: Sage.

Wasko, Janet, Murdock, Graham and Sousa, Helena (2011). "Introduction: The Political Economy of Communications Core Concerns and Issues." In *The Handbook of Political Economy of Communications*. Edited by Janet Wasko, Graham Murdock, and Helena Sousa, West Sussex: Wiley-Blackwell.

Wayne, Mike and O'Neill, Deirdre (2013). "The Condition of the Working Class: Representation and Praxis." *WorkingUSA: The Journal of Labor and Society*, 16: 487–503.

Wessels, Bridgette (2014). *Exploring Social Change: Process and Context*. Hampshire: Palgrave Macmillan.

Winlow, Simon and Hall, Steve (2013). *Rethinking Social Exclusion: The End of the Social?* London: Sage.

Wolfson, Todd and Funke, Peter, N. (2013). "Communication, class and concentric media practices: Developing a contemporary rubric." *New Media & Society, first published on April 9, 2013*, http://nms.sagepub.com/content/early/2013/04/05/1461444813481199, doi: 10.1177/1461444813481199.

Part III

TECHNOLOGY AND INEQUALITIES

Chapter Eight

Creating the Myth of a Better Future

Technological Determinism and Reproducing Social Inequalities

Banu Durdağ

The idea of technology as a panacea that fixes social problems recurs every time when a new technology emerges. This conception of technology, known as "technological determinism" and offering an idea of social reality and social change that is technologically determined, can be considered as one of the most influential discourses. It acts as a pivot in justifying the reproduction of the capitalist system and inequalities it engenders. The theories that can be gathered under the title of "information society," due to their emphasis on information and communication technologies (ICTs) in explaining the changes of the advanced capitalist countries in the late twentieth century, are prominent examples of technological determinism. With concepts such as "global village," "post-industrial society," "service economy," "network society," and "information age," these theories provided a discursive basis for the restructuring of capitalism in the 1970s and afterward. They moved beyond the realm of theory and shaped social reality with their influence in policy processes. Although the concept of information society, which can be seen as a cornerstone of neoliberal ideology, was criticized extensively in the 1990s and 2000s even today it has an incontrovertible hegemony on policy making in developing countries, such as Turkey. It has a crucial role in the articulation of these countries to neoliberalism with a mystified technology and social change perception that conceals social inequalities.

In this framework, the technological determinist conception of social change of information society theories will be discussed by focusing on "internal relations" of Marxist philosophy and Marx's critical conceptualization of technology and communication in order to find out which connections that constitute social reality are ignored and to highlight a critical way of thinking rather than a mystified one. Another purpose of this chapter is to analyze which implications this one-dimensional and linear model of history and social change has in the reproduction of social inequalities. In order to illustrate the argument two important policy documents, which represent technology and social development strategies of Turkey, are selected. The first one is entitled *Vision 2023* and prepared by The Scientific and Technological Research Council of Turkey (TÜBİTAK) as a national science and technology foresight exercise. The other one is *Information Society Strategy (2006–2010)*, prepared for the Turkish State Planning Organization (SPO) as a future projection for transition to the information society.[1]

TECHNOLOGICAL DETERMINISM

Technological determinism presumes technology as the driving force of social change (Chandler 2012; Servaes 2014). Technology is seen as an external and independent variable, like a *deus ex machina*, that changes and transforms society at every level with its own autonomous logic and trajectory. While technology is attributed with such an autonomous force, existing social conflicts and inequalities are excluded (Preston 2001). This gives the image of a headless society which hides the mechanisms that (re)produce fundamental social contradictions and inequalities.

Nevertheless, every time when a new technology emerges, technological determinism recurs in minds. It is one of the most powerful views to understand the nature of social change (Williams 2003). The reason of its hegemony is that it provides a simple and persuasive way of interpreting the complex social reality, eliminating the necessity of questioning other social factors and interactions. Though this simple perspective seems quite consistent in itself, it presents a distorted image of social reality. It reduces complex social reality to the effects of one part upon the whole and other parts of the whole in a linear and one-dimensional way.

This can be associated with the idea of *progress* that draws a fixed path for social development, and the efforts to rationalize and organize social change (Kumar 1986: 301; Marx 1993: 5–9). Following the development of the methods of natural sciences, positivism became the dominant *paradigm* of social sciences in the nineteenth century. Technological determinism is largely based on the legacy of this scientific stance which applies a *mechanistic* mode of explanation to social phenomena (Servaes 2014). While it heralds fundamental changes in society by focusing on particular quantitative changes and transformations, it ignores the complex fabric of social change.

There are two tendencies in the studies criticizing technological determinism. In the first one, it is argued that there are several forms of technological determinism that lie on a spectrum from "hard" to "soft" extremes (Smith &

Marx 1995: 111–5). In the "hard" one, technology is posited as an independent agent or "prime mover" of history regarding to its alleged impacts on society. These impacts can be seen as optimistic, offering a static path of transformation to a better society, or pessimistic, associating technology with an undesired society. But in both cases, technology is considered as the result of an isolated research and development process.

Concerning the "soft" version(s) of technological determinism, Raymond Williams gives an idea; even he calls it as "symptomatic technology view" rather than soft technological determinism (Williams 2003: 3–7). In the view of symptomatic technology, other "causal" factors are also emphasized in the process of social change. Technology is divested of its alleged autonomous power initiating change while other factors are embedded. Nevertheless, emergence of technologies is assumed as self-generated, just like in the "hard" one. In this context, both views miss the complexity of the relationship between technology and social change.

In contrast, the other tendency suggests that there is a "precise" interpretation of technological determinism, rather than "hard" and "soft" versions. According to Bruce Bimber (1995), to qualify a view as technological determinist, it should be both "technological," seeing technology as an artifact or a machine that shapes the course of human events, and "deterministic," referring a fixed path of progress through which every society would necessarily pass. Bimber tries to distinguish different versions of technological determinism in order to answer which one can be clarified as "truly technological deterministic" and categorizes three accounts: the normative, the nomological and the unintended consequences. The normative account is defined as the most familiar face of technological determinism because, while it focuses on norms and ethical issues in the development of technologies, it excludes larger sociopolitical context.[2] However, it is declared as the least specific and precise account of technological determinism due to its emphasis on human attitudes and norms. In the nomological account, "technological processes, once begun, require forms of organization or commitments of political resources, regardless of their social desirability or of previous social practices" (Bimber 1995: 83).[3] In the unintended consequences account, emerged technologies are assumed as having uncertain and uncontrollable outcomes on society. Thus, technology gets an autonomous position on social practices. Though Bimber distinguishes versions of technological determinism, he comes to the conclusion that only a nomological account meets both being "technological" and "deterministic."

These tendencies define the framework of technological determinism: Technology is seen as an artifact or a tool and considered as autonomous and external to the social sphere; social change and development is determined by technology; and there is a single set of patterns and a fixed path both for technological development and social progress (Bijker 1995). But there is still a question that needs to be answered: How can a holistic and critical way of thinking in the relationship of technology and social change be built?

MARX'S ANALYSIS OF "TECHNOLOGY" AND THE PHILOSOPHY OF "INTERNAL RELATIONS"

Karl Marx offers an adequate starting point for a robust analysis of the relationship between technology and society (Rosenberg 1976). David Harvey stresses that Marx's conceptualization of technology within its social and historical context "provides a general framework for dialectical and historical materialism" (Harvey 2010: 189). This is also a clear example of the philosophy of internal relations: "Technology reveals the active relation of man to nature, the direct process of the production of his life, and thereby it also lays bare the process of the production of the social relations of his life, and of the mental conceptions that flow from those relations" (Marx 1990: 493).

This demonstrates that "Marx's abstractions are not things but processes" (Ollman 2003: 68). Just like in his analysis of capital as an interrelated process, involving means of production, relations of production, labor-power, value, exchange, property and even more, technology is also abstracted as a process rather than a tool. This gives a vivid picture of the dialectical interactions between technology, humans, nature, actual process of production, production and reproduction of social life, and mental conceptions. All of these phenomena are internalized with each other, creating wholeness in an interaction. Thus, technology does not have a "deterministic" position on other social phenomena; but it "reveals" all others, and mediates between humans and their relationship with the material world (Harvey 2010: 193). At the same time, by acting on material world, humans not only change and transform it for their purposes and needs, but also change and transform their own natures (Marx 1990: 283). Therefore, it is a dynamic and an evolving process of both transformation of the world and a self-transformation of human beings.

Marx uncovers not just what the appearance of technology has in capitalism, but also the underlying reason of this particular appearance. This sheds light on why capitalism has to be so technologically dynamic, "whereas all earlier modes of production were essentially conservative" (Marx 1990: 617). Under capitalism, technology is primarily employed to increase the production and minimize the cost of labor-power; in other words, to augment the exploitation of surplus-value. The coercive laws of competition also compel capitalists to seek and adopt new production methods, or superior technologies improving productivity. Providing novelty in methods or technologies is also important to control and discipline labor, and to reduce the need for necessary labor. This is why capitalists have a constant tendency spurring the productive forces on to develop (Marx 1969: 93).

However, improvement of productive forces refers to a fundamental contradiction: "At a certain stage of their development, the material forces of production in society come in conflict with the existing relations of production" (Marx 1904: 12). Within this contradiction, while the relative power of classes dominate the direction of the development of the productive forces, the productive forces also affect the relative positions of classes that would either reproduce the existing relations of production or reveal an emancipatory potential for changing and transforming them. Therefore, under capitalism, technology is a field of class struggle. Technological possibilities are limited and marked by the priorities of the dominant groups but can also be shaped by social struggles in an evolving process.

Marx's analysis of technology neither considers technology as neutral nor posits it as an autonomous force. He gives a far richer mode of analysis within its historical and social context that is characterized by dialectical interactions within a totality. While Marx exposes the existing state of things, he also displays how these can be denied and transformed through struggle. What distinguishes Marx's use of dialectic is his abstraction process, which is underpinned by his "materialistic" philosophy of internal relations (Ollman 2003: 68). Primarily, the internal relations of Marxist philosophy enable us to avoid static, partial and one-dimensional understandings of reality, while "the common sense of our time and place, most social ties are thought about in abstractions that focus on the parts one at a time, separately as well as statically" (Ollman 2001: 68). And, there is not an assumption of finite parts in themselves or attribution of "absolute" predominance of the whole over the parts. Neither the whole simply consists of the sum of the parts, nor are the parts independent or isolated from the whole. Parts internalize with each other and the whole as well; and there is an organic tie between them. While "the whole gives meaning and relative importance to each part," parts also "forge the contours and meaning of the whole" (Ollman 2003: 140). This is why Marx's conceptualization and analysis of technology refer to the whole of social relations and fundamental social contradictions, tendencies and potentials for future possibilities are also uncovered.

There may be objections that Marx's analysis gives a materialist position on merely production technologies. As it is alleged by Marshall McLuhan (1994), did Marx really miss the communication bus? Yves de la Haye (1980) disproves such claims by addressing the issue from a materialist perspective that allows us both to understand communication and communication technologies in a critical way and to challenge the hegemonic position of technological determinism.

MATERIALIST POSITION ON COMMUNICATION AND COMMUNICATION TECHNOLOGIES

By focusing on the works of Marx and Friedrich Engels, Yves de la Haye puts the "communication question" in a broader perspective that contains "the material transportation infrastructure, the means of locomotion which favored passenger travel and the conveyance of commodities, and finally, the instruments for transmitting information which accelerated the diffusion of messages and increased their importance" (de la Haye 1980: 12). At first glance, this perspective may seem to be composed of just the means of communication and transportation, but it inserts the questions of exchange relations, the role of ruling class, class struggle, material and symbolic dimensions of communication and communication technologies into the analysis because the communication question is situated in the center of "the production-circulation dialectic" (de la Haye 1980: 12).

The framework of the production-circulation dialectic can be found in *Grundrisse*: "The more production comes to rest on exchange value, hence on exchange, the more important do the physical conditions of exchange—the means of communication and transport—become for the costs of circulation" (Marx 1993: 524). This highlights the vital role of the means of communication and transportation in the realization process of capital itself. The quest for more advanced and cheaper communication and transportation technologies is related to the basic requirements of the capitalist who needs to control, dominate, and foresee supply and distribution in order to go beyond the narrow circle of the local market. This is why the communication network, which was an unorganized and peripheral phenomenon within feudalism, became a necessary element from the very beginning of the expansion of the capitalist system.

De la Haye (1980: 25–34) stresses the dual role of the means of communication with references to Marx. Accordingly, the first role is related to the creation of communication networks that is based on the tendency of capitalism to expand the market and also on the needs of each capitalist to arrange his strategies and to measure his strength against the rest of the actors in order to survive within such an extended competition and an enlarged market. Besides being a force in the production, the means of communication also serve a vital role in the creation of social relations of production adequate to meet production level reached by society. During the development of capitalism, it appeared also "modern" means of communication, such as popular press, that create the symbolic conditions of exchange with systems of representations or ideologies that incorporate people into the market system. So, creating the symbolic conditions of exchange is the second role of the means of communication. Therefore, the development of communication technologies cannot be understood without considering the requirements of capitalism in order to consolidate the material and symbolic bases of the mobility of capital. De la Haye indicates a broader importance of communication technologies that accompanied development of societies' at all times as inherent parts of (re) production of social relations. And this is why those technologies, networks, not only serve this dual role, but also provide "communality." Hence, even they are marked by the interests and priorities of the dominant groups, they have emancipatory and revolutionary potentials which make them a field of social struggles.

Such a materialist position makes possible to demonstrate how social reality is distorted, and relations and mechanisms (re)producing the existing social inequalities are concealed by technological determinism. In this context, making a critical inquiry on the theories of "information society" which can be considered as one of the outcomes of technological determinist understanding of the current historical moment seems important.

THEORIES OF INFORMATION SOCIETY

Since the end of the 1950s, analyses that emphasized the growing importance of knowledge and information in the economy of the United States had been made due to the remarkable increase in the significance of scientific knowledge which was underpinned by the military-technical competition during the Cold War (Kumar 2005). Those analyses gave rise to the works that herald a new emerging society, "information society," that goes beyond the "industrial society" and its class conflicts through the appearance of "information" as the source of value by the development of ICTs. The concept of information society creates a "myth"[4] of a desirable and better future that indicates a break with previous social inequalities and assumes a "technological fix" for social problems. This concept and its "*belief in the omnipotence of technology*"[5] transcended its descriptive dimension and realm of theory, when the concept has taken a center position on the political agendas of both developed and developing countries during the restructuring of capitalism in the 1970s and afterward. Thus, as was stated by Jan Servaes (2003: 18), "information society vision have clearly become such a *new narrative*" whereas the "great narratives" are said to be vanishing.

The concept of information society and its current versions such as "network society," "new economy," and "digital age" are largely influenced by Daniel Bell's (1999) conceptualization of "post-industrial society" (Garnham 2001). In the late 1990s by Manuel Castells' (2000, 2001) trilogy, *The Information Age*, the concept has been moved into its current direction. While Bell and Castells provided the most sophisticated versions of those theories, serving as a basis for a hegemonic discourse for political elites, Alvin Toffler (1971, 1981) and Marshall McLuhan, in the 1970s and 1980s, popularized this conception (Webster 2006). Thus, focusing on those names is suitable both to periodize the theories of information society and to make a critical inquiry.

ICTS AS *DEUS EX MACHINA* OF THE INFORMATION SOCIETY

Information society theorists claim that, in the late 1960s and the early 1970s with the development of ICTs, structural changes happened in the leading capitalist countries, especially in the United States of America, and a "new" society, in which exhausting industrial works is being replaced by information processing as the new source of value, was born. Thus, "machines will increasingly perform the routine tasks; men the intellectual and creative tasks" (Toffler 1971: 402). Given the "collective good" character of information, it is unnecessary to maintain a "competitive" strategy (Bell 1999: 220). So, men will be "nomadic gatherers of knowledge" within a new egalitarian "global village" (McLuhan 1994: 5). From this perspective, property relations, power and exploitation will be anyway of lesser importance, and ownership will become "*a legal fiction*" (Bell 1973: 294–295).

According to Toffler, "behind such prodigious economic facts lies that great, growling engine of change—technology" (Toffler 1971: 25). Similarly, McLuhan (1994) posits technology as the real force of social change, while he heralds that the world is becoming a village by the development of technology. Although those two names give an obvious example—"hard" version—of technological determinism, Bell (1973) is cautious in explaining the reason for change. According to him, the reason for change is the increase in productivity with the "rationalization of production" that permits employees to shift from industry to services, and makes possible to produce enough goods with fewer workers. This is Bell's interpretation of Max Weber's "rationalization" as "the growth of an ethos of 'more for less'" (Webster 2006: 44). In his explication, "soft" tones of technological determinism can be discerned: "Technology [. . .] is the basis of increased productivity, and productivity has been the transforming fact of economic life" (Bell 1973: 191). So, though rationalization is claimed as the reason for change, technology lies as the driving force behind rationalization.

Manuel Castells also describes and celebrates a new phase of history: "A technological revolution, centered around information technologies, began to reshape, at accelerated pace, the material basis of society" (Castells 2001: 1). He conceptualizes the emerging society as "informational society" which is driven and explained by the development of ICTs, then, he defines the key feature of it as "the networking logic" and uses the concept of "network society" (Castells 2001: 21). He also explains that the concept of network society "does not exhaust all the meaning of the 'informational society'" (ibid.), and finally uses the concept of "information age" as the overall title of his trilogy.

According to Castells, the emerging society is "a specific form of social organization in which information generation, processing, and transmission become the fundamental sources of productivity and power because of new technological conditions emerging in this historical period" (ibid.). He associates this new social structure with "the emergence of a new mode of development, informationalism, historically shaped by the restructuring of the capitalist mode of production" (ibid. 14). Nevertheless, he notes that the restructuring of capitalism and the rise of informationalism are distinct processes. And, he claims that the development of ICTs is the outcome of an "autonomous dynamics of technological discovery and diffusion" (ibid 59). There are two separate and autonomous processes, just like in Bell's understanding of "realms." According to Bell, there are three independent realms as social, politics and culture; and the realm of social structure, which includes economy and technology, brought the changes that engendered the information society. Those are explicit examples for an atomistic understanding of social reality. Hence, questioning the role of other interrelated social factors—such as politics, culture, class conflicts, power, and property relations—become unnecessary because the new technology has arrived and its "silver-bullet" will solve all social problems for us. Even though Castells attempts to insert the growing importance of social movements and local forms of resistance in his analysis, at the end, he attributes all of them to the power of technology. This is the reification of technology that sublimes technology as an autonomous, objective, rational, and driving force of social change.

Adopt and Adapt: Where Are Those Who Cannot Adapt?

According to Toffler, the fact that quickly processing information is vital for coping with rapid changes is incompatible with cumbersome hierarchies: "This silent but significant deterioration of hierarchy, now occurring in the executive suite as well as at the ground level of the factory floor, is intensified" (Toffler 1971: 139). Furthermore, as ICTs multiply choices and options for everyone, demassification and destandardization of cultural outputs become real. Indicating a diminishment of inequalities, Bell emphasizes that ICTs provide expanded employment opportunities, especially for women and those who are unable to participate in industrial production. It is also assumed that everyone's voice can be easily heard by developing ICTs. From this perspective, social problems and inequalities can be fixed, and barriers and limits to full democratic participation can be removed by ICTs. It is also presumed that ICTs provide new opportunities both for poorest and richest nations.

As the development of ICTs is considered as self-generated and those technologies are seen to possess an autonomous logic and trajectory that bring revolutionary changes, there is only one option left for people: adopt and adapt (Hamelink 1988: 12). To accept those allegedly "neutral" technologies with docility is the key for social progress, in which ICTs and information are assumed as available and accessible to everyone. It is presumed that adoption and adaptation of ICTs bring necessarily a transition to information society. What is missing in the analyses of Toffler and Bell is the people who cannot adapt. Contrary to Toffler and Bell, McLuhan mentions that: "In that rapidly approaching future, what about the person who has not role-played well enough to attain continual creditworthiness? He will then, as he is now, be a non-person (And as we all know, non-persons pay cash.)" (McLuhan & Powers 1989:114).

In Castells' new society, there are two distinct but simultaneously existing spaces: "space of flows" and "space of places." The space of flows is centered on "global cities," such as New York, London, and Tokyo, where services are advanced, wealth is created by information processing (Castells 2001: 407–9). In this space, global elites, having access to ICTs and information, and ability to cope with the speed of "information age," readapt themselves to new conditions (Castells & Ince 2003: 55–9). Those who are excluded from information processing or unable to access to ICTs and to get qualifications to process information inhabit the space of places in which poverty goes around. This new geography of social exclusion is made up of multiple "black holes" and includes much of Sub-Saharan Africa, American inner-city ghettos, rural areas of Latin America, Asian mega-cities' shanty towns and French banlieues. Their problem is failing to adapt to "information age" and its demands because this new society holds promises only for those who have capacity to connect and access to the "network." This perspective reduces social inequalities to being included in network and being excluded from network, preventing to notice relations of exploitation and social inequalities within the network (Prey 2012).

While ICTs inevitably bring about information society to people adapting themselves to this new "better society," "natural selection" works for the rest. This is a combination of technological determinism with "social-Darwinism," concealing social forces, conflicts, competing interests and inequalities behind social changes. This combination also facilitates the articulation of neoliberal free market ideology in information society discourse. It is *the myth of a better future*: To become a winner of this selection process and not to be left behind, it is necessary to remove cumbersome State out of the economy, to free market competition. This is the way of catching up with technological change, and then shifting to information society.

DEPLOYING THE MYTH OF A BETTER FUTURE: TURKEY'S POLICIES ON INFORMATION SOCIETY

In the 1990s and afterward, information society became "a brand new 'grand societal project'" (Servaes 2003: 12). In accordance with the global initiatives, developing countries also took the same direction in order to diminish the gap and leapfrog advanced countries. The first attempt for building information society in Turkey came from the World Bank in 1993 with *Turkey: Informatics and Economic Modernization* report that recommended free-market-oriented neoliberal reforms, especially emphasizing privatizations. As a reaction to neoliberal policies, in 1999 TÜBİTAK prepared *The Turkish National Information Infrastructure Master Plan* (TUENA) and stressed the importance of local technological production and maximizing social and economic benefits of the information infrastructure. The document was not found market-oriented and in harmony with the global neoliberal ICT policies and discarded (Geray & Özdemir 2011: 607). When the European Union (EU) started the Lisbon Strategy in 2000 to become the most competitive and dynamic knowledge-based economy in the world,[6] Turkey's initiatives gained momentum by being included in *eEurope+*, the action plan for EU candidate countries.[7]

Neoliberalism and protectionism are main but contradicting positions related to information society among Turkish policy makers (Yüksel 2015). The documents that will be analyzed in this study also reflect these positions. On the other hand, though they seem to be contradicting, they share a similar technological determinist view.

Vision 2023

In order to have a more equitable, prosperous, peaceful, democratic, participatory and scientifically capable country in 2023,[8] the document recommends to increase Turkey's competence in eight strategic technology areas, such as information and communication technologies; biotechnology and genetic technologies; material technologies; nanotechnology; design technologies; mechatronics; production processes and technologies; energy and environmental technologies. Accordingly, this increased competency will provide competitiveness to capture a greater share from international markets and pave the way for prosperity. It can be said that market priorities are at the center in determining science and technology areas.

Moreover, technology is considered as an autonomous variable and the main reason of social changes:

With a technological determinist view, the document ignores social conditions, disclosing and underpinning technological developments, and complex fabric of social change. In addition, a stress on "threat/opportunity" binary can be noticed at the first pages of the document. Accordingly, by the scientific and technological developments in international level, Turkey has reached a crossroad where taking rapidly right decisions is vital for gaining competitiveness and prosperity, and for not being a passive member of the international community seeking to survive because of wrong decisions and delays. Instead of importation, the document underlines protectionism for science and technology development, so much so that it can be considered as neo-mercantilist.

Given that the solution of social inequalities is associated with competitiveness in the international market, the document has a narrow perspective. Inequalities and uncertainties created by the market itself are ignored. For example, the impacts of technology on employment are not examined. On the other hand, the lack of computer literacy, which is considered as one of the important issues of the debates of information society, finds its shortcut solution: "Instead of people keeping up with computers, computers keep up with people; in other words, computers with 'human literacy' have to be built" (TÜBİTAK 2003: 73). So is bypassed the inequality in adaptation process. The fact that people with access are not equal at all is ignored as well. From this perspective, transition to information society is an objective, rational, and desirable process, and requires getting competence in strategic technology areas, gaining competitive advantage and creating public awareness.

INFORMATION SOCIETY STRATEGY (2006–2010)

The document also posits ICTs as "prime mover" of social change: "Innovations in ICTs have an important effect on [. . .] all segments of the society and deeply affect [. . .] daily lives. In other words, these innovations cause a social transformation. These technologies already put their mark on the twenty-first century and laid the foundation for a new social transformation toward 'information society'" (SPO 2006: 1). The next emphasis is on efficiency and competitiveness given that Turkey's vision for transformation to information society is defined as follows: "To be a country that has become a focal point in the production of science and technology, that uses information and technology as an effective tool, that produces more value with information-based decision-making processes and that is successful in global competition, with a high level of welfare" (SPO 2006: 1–2). Thus, social welfare is identified with market mechanism and gaining competitive power with ICTs and information processing: "It is imperative to use ICT effectively in all areas of the economy and social life to ensure sustainable growth and competitiveness" (SPO 2006: 3).

The "threat/opportunity" binary is also emphasized: "If the less developed countries can make use of this period, it would provide an opportunity for these countries to leapfrog the more advanced countries. If, on the contrary, the countries lagging behind fail to benefit from this period, they may risk being pushed back fast even further from their current positions" (SPO 2006: 1–2). Transformation to information society becomes a must, just like in *Vision 2023*, not only to achieve social welfare through market mechanism but also not being subject to natural selection; because information society is considered as an irresistible and irreversible process.

The document indicates a number of actions based on two main axes in order to establish information society. The first axis is based on market demands and stresses strengthening the infrastructure of ICTs, developing new products and services, and reducing taxes in communication services to a reasonable level for the augmentation and sustainability of the competitive environment. The latter axis is based on adaptation: After strengthening the free-market conditions that will provide adequate context for the transition, it is necessary to create the adaptation of citizens. For this aim, development of human resources, life-long learning and e-learning are also highlighted. Additionally, "public internet access points" is suggested as a solution for "digital divide" (SPO 2006: 22). From this perspective, the problem of inequality is about getting access to ICTs and information. The document mentions nothing about inequalities of people with access and the destiny of those who cannot adapt. Briefly, the whole point is reduced to being included in network and excluded from network, as was the case in the theories of information society.

CONCLUSION

From a materialist position it is necessary to understand the relationship between technology and social change as a dialectical process which is shaped by social *praxes*, contradictions, and conflicts. Thus, it involves contingency and emancipatory potentials as well. This position also allows us to show

how social reality is distorted, and relations and mechanisms (re)producing the existing social inequalities are concealed by the explanations assuming a one-dimensional and linear relationship between technology and social change. The concept of information society gives an explicit example of those explanations. It heralds an emerging society through the lens of technological determinism. Thus, technology has come to be viewed as an autonomous variable and an external force, having its own trajectory and necessarily bringing about this allegedly new society. It is the reification of technology which sets technology apart and above human affairs and attributes to it an external force, affecting society from outside and determining events to which people have to adjust. In fact it is not surprising, as was stated by David F. Noble (2001: xi), "in a society [. . .] which long ago abandoned social purpose to the automatic mechanism of the market, and attributed to things a supremacy over people [. . .], technology has readily assumed its fantastic appearance as the subject of the story."

The reification of technology, as is the case in the concept of information society, also serves to divert attentions and to conceal the existing fundamental contradictions and inequalities. Free market ideology and social Darwinism are easily articulated in the discourse of information society. Therefore, it becomes a myth of a better future in which people will get wholly new opportunities if they succeed to adapt themselves to the new society and to meet its demands. Such a linear model of history and social change in which only people adjusting and readapting themselves to an emerging new society, undermines efforts against social inequalities, and depoliticizes debates on the conditions of the people who are unable to adapt themselves to this allegedly irreversible *progress*. This is why in the descriptions of Bell and Toffler, everyone seems to have adapted well to information society. Even though Castells recognizes the people who are unable to meet the demands of the new society, in his "network society" there is no exploitation or social inequalities for people who succeed to adjust.

The policy documents are largely based on this discursive stance provided by the theories of information society. As a result of this, the debate on social inequalities is limited to improving the conditions of people who are defined as disadvantageous. Certainly, it cannot be expected from policy documents, especially the ones subliming the market mechanism, to have a Marxist perspective on both the relationship between technology and social change, and the issue of social inequalities. But the point is that such kind of narrow perspective makes it impossible to see the relations and mechanisms producing and reproducing social inequalities at global/local level. Moreover, it ratifies the status quo which reduces structural inequalities to the natural law, in other words to fatalism.

NOTES

1. These are two of the last three policy papers of Turkey and have widely influenced its efforts in the last decade. This is the reason for choosing them to analyze. The last policy paper is relatively new and was published in March 2015, during the preparation of this study, with the title *2015–2018 Information Society Strategy and Action Plan*. It is available on (in Turkish) http://www.bilgitoplumustratejisi.org/tr/doc/8a9481984680deca014bea4232490005 (accessed 10 May 2015). The policy paper for the period between 2010 and 2014 has never been published without making explication. Furthermore, the last document was published with one year delay. This is why it covers the period between 2015 and 2018. In its introduction, it qualifies *Information Society Strategy (2006–2010)* as a fundamental policy paper.

2. Bimber associates this account with Jürgen Habermas' *Toward a Rational Society* and Jacques Ellul's *The Technological Society*.

3. This account is mainly rested on the arguments of G. A. Cohen and Richard Miller, and is associated with Robert Heilbroner's article "Do Machines Make History?"

4. Cees J. Hamelink considers the concept information society as a myth that offers an explanation of the late twentieth century and legitimizes the interests of a particular social group. Also Alvaro de Miranda (2009) discusses information society theories as a myth.

5. Ernest Mandel, states that "*the belief in the omnipotence of technology is the specific form of bourgeois ideology in the late capitalism*" and "the notion of 'post-industrial society' [...] corresponds to the same ideological trend" (Mandel 1976: 501).

6. See The European Council (EC), *Lisbon European Council 23 and 24 March 2000 Presidency Conclusion*, (2000), http://www.europarl.europa.eu/summits/lis1_en.htm (accessed July 10, 2014).

7. SPO, *Information Society Strategy (2006–2010)*, (July 2006), 1. http://unpan1.un.org/intradoc/groups/public/documents/unpan/unpan025636.pdf (accessed 21 May 2014).

8. TÜBİTAK, *Vision 2023, National Science and Technology Policies: 2003–2023 Strategy Document*, (in Turkish), (2 November 2004), 9. http://www.tubitak.gov.tr/tubitak_content_files/vizyon2023/Vizyon2023_Strateji_Belgesi.pdf (accessed June 11, 2014).

REFERENCES

Ampuja, Marko, and Juha Koivisto (2014). "From 'Post-Industrial' to 'Network Society' and Beyond: The Political Conjunctures and Current Crisis of Information Society Theory." *tripleC* 12, no. 2 (2014): 447–463.

Bell, Daniel (1999). "The Coming of Post Industrial Society." In *Modernity, Critical Concepts*, Vol. IV, edited by Malcolm Waters, 213–224. London and New York: Routledge, 1999[1976].

Bell, Daniel (1973). *The Coming of Post-Industrial Society: A Venture in Social Forecasting*. New York: Basic Books, Inc., Publishers.

Bijker, Wiebe E (1995). "Sociohistorical Technology Studies." In *Handbook of Science and Technology Studies*, edited by Sheila Jasanoff et. all, 229–256. Thousand Oaks, London and New Delhi: Sage Publications.

Bimber, Bruce (1995). "Three Faces of Technological Determinism." In *Does Technology Drive History?*, edited by Merritt Roe Smith and Leo Marx, 79–100. Cambridge, MA: The MIT Press.

Castells, Manuel, and Martin Ince (2003). *Conversations with Manuel Castells*. Oxford: Blackwell.

Castells, Manuel (2001). *The Rise of the Network Society: The Information Age, Economy, Society and Culture,* Vol. I, 2nd ed. Oxford, Massachusetts: Blackwell, 2001.

Castells, Manuel (2000). *End of Millennium, The Information Age: Economy, Society and Culture*, Vol. III, 2nd ed. Malden, Oxford, Victoria: Blackwell.

Chandler, Daniel (2012). "Technological or Media Determinism." http://visual-memory.co.uk/daniel/Documents/tecdet/tdet03.html (accessed 14 December 2012).

De la Haye, Yves (1980). *Marx and Engels on the Means of Communication: The Movement of Commodities, People, Information and Capital*. New York: International General.

De Miranda, Alvaro (2009). "Technological Determinism and Ideology: Questioning the 'Information Society' and the 'Digital Divide.'" In *The Myths of Technology: Innovation and Inequality*, edited by Judith Burnett et al., 23–37. New York: Peter Lang.

Garnham, Nicholas (2001). "The Information Society: Myth or Reality." *2001 Bugs: Globalism and Pluralism*. http://www.infoamerica.org/teoria_articulos/garnham01.pdf (accessed September 17, 2014).

Geray, Haluk, and Funda Başaran Özdemir (2011). "Reproducing Dependency: How Hegemonic Discourse Shape ICT Policies in the Periphery." In *Handbook of Research on Information Communicaton Technology Policy: Trends, Issues and Advancements*, Vol. II, edited by Esharenana E. Adomi, 599–615. Hershey, New York: Information Science Reference.

Hamelink, Cees J. (1988). "Is There Life After the Information Revolution?" In *The Myth of the Information Revolution: Social and Ethical Implications of Communication Technology*, edited by Michael Traber, 7–34. London: Sage.

Harvey, David (2010). *A Companion to Marx's Capital*. London, New York: Verso.

Kumar, Krishan (2005). *From Post-Industrial to Post-Modern Society: New Theories of the Contemporary World*, 2nd ed. Malden, Oxford and Victoria: Blackwell.

Kumar, Krishan (1986). *Prophecy and Progress: The Sociology of Industrial and Post-Industrial Society*. London: Penguin.

Mandel, Ernest (1976). *Late Capitalism*. Translated by Joris De Bres, London: NLB.

Marx, Karl (1993). *Grundrisse: Foundations of the Critique of Political Economy*. Translated by Martin Nicolaus, London: Penguin Classics.

Marx, Karl (1990). *Capital: A Critique of Political Economy*, Vol. I. Translated by Ben Fowkes, London: Penguin Classics.

Marx, Karl (1969). *Theories of Surplus-Value, Part I*. Translated by Emile Burns, London: Lawrence and Wishart.

Marx, Karl (1904). *A Contribution To The Critique of Political Economy*. Translated by N. I. Stone, Chicago: Charles H. Kerr & Company.

McLuhan, Marshall (1994). *Understanding the Media: The Extensions of Man*. Cambridge, MA: The MIT Press.

McLuhan Marshall, and Bruce R. Powers (1989). *The Global Village: Transformations in World Life and Media in the 21st Century*. New York and Oxford: Oxford University Press.

Noble, David F. (2001). *Forces of Production: A Social History of Industrial Automation*. New Brunswick and London: Transaction.

Ollman, Bertell (2003). *Dance of the Dialectic: Steps in Marx's Method*. Urbana and Chicago: University of Illinois Press.

Ollman, Bertell (2001). *Alienation: Marx's Conception of Man in Capitalist Society*. Cambridge: Cambridge University Press.

Preston, Paschal (2001). *Reshaping Communications: Technology, Information and Social Change*. London: Sage.

Prey, Robert (2012). "The Network's Blindspot: Exclusion, Exploitation and Marx's Process-Relational Ontology." *tripleC* 10, no. 2 (2012): 253–273.

Rosenberg, Nathan (1976). "Marx as a Student of Technology." *Monthly Review* 28, no. 3 (July-August 1976): 56–77.

Servaes, Jan (2003). "The European Information Society: A Wake-Up Call." In *The European Information Society: A Reality Check*, edited by Jan Servaes, 11–32. Bristol and Portland: Intellect, 2003.

Servaes, Jan (ed.) (2014). Technological Determinism and Social Change. Lanham: Lexington Books.

Smith, Merritt Roe, and Leo Marx (eds.) (1995). *Does Technology Drive History?*. Cambridge, MA: MIT Press.

SPO, *Information Society Strategy (2006–2010)*, (July 2006). http://unpan1.un.org/intradoc/groups/public/documents/unpan/unpan025636.pdf (accessed 21 May 2014).

Toffler, Alvin (1981). *The Third Wave*. New York: Bantam Books.

Toffler, Alvin (1971). *Future Shock*. 21st printing. Toronto, New York and London: Bantam Books.

TÜBİTAK (2004). *Vision 2023, National Science and Technology Policies: 2003–2023 Strategy Document*. (in Turkish), (November 2, 2004). http://www.tubitak.gov.tr/tubitak_content_files/vizyon2023/Vizyon2023_Strateji_Belgesi.pdf (accessed June 11, 2014).

Webster, Frank (2006). *Theories of the Information Society*. London and New York: Routledge.

Williams, Raymond (2003). *Television: Technology and Cultural Form*. London and New York: Routledge.

Yüksel, Hakan (2015). "Creating Dependency Instead of Prosperity: A Critique of Information Society Policies in Turkey." In *Proceedings of the ISIS Summit Vienna 2015*, June 3–7, 2015; Vienna, Austria, S3020, http://sciforum.net/conference/isis-summit-vienna-2015/paper/2857 (accessed June 26, 2015).

Chapter Nine

Digital by Default

Consequences, Casualties and Coping Strategies

Ilse Mariën, Rob Heyman,
Koen Salemink, and Leo Van Audenhove

INTRODUCTION: THE MYTH OF A FREE DIGITAL CHOICE

The overall question throughout research on digital inequalities has mainly been what hinders or prevents individuals from engaging voluntarily with ICTs by examining differences in access and usage. This is quite logic because initially ICTs were—similar to television or telephones—not much more than new and emerging technologies ready to be diffused and adopted (Rogers 2003). Digital divide research consequently focused on studying socio-demographic characteristics in relation to patterns of diffusion, adoption and usage (Barzilai-Nahon 2006; Hanafizadeh et al. 2009). This explains why the first findings pointed at a lack of physical access as a first and foremost characteristic of digital inequalities (NTIA 1999). Nowadays, many researchers assume ubiquitous connectivity as an enabling force for all. The overall picture for digital inclusion has become more complex, and a lack of motivation to engage with ICTs, insufficient digital skills, scarce resources and support, and limited opportunities regarding training, learning, or usage have additionally been identified as key barriers (Brotcorne, Mertens and Valenduc 2009; Helsper 2012; Mariën and Van Audenhove 2011; Mertens and Servaes 2011). However, what has not evolved in the current theoretical frameworks and measurement schemes is the premise of the voluntary engagement with ICTs. The main focus still is if and to what extent people are choosing or willing to adopt and use ICTs (Tsatsou 2011).

Our research, on which we build this chapter, has shown that this voluntary basis of engaging with ICTs is less and less valid in today's Western societies (Mariën and Prodnik 2014; Mariën et al. 2013). Services are digitized at an ever-faster pace. Innovation cycles are succeeding rapidly and endlessly, leading to a continuous stream of new ICTs, applications and services. Access to institutional processes, information streams, and employment or education opportunities, are increasingly being transformed into *digital by default* (Helsper 2011). Moreover, the use of ICTs is clearly set as the overall normative stance of how today's Western societies are organized. Problematic in this regard is that, at first sight, public and private institutions are implementing the majority of these digitization processes without an in-depth consideration of those who are being victimized and set aside (Mariën and Prodnik 2014). This implies that the crucial question of research on digital inequalities is not who chooses to engage with ICTs and who does not, as if it were predetermined by choice, but instead at which levels the digitization of society in all its forms is reinforcing or creating mechanisms of social exclusion. Ongoing digital developments are regarded as an important contributor to social stratification. In this sense, one has to follow the digital default or face social exclusion (Mariën and Prodnik 2014; Crang et al. 2007).

Digital inequalities today transcend the idea of what Helsper (2008) has referred to as *a free* and *informed digital choice*, conceptualized as the freedom of individuals to choose whether they engage with ICTs or not according to their own beliefs, desires, wants, and needs. Digital inequalities evidently also apply to *self-excluded non-users* who voluntarily choose not to engage with ICTs, in spite of appropriate levels of access and skills. They are characterized by an overall lack of motivation and a negative attitude toward ICTs (Haddon 2000). Particular in this regard is that many self-excluded non-users might indirectly be considered as users because they tend to rely on *proxy-users* to resolve their digital needs: other individuals—very often family members or friends—are using the Internet, digital services or other ICTs on their request (Gilbert 2010; Helsper 2008). However, whereas individuals might believe they are making a free digital choice, in reality their engagement with ICTs is determined by contextual factors such as the available infrastructure, pricing schemes or policies within a region, or cultural and social influences of one's immediate surroundings (Helsper 2008; Townsend et al. 2013; Witte and Mannon 2010). In fact, this especially applies digitally excluded non-users living in poverty and in poorly connected rural areas (Michailidis et al. 2011). These individuals are non-users *by force*, but often—because of societal pressure and expected societal norms—prefer to claim they are non-users *by choice* instead of acknowledging their personal flaws and their inability to adapt to the overall digital norm of society (Witte and Mannon 2010).

The assumption can thus be made that non-engagement, and the idea of making a free digital choice, has become nearly impossible in today's Western societies, due to the in-depth entanglement and ubiquity of ICTs within daily practices, routines, and common public and private services. This implies that the premise of choosing to engage or not engage with ICTs is becoming oblivious and should no longer be considered as a valid entry point for studying digital inequalities. Consequently, theoretical models based upon appropriation theory or the diffusion of technologies are outdated and the need for a new approach is emerging. Also, it implies that merely using the perspective of *digital inequalities*—that is, studying differences in access, usage, skills, and other barriers—is insufficient and that additional examinations are needed of how, where and to what extent mechanisms of *digital exclusion*—that is, immediate societal disadvantages caused by digital inequalities—are at play. Therefore, this chapter approaches digital inequalities from a human rights perspective—such as, the various rights that individuals are entitled to because they are necessary to ensure full participation in society. As such, this contribution adds a new dimension to the current investigations of digital inequalities. Instead of looking at individual flaws, and the dynamics behind these, this chapter examines the processes that are hindering or enabling commonly accepted entitlements. It will do so by analyzing the following aspects:

1. A theoretical comparison of at-risk indicators of social versus digital exclusion, distributed across five types of resources: economic, cultural, political, social, and personal.
2. A critical view on the added value of a human rights perspective, and the referral to ICTs as entitlements.

As such, this chapter will provide a critical and in-depth analysis of how, in what life domains, in what particular spatial contexts, and among which population groups old and new mechanisms of exclusion are being created by the digitization of society.

FROM DIGITAL TO SOCIAL EXCLUSION AND BACK: A FUNDAMENTAL QUESTIONING

Throughout the last decade, leading scholars have shown that digital exclusion is a highly complex and multidimensional phenomenon that is defined by various technology-related barriers and social exclusion mechanisms, both on individual and institutional level (Gilbert 2010; Helsper 2012; Tsatsou 2011; Witte and Mannon 2010; Zillien and Hargittai 2009). On the one hand, ICT-related barriers such as a lack of physical and qualitative access, low levels of digital skills, little to no opportunities of use or a systemic lack of motivation to engage with ICTs have been identified as key disablers (Tsatsou 2011; van Dijk 2005; Mariën and Van Audenhove 2011). On the other hand, digital exclusion has been identified as a structural issue that is highly intertwined with mechanisms of social exclusion and as such, is related to aspects of social status, class and social stratification (Witte and Mannon 2010). According to van Dijk (2003, 2005) the so-called *Matthew effect* is clearly at play as advantaged groups within society continuously and systematically succeed in using ICTs to their immediate societal advantage whereas this is not or less the case for disadvantaged groups, thus reinforcing mechanisms of social exclusion and stratification. Moreover, the relation between digital and social exclusion is claimed to be bidirectional, stating that digital exclusion leads to social exclusion and vice versa. Thus creating a vicious cycle of exclusion mechanisms: "*Social exclusion leads to digital exclusion, which in turn perpetuates and exacerbates that social exclusion*" (Warren 2007: 379).

Notwithstanding that large-scale quantitative studies seem to confirm the nature of the mutual relation between determinants of digital and social exclusion, doubt remains about the causality between both (Helsper 2008; van Deursen 2010). Whereas quantitative research indicates that socio-economic status characteristics—age, gender, income, job status, ethnic background . . .—are among the main indicators for digital exclusion, more contextualized and often qualitative studies show a slightly different picture and draw attention to the distribution of support mechanisms and other types of economic, social, and cultural resources. Moreover, these studies highlight that not all disadvantaged individuals are confronted with a high number of ICT-related barriers. On the contrary, they show that a vast part of these socially disadvantaged groups succeed rather well in using ICTs to their immediate advantage (Gilbert 2010; Mariën 2012; Schurmans and Mariën 2013). Simultaneously, other research indicates that mechanisms of digital exclusion are even so present among advantaged—and thus unexpectedly digitally excluded groups—such as young people, high-educated elderly, or middle-class families (Brotcorne et al. 2010; Haché and Cullen 2010; Hargittai 2010; Livingstone and Helsper 2007).

Consequently, the relation between digital and social exclusion is not as one-dimensional and straightforward as presumed and a revision of the causal relation between both is called for. Therefore, this chapter entails a critical comparison of the characteristics of at-risk factors of digital and social exclusion; based upon the results of several theoretical and empirical studies realized by the authors, that focused on the conceptual evolution of the digital divide to digital exclusion (Mariën et al. 2010); the modeling of a multidimensional framework for digital exclusion and digital inclusion policies (Mariën and Van Audenhove 2011; Mariën and Van Audenhove 2012a, 2012b, 2012c); the exploration of the mutual dynamics and processes between digital and social exclusion (Mariën et al. 2013); the structural causes of user disempowerment (Mariën and Prodnik 2014) and qualitative user-oriented research among several vulnerable groups, for example NEETs, people living in poverty, low-educated, unemployed, and ethnic minorities (Mariën and Van Audenhove 2010; Mariën 2012; Salemink and Strijker 2014; Schurmans and Mariën 2013).

To facilitate and structure this analysis, the at-risk factors and characteristics of digital and social exclusion were classified across Helsper's (2008) categorization of five vital resources that are needed to ensure full digital and societal participation, namely personal, social, cultural, economic, and political resources. These five resources are based upon Bourdieu's (1986) interpretation of human capitals and represent a simplified and manageable approach to studying mechanisms of inequality because they cover both macro and micro aspects. As such, the comparison and analysis of at-risk factors and characteristics across these five types of resources—*for a detailed overview see annex 1 to 5*—allows identifying if and how mechanisms of social and digital exclusion are intertwined.

The overview as presented in figure 9.1 provides an in-depth understanding of the influential relation between social and digital exclusion and indicates, per type of resource, which at-risk factors coincide with one or more of

Table 9.1. Five Types of Resources

Personal resources	Individual attributes that impact one's ability to master ICTs or influence one's societal status—e.g., well-being, personal values and attitudes, communication skills, soft skills, and cognitive skills. (See annex 1)
Social resources	Rooted within one's broader level of participation and compliance within society and one's embedding in social capital networks—e.g., family composition, social support networks, societal norms. (See annex 2)
Cultural resources	Related to or originated in one's personal cultural background—e.g., gender, age, ethnicity, language—and to one's cultural practices and norms, often influenced by the imminent and dominant culture within one's immediate social environment. (See annex 3)
Economic resources	The various aspects that have a decisive influence on one's financial situation, such as employment, income, education and training opportunities, financial skills, or economic opportunities. (See annex 4)
Political resources	The regulatory framework in place—e.g., policies, infrastructure, social rights, and socio-spatial characteristics—and one's potential participation within decision-making processes and bodies. Consequently, it also comprises reflections related to agency and structure. (See annex 5)

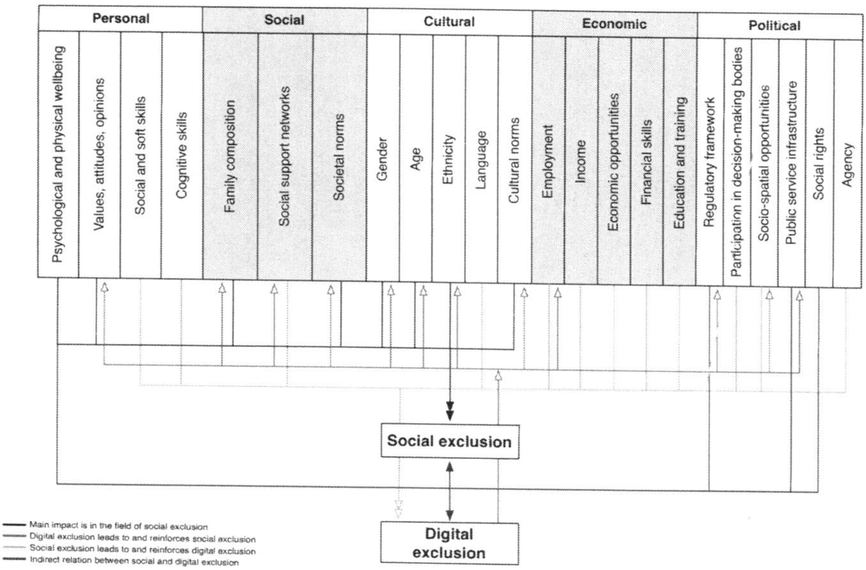

Figure 9.1. Dynamics of Social and Digital Exclusion: An Overview

the following dynamics: (1) social and digital exclusion are indirectly related (i.e., blue lines); (2) social exclusion is more prominent than digital exclusion (i.e., black lines); (3) social exclusion creates digital exclusion (i.e., green lines); and (4) digital exclusion reinforces social exclusion (i.e., red lines). The graphic overview also shows that indirect relations between social and digital exclusion are significantly less present than direct relations.

INDIRECT CAUSES AND CONSEQUENCES: DEFINING POTENTIAL EXCLUSION MECHANISMS

Indirect relations initially appear to apply to policy-related at-risk factors. Four at-risk indicators are at play with regards to both social and digital exclusion, namely: impact of regulatory framework, public service infrastructure, social rights, and well-being. The concrete characteristics are however distinct. For example, for the at-risk indicator *well-being* (see annex 1, personal resources) the characteristics of social exclusion are a lack of availability and access to care infrastructure and support, subject to substance abuse and a higher poverty risk among chronically ill individuals (Daly et al. 2008; Jehoel-Gijsbers and Vrooman 2007; Liamputtong 2007; Salemink and Strijker 2012; Warren 2007). Digital exclusion on the other hand is characterized by a lack of usability standards, a lack of available and affordable adaptive technologies or a limited take-up of ICT-solutions for health issues (Boeltzig and Pilling 2007; Communities and Local Government 2008). Though both are grounded in the specific needs and requirements of individuals dependent on some kind of care and support, there appears to be no direct cause-effect relation. The lack of care infrastructure is no direct cause of design inequalities and vice versa. There is however an indirect influence. Regulating usability standards and the affordability of adaptive technologies would significantly improve the care and support infrastructure as they imply solutions to immediate ICT-related barriers and enable a larger societal participation of populations with special needs (Bianchi et al. 2006). Similar dynamics can be identified with regards to the overall regulatory framework that applies to public service infrastructure and social rights (see political resources, annex 5). For example, the lack of a pro-active *poverty check* alongside new regulatory measures goes hand in hand with a lack of reflection about social exclusion mechanisms that are potentially caused by digitization processes of public and commercial services. Also, the absence of a social tariff for ICTs and the lack of recognition of ICT-access as a social right are an indirect aspect of the overall lack of social service infrastructure and mediation by professionals to enhance access to these infrastructures and resources.

Indirect relations are also present with regards to the following at-risk factors: family composition, personal characteristics (i.e., gender, age, ethnicity), and normative injunctions (i.e., societal norms, cultural norms, values, attitudes and opinions). The comparison shows that these at-risk factors have a more stringent impact on social than on digital exclusion; yet they indirectly define one another. Characteristics such as family breakdown, substance abuse, a defiant social identity, a lack of self-determination or a criminal or unstructured lifestyle are brought to the fore as direct causes and consequences of social exclusion (Communities and Local Government 2008; Haché and Cullen 2010; Helsper 2008; Emmel et al. 2006). Belonging to an ethnic minority, being a woman or an elderly person in many cases coincides with an increased risk of being socially excluded from various life domains (Jehoel-Gijsbers and Vrooman 2007; Warren 2007). Experiencing social exclusion is also characterized by a lack of sense of belonging to society, the inability to live according to common societal and cultural norms or a lack of life satisfaction and overall well-being (Helsper 2008; Jehoel-Gijsbers and Vrooman 2007; Lager et al. 2013; Witte and Mannon 2010). In the digital field, however, the effect of these at-risk factors is indirect, complex, and contradictory in nature. The influence of cultural resources (i.e., gender, age, and ethnicity) on digital exclusion remains fairly limited as they mainly define the context, diversity, and intensity of usage patterns, without direct societal consequences (Brotcorne et al. 2010;

Hargittai 2007). Gender defined ICT-use patterns imply that women use ICTs in a different way than men, which as such, is not a problem, as long as these use patterns are accompanied by societal advantages (Brandtzaeg et al. 2010; van Dijk 2003). The situation is similar with regards to age and ethnicity: usage patterns are developed according to daily wants and needs, or common cultural practices. Offline behavior, lifestyle, life choices, daily practices or a rejection of digital as the overall accepted normative stance, undoubtedly define (non-) engagement with ICTs (Doyle 2008; Haché and Centeno 2011). Differences in usage do not imply that mechanisms of exclusion are present, but with the growing importance of digital participation this is becoming ever more likely. Or as Livingstone and Helsper (2007: 424) emphasize:

> "People may approach learning, careers advice, participation or any other social benefit through both online and offline means, with the balance of resources still greatly favouring offline routes to inclusion. If and when this balance alters, online routes to inclusion will become more important, and the costs of digital exclusion will become more apparent."

On the other hand, participating and living in today's society with no or very limited engagement with ICTs is still possible. Moreover, non-use can easily go hand in hand with an overall sense of well-being (Brants and Frissen 2003; Servaes and Heinderyckx 2002; van Deursen 2010). This implies that being digitally excluded can coincide with being socially included. Hence, the reasoning that personal characteristics and normative injunctions based upon individual choices or shaped by the social and cultural context have a more stringent impact on social than on digital exclusion.

DIRECT CAUSES AND CONSEQUENCES: REDEFINING OLD AND NEW EXCLUSION MECHANISMS

Our analysis indicates that the direct relation between social and digital exclusion is twofold. On the one hand social exclusion mechanisms are transmitted to digital exclusion. On the other hand digital exclusion mechanisms are reinforcing old and creating new mechanisms of social exclusion. The at-risk factors of social exclusion that are continued, and moreover amplified in the digital field are related to skills (i.e., cognitive, social, soft, financial, language, and education), financial strength (i.e., employment, income, and economic opportunities), social support networks, socio-spatial inequalities and self-determination (i.e., agency, participation in decision-making bodies). For social and digital exclusion, these at-risk factors and their characteristics are identical. In other words, regarding skills, financial strength, support networks, socio-spatial inequalities, and self-determination, the old and deep-rooted mechanisms of social exclusion are transposed to digital exclusion. For example, unemployment and poverty hinder people from acquiring a certain degree of financial independence and stability. Logically, this causes a limited capacity to acquire qualitative and sustainable home access to ICTs, pay for the secondary costs that go hand in hand with the use of ICTs or take advantage of package deals or bundling of services (Brotcorne et al. 2010; Livingstone and Helsper 2007; Pena-Lopez 2009; van Deursen 2010; van Dijk 2005). Lack of compliance with formal education, negative learning experiences, poor educational achievement, lack of recognition of certification schemes, differing learning styles, and learning needs hamper engagement in formal and lifelong education in general, but also in additional ICT-related courses (Brotcorne et al. 2009; Heeley and Damodaran 2009; Mariën and Van Audenhove 2008). These mechanisms of limited participation in education seem to coexist and apply to learning trajectories in general, disregarding the field, focus and topic of the course or training (Salemink and Strijker 2014). Low levels of self-esteem, confidence, self-efficacy, communication competences and problem-solving capabilities hamper social interactions and autonomy in daily life, and also limit interaction with or about ICTs. Moreover, they go hand in hand with so-called *button anxiety*—for example, being subject to feelings of fear and anxiety when having to deal with ICTs (van Dijk 2006). Low levels of agency, self-efficacy, and problem-solving skills also hinder an autonomous use of ICTs and the development of digital skills through trial-and-error and other autodidact ways (Haché and Cullen 2010; van Dijk 2005). Consequently, a lack of social, soft, and cognitive skills increases the need for support, creates more dependency on others and reinforces feelings and mechanisms of disempowerment. An underlying hypothesis is that, in today's digital society, autonomy leads to empowerment whereas a lack of autonomy leads to vulnerability (Pierson 2012).

The reinforcement of old and the creating of new mechanisms of social exclusion due to digital exclusion mechanisms mainly applies to at-risk factors related to cultural characteristics (i.e., gender, age, and ethnicity), normative injunctions (i.e., values, attitudes and opinions, societal norms, cultural norms) and political resources (i.e., regulatory framework, socio-spatial opportunities and public service infrastructure). Moreover, the digital norm implemented within a society and the ability of individuals to access, find, and benefit from opportunities and support networks have a decisive influence. The rapid and ongoing digitization of public and private services in all life domains is pushing toward the obligatory use of ICTs, thus creating mechanisms of user disempowerment, limiting the individual ability to make free digital choices and thus leading to diminished feelings of well-being

(Crang et al. 2006; Helsper 2008; Mariën and Prodnik 2014). Those who do not wish to use ICTs or those who do not have the ability and opportunity to easily engage with ICTs are increasingly being excluded from commonly accepted entitlements such as services, work, education, or information (Mariën and Prodnik 2014). People who live in "underserved" rural areas especially face difficulties in acquiring access to public services (Salemink and Strijker 2012). The spatial factor of rurality can even result in a so-called rural penalty: people who live at a distant from services—in some cases by choice, in some cases as a given fact—have limited access to these services. Their physical remoteness is reinforced by their limited access to digital connections, thereby putting these people at risk of digital and social exclusion (Malecki 2003; Townsend et al. 2013). Or as van Deursen and van Dijk (2010: 909) explain more profoundly:

> ". . . there are strong indications that large parts of the population will be excluded from actual and effective Internet use . . . In the beginning, groups with fewer internet skills will be persuaded in negative ways; flights will be booked, concerts will be sold out, jobs will be given away, and dates will primarily be granted to those having access. Continuing the transformations towards the Internet in the most important domains of life will eventually lead to serious problems the lack of internet skills among large parts of the population is not accounted for."

In particular, this occurs when there is a discrepancy between individual proficiency levels, cultural and context defined usage patterns and the level of digitization within society. Negative consequences occur when individuals are disabled or prevented from grasping the fundamental added value of ICT-usage (Brotcorne et al. 2010; Hargittai 2010; Witte and Mannon 2010; Zillien and Hargittai 2009). Or yet, when one individual or population group, more than another, succeeds in taking immediate added value out of their ICT-use (Hüsing and Selhofer 2004; van Dijk 2005). Mechanisms of social exclusion also apply when and where individuals are disabled from benefiting from the added value of different networks in terms of support or opportunities (Crang et al. 2007; Warren 2007). Support networks provide opportunities of use, stimulate the development of digital skills and deliver vital information about new and valuable applications. More and more, support networks (i.e., social and cultural capital communities) are transferred to online environments, incapacitating non-proficient or limited users to make part of or rely on these digitized networks (Brotcorne et al. 2010; Graham 2002; Haddon 2006; Stewart 2007; van Dijk 2005). In other words, the ongoing digitization of our daily routines and practices, in all life domains, proportionally increases the risk of reinforcing existing and creating new mechanisms of social exclusion.

ICTS AS ENTITLEMENT: A HUMAN RIGHTS PERSPECTIVE

When reflecting about renewed approaches for studying digital inequalities, ideas on integrating a human rights perspective always submerge. This is quite logic, seen how extensively digital inequalities are interwoven with social inequalities, and consequently how solutions are intertwined with social inclusion policies (Haché and Cullen 2010; Martinez and Mesa del Olmo 2010; Mertens and Servaes 2011; Tsatsou 2011). More yet—especially in the field of digital inclusion policies and practices—human rights and the social, economic, and cultural participation they entail are brought to the fore as the overall normative stance for identifying solutions (Bianchi et al. 2006; Steyn and Johanson 2011). Mansell (2002), for example, proposes a rights-based approach for redefining new media policies in order to enable individuals to become empowered, active, and capable media users. Peters (2014) gives a comprehensive and critical overview of how human rights principles are being and should be applied to the Internet. Selwyn (2003), in turn, uses various dimensions of participation in society as a potential framework for defining key digital inclusion policy priorities. Bianchi et al. (2006) take that approach one step further and frame inclusion as:

> "a normative imperative, consisting of a set of individual entitlements to fundamental human freedoms, autonomy, dignity and equitable participation in society. Each citizen should be able to claim these entitlements on the basis of the universally agreed canon of human rights." (Bianchi et al. 2006: 1–2)

Moreover, various scholars highlight the promising potential of ICTs for developing broader societal goals such as improving health, stimulating learning or enabling economic opportunities and societal participation (Bianchi et al. 2006; Haché and Cullen 2010; Notley and Foth 2008; Servaes 2014; Steyn and Johanson 2011). It is among others this potential for empowerment, inclusion, and participation that has initiated the idea of considering access to ICTs as a human right and an entitlement to be strived for, see for example, the discussion paper by UNESCO (2013) on Internet universality.

However, taking access to ICTs as a human right, and consequently the idea of *Universal Access* as a starting point of reflection and policies, is accompanied by a number of risks and potentially perverse effects (Witte and Mannon 2010). It neglects two important questions. First, is everybody capable of using the Internet and secondly does this increase their autonomy or freedom? If we invest in diffusing new media, can we make sure that civilians are more free or empowered, and increase their overall societal inclusion and participation? Or are we merely helping capital to find new markets through self-fulfilling prophecies of connectedness (van Dijck 2013) resulting in more subsumption of the prosumer commodity (Fuchs 2012). Or is like Mansell (2002: 6) indicates, another approach needed, that focuses on skills and capabilities:

> "Once connected, there are no grounds for simply assuming that citizens will be empowered to be able to conduct their social lives in meaningful ways. There is, therefore, a growing need to examine whether the deployment of new media is consistent with ensuring that the majority of citizens acquire the necessary capabilities for interpreting and acting upon a social world that is intensively mediated by the new media."

Such reflections are consistent with the findings brought to the fore by civil society organizations in the field of digital inclusion. Delivering mere ICT-access to individuals does not lead to an automatic amelioration of their societal position (Bianchi et al. 2006). Instead, a comprehensive approach is needed with a focus on combating the various ICT-related barriers (i.e., access, skills, attitude, opportunities of use, support resources . . .) while framed within social policy initiatives (Notley and Foth 2008; Wright and Wadhwa 2010).

SEN'S CAPABILITIES AND FREEDOM FRAMEWORKS: LESSONS LEARNT

In order to bring focus to these broader, yet highly individualized goals of empowerment, participation, and inclusion, Sen's capability approach (1993, 2001) is increasingly being applied to frame media entitlements in a more comprehensive way that exceeds mere access and usage (Bianchi et al. 2006; Mansell 2002; Garnham 1997). Claims are made that the capability approach places the individual at the center of inclusion policies (Bianchi et al. 2006). Or, that stimulating the development of capabilities, allows individuals to make *free and informed choices* about their (non-) engagements with ICTs (Helsper 2008; Nussbaum 2000; Selwyn and Facer 2007). Consequently, one of the central questions of digital inclusion initiatives has become how the overall capabilities of socially and digitally excluded individuals can be developed so as to allow an autonomous, empowered, and self-conscious (non-) use of ICTs. Obviously, Sen's framework has dealt with the same questions for development. What needs to be measured and improved in order to increase autonomy and empowerment? Previous development theories looked at utility, measured in money as a proxy for utility or directly by mapping access to certain resources. The problem with access is that it is relative to ones' position and the society one is in. More yet, not all resources are equally required by the same person:

> "For example, a poor person with a parasitic stomach ailment may prefer two kilos of rice over one, in much the same way that another person—equally poor but with no ailment—may, but it would be hard to argue that both do equally well with, say, one kilo of rice." (Sen 2001: 69)

Also, actors may be free to refrain from consuming these resources, which is different from not being able to consume them. For example, a person fasting may have access to food, but chooses not to. This last example is similar to the digitally self-excluded. In these cases access to goods and capital are bad parameters for freedom. Societies on the other hand, create particular expectations with regard to necessary goods and services:

> "By necessaries I understand not only the commodities which are indispensably necessary for the support of life, but whatever the custom of the country renders it indecent for creditable people, even the lowest order, to be without." (Sen 1981:18 in Garnham, 1997)

So, a society has certain "necessaries" that are required to coincide with the overall common normative standard in society. Necessaries may at firsthand seem physical resources, but they should be more broadly interpreted, as they can also consist of, for example, access to information or education.

Sen proposed to stop measuring factors that were only indirectly related to well-being by focusing on functionings or *"the various things a person may value doing or being"* (Sen 2001: 75). A person's well-being could than be evaluated by analyzing the various functionings achieved in that person's life. It is however important to note the difference between well-being and agency. Because not all functionings are achieved by one isolated person. Being able to vote for example, or having food is usually not achieved by one person only (Robeyns 2005). However, a focus on mere functionings would be similar to utilitarian approaches. Individuals may still choose to disregard these life goals because they favor other goals or are unable to change resources in functionings due to lack of particular resources, which are indirectly related to a good. To escape the shortcomings of utilitarian approaches and account for individual heterogeneity, Sen introduces capability sets that constitute all feasible functionings available to a person (Sen 2001: 75), including freedom of choice. Individuals can still decide not to convert a possible functioning into an achieved functioning. This means that a capability is a potential functioning if all conversion factors are present (Robeyns 2005). Robeyns (2005: 99) has deepened and diversified the definition of conversion factors by identifying three groups: (1) personal conversion factors (e.g., metabolism, physical condition, sex, reading skills, intelligence) influence how a person can convert the characteristics of a commodity into a functioning; (2) social conversion factors (e.g., public policies, social norms, discriminating practices, gender roles, societal hierarchies, power relations); and, (3) environmental conversion factors (e.g., climate, geographical location). According to Sen the ultimate goal of development is freedom that can either be instrumental or intrinsic. Instrumental freedoms are basic freedoms required to develop and enable other types of freedom that in turn can again be instrumental or intrinsic. The ultimate goal of Sen's framework for development is intrinsic freedom, or in other words, to have a *complete capability set*. A major shortcoming of Sen's work, however, is that he refrains from defining intrinsic capabilities because they depend on individual and cultural preferences. Nussbaum criticizes Sen's lack of fundamental freedoms, these are required to create: "*fundamental entitlements that are to some extent independent of the preferences that people happen to have, preferences shaped, often, by unjust background conditions*" (Nussbaum 2003: 48).

ICTS AS ENTITLEMENT: REALLY?

In spite of a broader approach on capabilities, the fundamental question for defining key priorities for digital inclusion remains whether ICTs can and should be considered as an entitlement and a basic human right. Translating Sen's approach to digital inequalities implies that ICTs can only be entitlements if they are not merely considered as functionings but also conversion factors for other functionings. This has to be the case to such an extent that individuals without this conversion factor—ICTs—are disadvantaged and unable to access particular capabilities. In other words, when these individuals are deprived of capabilities because access to ICTs is an instrumental freedom. Consequently, ICTs should only become an entitlement if benefits for a majority result in deprivations for a minority with regard to other important freedoms. For example, it is no longer possible to find jobs without ICTs, in that case, ICTs have become an irreversible part of job hunting for non-users. In this regard Mansell (2002) adds that access is not enough, and that other conversion factors such as skills should additionally be incorporated as entitlements.

A crucial question in this regard is whether the continuous and rapid digitization of society is currently creating such a situation in which a majority has all the advantages while a minority is living a worst-case scenario. The results of the comparison of at-risk factors and their characteristics confirm the reality of the Matthew-effect in the field of digital exclusion, as already indicated several years ago by van Dijk (2003, 2005). Some advantaged groups are in other words, continuously able to improve their societal position, whereas disadvantaged groups are not. However, it remains unclear whether there's a fundamental imbalance within today's Western societies between these advantaged and disadvantaged groups. The reality is that adoption figures of access, use, and skills tend to show overtly positive evolvements. Whereas research on digital exclusion clearly indicates that a vast part of individuals is not following the digital (r)evolution. Consequently, starting to consider ICTs as entitlements is only possible if one recognizes the potential benefits on the one hand, and the concrete deprivations on the other hand. According to Garnham (1997: 123) this means that one has to see what capabilities people without ICTs are deprived from: "*For instance, while I personally hate the mobile phone, we have to recognize that mobility widens the capability set and is a functioning that is increasingly widely available. Are those without it now sufficiently disadvantaged to make it an entitlement?*" It also implies that it is important to invest in longitudinal research on the convergence between human rights, entitlements and digital inequalities and how each of these aspects is influenced by the ongoing digitization of services and society in general.

But these reflections on ICTs as entitlements should also be reframed more critically. If a society has to rely on a technology it does not control, such as the Internet or social media, should we strive to make it an entitlement? Especially if this technology in itself is not yet finished or stabilized (Feenberg 2009). Defining unfinished ICTs as entitlements is a dangerous game where one risks to drive capitalist expansion while at the same time increasing digital(ized) conversion factors for fundamental freedoms. It means that entitlements are used to primarily drive economic considerations and only secondly fundamental freedoms. Also, non-users, whether by choice or not, beg the question if ICTs should ever be taken as the overall normative stance within society. These non-users may have valid arguments to resist progress and these are nullified if digital by default is set as the overall norm or better said as an *unwanted* entitlement. One might argue that many self-excluded users rely on proxy-users, but they are particular and spontaneous. It is impossible to depend on the benevolence of proxy-users in a universal human rights perspective. An ICTs-as-entitlements approach should make claims about the right to proxy-technologies or proxy-conversion factors. In other words, an entitlement approach has to question the digital by default instead of vindicating this default.

CONCLUSION: SOME FUNDAMENTAL QUESTIONS FOR DIGITAL INEQUALITY RESEARCH

The analysis and comparison of at-risk factors and their characteristics, spread across personal, social, cultural, economic, and political resources, has undoubtedly shown that social and digital exclusion mechanisms are intertwined. Moreover, it emphasizes that distinct spheres of influences between social and digital exclusion are a reality. Digital exclusion is embedded in offline social exclusion, and with the ongoing digital developments, the digital realm starts to substantially affect the offline realm. However, the relation between social and digital exclusion is linear, circular, and in that sense not straightforward.

In the first place, this chapter points out that social inequalities do not at all times and under all circumstances lead to digital inequalities, as is too often and easily presumed. It clarifies that such a direct and unilateral cause-effect relationship foremost applies to skills, financial strength, social support networks, and socio-spatial characteristics. Consequently, resolving digital exclusion mechanism related to each of these aspects must automatically consist of simultaneously resolving the underlying mechanisms of social exclusion. For providing qualitative and sustained access, it implies increasing the limited financial means of socially excluded individuals, or lowering the current costs of ICTs by way of alternative solutions such as a social tariff for Internet access. For skills, this means that an increased focus is needed on the development of soft and social skills to increase confidence, self-efficacy, and autonomy. Increasing people's soft skills is often a more necessary intervention than the actual provision of material goods such as access to ICTs. An ICT-ready mind is an important step toward adoption and actual sustainable usage. Also, additional research is needed to unravel and test (a) the hypothesis that autonomy leads to empowerment and that a lack of autonomy leads to vulnerability; and (b) the hypothesis that a lack of soft skills leads to mechanisms of self-exclusion by not asking, not going after what one is entitled to, by not taking the necessary steps toward engagement in social networks, employment or other life domains. To sum up, this chapter has highlighted that the debate so far has created substantial knowledge about individual capabilities and motivations, but *the debate should now aim at understanding structures and mechanisms at meso and macro levels*.

In the second place, this chapter highlights the growing risk of becoming socially excluded due to mechanisms of digital exclusion. It suggests a justified fear that the willingness and ability of individuals to engage with ICTs will not continue to collide with the future and relentless digitization of society. The hypothesis is that the more processes and practices are digitized by default, the higher the risk will be of reinforcing existing and creating new mechanisms of social exclusion. In other words, the expectation is that new mechanisms of social exclusion will become more prominent in the future because formerly socially included groups will also become excluded. Consequently, the question "*when, with whom and how are digitization processes creating new mechanism of social exclusion*" is a crucial aspect of future digital inequality research.

This chapter also articulates a fundamental need to further examine the idea of recognizing ICTs as entitlements from a human rights perspective. Do digitization processes negatively influence internationally accepted entitlements and basic human rights such as employment, social security, housing or education? And, even though the question "*what ICTs should be entitlements*" is medium determinist and in favor of a status quo, the reverse question "*what happens if ICTs have become entitlements*" is more critical and adds not only the inclusion of soft skills surrounding ICTs, but also the need to look for alternative conversion factors to guarantee instrumental freedoms. In other words, the fundamental point of reflection of solutions for digital inequalities should not be how to ensure that individuals are given the material goods they are entitled to for living according to the commonly accepted norms within a society, but instead, how individuals can be enabled to develop their capabilities and alternative resources so they can move autonomously and self-consciously toward their own pre-set goals.

REFERENCES

Barzilai-Nahon, Karine (2006). "Gaps and bits: Conceptualizing measurements for digital divide(s)." *The Information Society* 22: 269–278.

Bianchi, A., Barrios, S., Cabrera, M., Cachia, R., Compano, R., Malanowski, N., Punie, Y., Turlea, G., Zinnbauer, D. and Centeno, C. (2006). "Revisiting eInclusion: From vision to action." Report European Commission, Joint Research Center (JRC), Institute for Prospective Technological Studies (IPTS). Sevilla: European Commission.

Boeltzig, Heike, and Pilling, Doria (2007). "Bridging the digital divide for hard-to-reach groups." Report e-Government Series, IBM Center for The Business of Government.

Bourdieu, Pierre (1986). "The Forms of Capital." In *Handbook of Theory and Research for the Sociology of Education*, edited by John G. Richardson. New York: Greenwood Press.

Brandtzaeg, Petter B., Heim, Jan, and Karahasanovic, Amela (2010). "Understanding the new digital divide: A typology of Internet users in Europe." *International Journal of Human-Computer Studies* 69(2011):123–138.

Brants, Kees, and Frissen, Valerie (2003). "Inclusion and exclusion in the information society." Final deliverable for The European Media and Technology in Everyday Life Network, 2000–2003.

Brotcorne, Périne, Mertens, Luc, and Valenduc, Gerard (2009). "Offline jongeren en de digitale kloof. Over het risico op ongelijkheden bij 'digital natives'" Report for POD Maatschappelijke Integratie by Fondation Travail-Université (FTU), Centre de Recherche Travail & Technology, Namen.

Brotcorne, Périne, Damhuis, Lotte, Lauren, Véronique, Valenduc, Gerard and Vendramin, Patricia (2010). "La fracture numérique au second degree." Report, Fondation Travail-Université ASBL, Namen.

Communities and Local Government (2008). "An analysis of international digital inclusion strategies: why develop a digital inclusion strategy and what should be the focus?" Report for Tech4i2, the Department for Communities and Local Government. London, UK.

Crang, Michael, Crosbie, Tracie and Graham, Steven (2006). "Variable geometries of connection: Urban digital divides and the uses of information technology." *Urban Studies* 43(13): 2551–2570.

Crang, Michael, Crosbie, Tracie, and Graham, Steven (2007). "Technology, time-space, and the remediation of neighbourhood life." *Environment and Planning A* 39: 2405–2422.

Daly, Anne, McNamara, Justine, Harding, Ann, and Yap, Mandy (2008). "Indicators of risk of social exclusion for children in Australian households: An analysis by state and age group." *Australasian Journal of Regional Studies* 14(2): 133–154.

Doyle, Kenneth O. (2008). "Introduction: Thinking differently about the new media." *American Behavioral Scientist* 52(1):3–7.

Emmel, Nick, Hughes, Kahryn, and Greenhalgh, Joanne (2006). "Developing methodological strategies to recruit and research socially excluded groups." Project report, ESRC Research Methods Programme. UK.

Feenberg, Andrew (2009). "Critical Theory of Communication Technology: Introduction to the Special Section." *The Information Society* 25 (2): 77–83.

Fuchs, Christian (2012). "The Political Economy of Privacy on Facebook." *Television and New Media* 13(2): 139–59.

Garnham, Nicholas (1997). "Amartya Sen's 'Capabilities' Approach to the Evaluation of Welfare: Its Application to Communications." *The Public* 4(4): 25–34.

Gilbert, Melissa (2010). "Theorizing Digital and Urban Inequalities: critical geographies of 'race,' gender and technological capital." *Information, Communication & Society* 13(7): 1000–1018.

Graham, Stephen (2002). "Bridging urban digital divides? Urban polarisation and Information and Communications Technologies (ICTs)." *Urban studies* 39(1): 33–56.

Haché, Alexandra, and Centeno, Clara (2011). "Under the radar: The contribution of civil society and third sector organisations to eInclusion." Report for the European Commission by the Institute for Prospective Technological Studies (IPTS), a Joint Research Center (JRC). Sevilla, Spain.

Haché, Alexandra, and Cullen, Joe (2010). "ICT and Youth at Risk: How ICT-driven initiatives can contribute to their socio-economic inclusion and how to measure it." Report for the European Commission by the Institute for Prospective Technological Studies (IPTS), a Joint Research Center (JRC). Sevilla, Spain.

Haddon, Leslie (2000). "Social Exclusion and Information and Communication Technologies: Lessons from Studies of Single Parents and the Young Elderly." *New Media and Society* 2(4): 387–406.

Haddon, Leslie. (2006). *Information and communication technologies in everyday life: A concise introduction and research guide*. Oxford: Berg.

Hanafizadeh, Mohammed R., Saghaei, Abbas, and Hanafizadeh, Payam (2009). "An index for cross-country analysis of ICT infrastructure and access." *Telecommunications Policy* 33: 385–405.

Hargittai, Eszter (2010). "Digital na(t)ives? Variation in Internet skills and uses among members of the 'Net generation." *Sociological Inquiry* 80(1): 92–113.

Heeley, Melanie, and Damodaran, Leela (2009). *Digital inclusion: A review of international policy and practice.* Loughborough University.

Helsper, Ellen, J. (2008). "Digital inclusion: An analysis of social disadvantage and the Information Society." Report for the Department for Communities and Local Government, London.

Helsper, Ellen, J. (2011). "The emergence of a digital underclass: digital policies in the UK and evidence for inclusion." Media policy brief 3 by the Department of Media and Communications. London: London School of Economics and Political Science.

Helsper, Ellen, J. (2012). "A corresponding fields model for the links between social and digital exclusion." *Communication Theory* 22(4): 403–426.

Hüsing, Tobias, and Selhofer, Hannes (2004). "DIDIX: A digital divide index for measuring inequality in IT diffusion." *IT and Society* 1(7): 21–38.

Jehoel-Gijsbers, Gerda, and Vrooman, Cok (2007). "Explaining social exclusion. A theoretical model tested in the Netherlands." Report for The Netherlands Institute for Social Research (SCP). The Hague.

Lager, Debbie, Van Hoven, Bettina, and Huigen, Paulus (2013). "Dealing with change in old age: Negotiating working-class belonging in a neighbourhood in the process of urban renewal in the Netherlands." *Geoforum* 50: 54–61.

Liamputtong, Pranee (2007). *Researching the vulnerable*. London, Thousand Oakes, New Delhi: Sage Publications Ltd.

Livingstone, Sonia, and Helsper, Ellen J. (2007). "Gradations in digital inclusion: children, young people and the digital divide." *New Media and Society* 9(4): 671–696.

Malecki Edward (2003). "Digital developments in rural areas: potentials and pitfalls." *Journal of Rural Studies* 19: 201–214.

Mansell, Robin (2002). "From Digital Divides to Digital Entitlements in Knowledge Societies." *Current Sociology* 50(3): 407–26.

Mariën, Ilse (2012). "Evaluatie van het Recup PC project van Stad Gent: Do's en Don'ts voor de toekomst." Research report commissioned by Digipolis Gent.

Mariën, Ilse, Van Audenhove, Leo, Vleugels, Chris, Bannier, Stijn, and Pierson, Jo (2010). "Digitale kloof van de tweede graad in Vlaanderen." Research report commissioned by the Instituut Samenleving & Technologie (IST). Brussels.

Mariën, Ilse, Baelden, Dorien, Bens, Jana, Schurmans, Dana, Van Audenhove, Leo, Smukste, Kristine, Pierson, Jo, Lemal, Marijke, and Goubin, Erik (2013). "Van digitale naar maatschappelijke participatie: Opportuniteiten en uitdagingen." In *De sociale staat van Vlaanderen 2013*, edited by Callens, M., Noppe, J. and Vanderleyden, L., 227–272. Brussel: Studiedienst Vlaamse Regering.

Mariën, Ilse, and Prodnik, Jernej A. (2014). "Digital inclusion and user (dis)empowerment: a critical perspective." *Info* 16(6): 35–47.

Mariën, Ilse, and Van Audenhove, Leo (2008). "e-Learning en e-inclusie initiatieven: Een kwalitatieve analyse van een aantal laagdrempelige e-learning en ICT-cursussen bij VDAB." Research report for the IBBT Acknowledge project.

Mariën, Ilse, and Van Audenhove, Leo (2010). "Embedding e-inclusion initiatives in people's daily reality: The role of social networks in tackling the digital divide". Paper presented at the Digitas Conference Digital Natives, Digital Immigrants, Digital Asylum-seekers: The Clash of Cultures, Sibiu, Rumania, June 21–23.

Mariën, Ilse, and Van Audenhove, Leo (2011). "Mediageletterdheid en digitale vaardigheden: naar een multidimensioneel model van digitale exclusie." In *Mediageletterdheid in een digitale wereld*, edited by Marie-Anne Moreas, and Jan Pickery, 99–137. Brussel: Studiedienst Vlaamse Regering.

Mariën, Ilse, and Van Audenhove, Leo (2012a). "Meetbaarheid van digitale inclusie." Research report commissioned by Digipolis and the City of Ghent.

Mariën, Ilse, and Van Audenhove, Leo (2012b). "Digitale inclusie en beleid in Gent." Research report commissioned by Digipolis and the City of Ghent.

Mariën, Ilse, and Van Audenhove, Leo (2012c). "Digitale inclusie: Het middenveld als structurele partners." In *Armoede en sociale uitsluiting. Jaarboek 2012: Lokale vormen van armoedebestrijding: een sociaal innovatieve* benadering, edited by Danielle Dierckx, Stijn Oosterlynck, Jill Coene, and An Van Haarlem, 317–332. Antwerpen: OASeS.

Martinez, Pedro M., and Mesa del Olmo, Adela (2010). "*Digital Divide and Digital Citizenship: Adapting the Social Policies to Promote e-Inclusion.*" Proceedings of the 10th European Conference on E-Government: National Center for Taxation Studies University of Limerick, Ireland, June 17–18.

Mertens, Stefan, and Servaes, Jan (2011). "ICT policies on structural and socio-cultural participation in Brussels," ADOMI E. (ed.), *Handbook of Research on Information Communication Technology: Trends, Issues and Advancements. Vol. 1*. Hershey-New York: IGI Global, 319–336.

Michailidis, Anastasios, Partalidou, Maria, Nastis, Stefanos A., Papadaki-Klavdianou, Aphrodite, and Charatsari Chrysanthi (2011). "Who goes online? Evidence of internet use patterns from rural Greece." *Telecommunications Policy* 35: 333–343.

National Telecommunications and Information Administration (NTIA) (1999). "Falling through the net: Defining the digital divide." Report for the U.S. Department of Commerce. Washington, D.C.

Notley, Tanya M., and Foth, Marcus (2008). "Extending Australia's digital divide policy: an examination of the value of social inclusion and social capital policy frameworks." *Australian Social Policy 7*.

Nussbaum, Martha (2000). "Women's Capabilities and Social Justice." *Journal of Human Development* 1(2): 219–247.

Nussbaum, Martha (2003). "Capabilities as Fundamental Entitlements: Sen and Social Justice." *Feminist Economics* 9(2–3): 33–59.

Pena-Lopez, Ismael (2009). "Measuring digital development for policy-making: Models, stages, characteristics and causes." PhD diss., Information and Knowledge Society Doctoral Programme, Internet Interdisciplinary Institute, Universitat Oberta de Catalunya.

Peters, Michael. A. (2014). "Internet Universality: Human Rights and Principles for the Internet." In *Knowledge Cultures* 2(3): 15–28.

Pierson, Jo (2012). "Online privacy in social media: a conceptual exploration of empowerment and vulnerability." *Communications and Strategies* 88(4): 99–120.

Robeyns, Ingrid (2005). "The Capability Approach: A Theoretical Survey." *Journal of Human Development* 6(1): 93–117.

Rogers, Everett M. (2003). *Diffusion of Innovations (5th Edition)*. New York: The Free Press.

Salemink, Koen, and Strijker, Dirk (2014). "Social and digital exclusion: The Case of Gypsy-Travelers in the Netherlands." Paper presented at the 25th European Regional Conference of the International Telecommunications Society, Brussels, June 22–24.

Salemink Koen, and Strijker Dirk (2012). "Breedband op het platteland." Rapportage voor Woon-en Leefbaarheidsbasisplan Oost-Groningen, RUG-FRW, Groningen.

Schurmans, Dana, and Mariën, Ilse (2013). "Naar gebruikersprofielen van kwetsbare jongeren: Over digitale media, sociale context en digitale ongelijkheden." Research report, in collaboration with Maks vzw and commissioned by Mediawijs.be, The Flemish Knowledge Center for Media Literacy. Brussel: Mediawijs.be.

Selwyn, Neil (2003). "Defining the 'digital divide': Developing a theoretical understanding of inequalities in the information age." Occasional Paper for the ESRC project Adults Learning @ Home.

Selwyn, Neil, and Keri Facer (2007). "Beyond the digital divide: Rethinking digital inclusion for the 21st century." Bristol: Futurelab.

Sen, Amartya (1993). "Capability and Well-being." In *The Quality of Life*, edited by Martha C. Nussbaum and Amartya K. Sen, 30–53. Oxford: Clarendon Press.

Sen, Amartya (2001). *Development as Freedom*. Oxford; New York: Oxford University Press.

Servaes Jan and Heinderyckx Francois (2002). "The 'new' ICTs environment in Europe: Closing or widening the gaps?" *Telematics and Informatics*19(2): 91–116.

Servaes, Jan (ed.) (2014). *Technological Determinism and Social Change. Communication in a Tech-Mad World*. Lanham: Lexington Books.

Stewart, James (2007). "Local experts in the Domestication of Information and Communication Technologies." *Information, Communication and Society* 10(4): 547–569.

Steyn, Jacques, and Johanson, Graeme (2011). *ICTs and sustainable solutions for the digital divide: Theory and Perspectives*. Hershey: Information Science Reference, IGI Global.

Townsend, Leanne, Sathiaseelan, Arjuna, Fairhurst, Gorry, and Wallace, Claire (2013). "Enhanced broadband access as a solution to the social and economic problems of the rural digital divide." *Local Economy* 28: 580–595.

Tsatsou, Panayiota (2011). "Digital divides revisited: What is new about divides and their research?" *Media, Culture and Society* 33(2): 317–331.

UNESCO (2013). "Internet Universality: A Means towards Building Knowledge Societies and the Post-2015 Sustainable Development Agenda." Discussion Paper.

van Deursen, Alexander J.A.M. (2010). *Internet Skills: vital assets in an information society*. Enschede: University of Twente.

Van Deursen, Alexander J.A.M., and van Dijk, Jan A.G.M. (2010). "Internet skills and the Digital Divide." *New Media and Society* 13(6): 893–911.

Van Dijk, Jan A.G.M. (2003). *De digitale kloof wordt dieper*. Amsterdam, Den Haag: SQM en Infodrom @ United Knowledge.

Van Dijk, Jan A. G. M. (2005). *The deepening divide. Inequality in the information society*. London, New Delhi: Sage, Thousand Oaks.

Van Dijk, Jan A.G.M. (2006). "Digital divide research, achievements and shortcomings." *Poetics* 34: 221–235.

Warren, Martyn (2007). "The digital vicious cycle: Links between social disadvantage and digital exclusion in rural areas." *Telecommunications Policy* 31: 374–388.

Witte, James C., and Mannon, Susan E. (2010). *The Internet and social inequalities*, New York, London: Routledge, Taylor & Francis Group.

Wright, David, and Wadhwa, Kush (2010). "Mainstreaming the e-excluded in Europe: strategies, good practices and some ethical issues." *Ethics Information Technology* 12: 139–156.

Zillien, Nicole, and Hargittai, Eszter (2009). "Digital distinction: Status-specific types of Internet usage." *Social Science Quarterly* 90(2): 274–291.

Chapter Ten

From Racial Capitalism to Democratic Capitalism

Historical Perspectives of Inequalities and Communication Technologies in South Africa

Toks Oyedemi

> The first man who, having enclosed a piece of ground, bethought himself of saying 'this is mine', and found people simple enough to believe him, was the real founder of civil society. From how many crimes, wars, and murders, from how many horrors and misfortunes might not any one have saved mankind, by pulling up the stakes, or filling up the ditch, and crying to his fellows: 'Beware of listening to this imposter; you are undone if you once forget that the fruits of the earth belong to us all, and the earth itself to nobody (Jean-Jacques Rousseau, *'Discourse on Inequality' in The Social Contract and Discourses, 1754, 1973: 76).*

South Africa today is inconceivable without its troubled past. To understand social inequalities in contemporary South Africa, one needs to engage the country's history and the implication it has in shaping contemporary South African society (Bundy 1993, Terreblanche 2005). Although current economic and political dynamics have implications on the nature of inequalities in South Africa, the general pattern of social inequalities is largely historical. Contrary to a popular global discourse of locating origin of South African social inequalities to apartheid, and the common practice in South Africa to exclusively blame the Afrikaners and apartheid (Louw 2004, Magubane 2001), the history of inequalities in South Africa is more complex and definitely goes back long before the birth of the apartheid policy. This chapter explores the nature of capitalism that shapes pre-apartheid pattern of inequalities, the inequalities during apartheid, and the current pattern of post-apartheid inequalities. This trajectory of inequalities manifests in the skewed access to many social and economic resources, including communication technologies.

RACIAL CAPITALISM AND THE HISTORY OF SOCIAL INEQUALITIES

Two key forms of capitalism shaped the historical and current patterns of inequalities in South Africa. The first is racial capitalism, which dominated a pattern of exploitation from 1652 to 1994. The second is the post-apartheid democratic capitalism and its neoliberal agendas. Racial capitalism started with the 1652 arrival of Jan Van Riebeeck and the Dutch East India Company (DEIC). The company was a huge commercial parastatal, a multinational commercial enterprise with ships traveling between Europe and its trading empire in Asia. DEIC planned to use the Cape in South Africa as a base to resupply its ships usually with milk and fresh meat from the indigenous Khoi people (Clark & Worger 2004, Magubane 2001). As Clark and Worger (2004) note, this operation changed when the Khoi objected to the unsatisfactory condition of terms of trade offered. This, and many other reasons, including a racist impression of the native Africans, for example, as recorded in Van Riebeeck's diary, as "dull, stupid and odorous" (Leipoldt 1936: 130), led the DEIC to embark on a series of genocidal wars driving the Khoi from their land and replacing them with commercial farms run by European settlers using imported slave labor.

The Dutch developed a colony in and around Cape Town that involved disparate groups, including Europeans settlers, slaves imported from different regions from Mozambique to the Malay archipelago, and offspring of European procreations with slaves and the indigenous KhoiKhoi women. The Dutch structured the Cape on a racial hierarchy with the DEIC employees at the top, followed by settlers, the mixed racial groups, and slaves at the bottom (Clark & Worger 2004). Individual rights were limited to racial designation.

The British arrived in South Africa in 1795, and consequently took over the Dutch Colony in Cape Town. This was an imperialist expansion motivated by the loss of the American colonies, the strategic location of the South African Cape in the British imperialist trading network, and the good soil and fine weather in the Cape. The British embarked on Anglicizing South Africa, starting from the Cape, and in 1807 banned slavery. This interference by the British made the Dutch farmers (Boers) leave the eastern Cape of South Africa in search of their own land often confronting tribal Africans in conflict on this migration, they appropriated land and made treaties with local chief to acquire land.

The British began the process of transforming South Africa with the vision of a grand empire; many British emigrants were encouraged to settle in the Cape. The British imperial campaign of dispossession involved many bloody frontier wars fought against the Xhosa nation in the eastern Cape

(Now the Eastern Cape Province) and with the Zulus, often resulting in the appropriation of large chunk of their tribal lands and talks of genocide and extermination.[1]

The discoveries of diamond in 1867 and gold in 1886 began a complex structuring of British interest in Africa, and the origin of an advanced modern racial capitalism. There were no more talks of African extermination, but rather the importance of this population as cheap labor in a new capitalist system brought about by the discoveries of precious minerals. Louw (2004) argues that the diamond and gold mining industries radically transformed South Africa, attracting foreign capital, entrepreneurs, and migrants. It stimulated growth of different economic sectors, such as agriculture, transportation, and government tax revenues. This also led to a racially divided labor force, within which the African workers became migrant workers who lived in closed compounds and provided very cheap labor. For the British capitalists, sourcing cheap labor among the Africans was very paramount to the success of mining industries. They conquered independent African states in the region, appropriated their land and impose taxation on nearly all resources of daily living; this eventually drove many Africans to the mines, White farms and factories in search of employment.

The British capitalist agenda led to migrant labor system, which brought cheap labor from the southern African states to the mining industry. This migrant cheap African labor underpins racial capitalism through the twentieth century (Louw 2004). The discovery of gold in the Transvaal Republic, an "independent" region occupied by Afrikaners, made this region potentially rich and attractive to the British imperialist. This became a major cause of the Anglo-Boer war. The end of the war brought a huge political and economy control of the British over South Africa. Race and class were tools used to structure the mining labor system for immense profitability with Africans doing the menial and manual heavy work. In the bid for a continuous supply of cheap labor, the British imported Chinese indentured labor. The 60,000 cheap Chinese laborers constituted a huge number of the workforce in the mines and they were paid less than African mineworkers and subjected to much more stringent discipline and control (Clark & Worger, 2004). At the height of racial capitalism in South Africa, many features of the system encompass the economic model that formed the roots of modern social inequalities in South Africa:

- Society was organized to service the needs of an Anglo-owned mining industry for maximum profit.
- The economy depended upon cheap Black African labor to facilitate industrialized deep-level mining.

- To guarantee an abundant supply of African labor, a migrant labor system was built covering all southern Africa. Since alternative forms of labor-intensive employment were a potential threat to labor flows to the mines, these were curtailed and managed. For example, Boer sharecropping practices were destroyed and the "surplus labor" was driven out of farming district. The 1913 Land Act, which created "black reserves," finally sealed this closure. This was a segregation law that restricted African ownership of land to 7 percent of the country. The law had a strong influence on the later system of apartheid with its white supremacist and oppressive workings.
- Autonomous African polities were perceived as dangerous; hence, they were turned into "reserves," which were overwhelmingly populated by women, children, and old people because males became migrant workers.
- A pass system limited the movement of Africans in the country. It regulated the flow of Africans into "white areas."
- Racial capitalism built an ethnic ranking system, with the British-born Anglos on top as the country's elite, then followed by Anglo colonials, and thereafter non-Anglo Whites, such as the Afrikaners, followed by the Indians, and Coloreds, then Africans—who constituted the majority population group in South Africa. (Louw 2004: 20).

This first phase of racial capitalism in South Africa resulted in a generational pattern of poverty among African population. The Land Act of 1913 was the most notorious of the segregation laws, and the most successful in impoverishing Africans. Africans are for most part of the twentieth century a disenfranchised and property-less group with very limited citizenship rights (Terreblanche 2005, Mugabane 2001). Discriminatory labor laws, such as the Mines and Works Act that reserved skilled jobs on the mines for whites and consequently prevented upward mobility for Africans on the mines, entrenched racial capitalism in South Africa from the early 1900s and began the trajectory of income inequality.

The second phase of racial capitalism constituted the period of apartheid. The roots of apartheid have been laid by the British segregation laws and African labor exploitation, however the institution and policy of apartheid was so destructive and oppressive to millions of Africans, and its legacy still haunts many social and economic issues in South Africa. Apartheid was introduced by the National Party (NP) government in 1948 with a philosophy of separate development for the different racial groups in South Africa. In practice apartheid was an oppressive and demoralizing institution that shaped the generation of inequalities in South Africa. Apartheid laws forced different racial groups to live separately and develop unequally depriving most Africans access to many quality social resources. The impacts of apartheid and its many oppressive and economically destructive laws affecting mostly the African majority population have been critically discussed in many academic works (cf Clark & Worger 2004, Terreblanche 2005, Guelke 2005, Louw 2004).

Apartheid operated as a system that involved: affirmative action policy through job reservations for Afrikaners to encourage an upward ranking of Afrikaners in employment structure; Africans were banned from skilled work, limiting them mostly to manual labor; Africans were expected to carry a "pass book" (a form of identity document) to monitor their movement into "white areas," mostly in the cities; separate public amenities such as housing, education and transportation were created for white population and non-white population—while amenities for whites were of high standard, the ones for non-whites were mostly sub-standard; there were forced removals of millions of Africans to designated group areas; African homelands were established and citizens of these independent states were declared aliens in South Africa.

The impact of apartheid policy was enormous and well documented: White South Africans enjoyed a standard of living, which was even higher than in most Western industrialized world. Overall white per capital income was ten times that of Africans. Not surprising, by the early 1980s South Africa had the most inequitable distribution of income in the world. This had implications on many other social sectors such as education and health. During this period, as many as 25 percent of African and Coloured[2] children died before their first birthdays (Clark & Worger, 2004: 63).

The most conspicuous impact of apartheid was the blatant racism that Africans and "non-white" confront daily, not only the limited access to resources that stunted their economic and social empowerment and led to high level of inequalities, but also the daily reminders of separate buses, schools, trains, restaurants, beaches, and so forth. These were constant reminders that the "non-white" population groups were second-class citizens in South Africa. The overall legacy of the history of oppressive and violent racial capitalism is mostly noted in generational poverty in South Africa:

> Poverty is normally a lifelong experience of multiple deprivations, and is accompanied by pain, destitution, humiliation, and squalor. For most of the 28 million South Africans (of whom 25 million were Africans) who in 1996 belonged to households that spent R1, 800 or less a month, poverty was not a new phenomenon but had been their destiny for many generations. The impoverishment and proletarianization of the Khoisan and the different African tribes was a long and relentless process that began in the late 17th century and continued uninterruptedly and increasing intensity until the 1980s . . . Given the power relations on which colonialism, segregation, and Apartheid were based, the empowerment and enrichment of whites were one side of the colonial coin, and the exploitation and impoverishment of African and Coloureds the other (Terreblanche 2005: 384).

This generational poverty trap was instituted through a combination of many forms of exploitation. Take labor for instance, prior to 1994, laws prevented Africans from doing skilled and highly paid jobs. They were paid lower wages even if they were employed in the same job categories as whites, they were prevented from joining organized labor, thereby depriving them the power of wage negotiation, and discriminatory laws prevented professional trainings, consequently condemning them to low-paid unskilled job (ibid).

POST-APARTHEID AND THE ERA OF DEMOCRATIC CAPITALISM

When apartheid collapsed in 1994 and a democratic government led by Nelson Mandela took over, it inherited a country with a large section having one of the most developed infrastructures in the world, and arguably the most developed in Africa. It also inherited one of the most unequal societies in the world with a huge poverty burden. Thabo Mbeki, the then former deputy president states:

> We therefore make bold to say that South Africa is a country of two nations. One of these nations is white, relatively prosperous, regardless of gender or geographic dispersal. It has ready access to a developed economy, physical, educational, *communication* and other infrastructure. This enables it to argue that, except for persistence of gender discrimination against women, all members of this nation have the possibility to exercise their right to equal opportunity . . .
>
> The second and larger nation of South Africa is black and poor, with the worst affected being women in the rural areas, the black rural population in general and the disabled. This nation lives under conditions of grossly undeveloped economic, physical, educational, *communication* and other infrastructure. It has virtually no possibility to exercise what in reality amounts to a theoretical right to equal opportunity (1998: 71–72, emphasis added).

The high level of poverty and inequality was a noticeable legacy of the system of racial capitalism. Racial capitalism shaped the unequal access to resources such as health services, shelter, education, water, energy/power, employment, income, and other issues of welfare and human rights. The legacy of colonization, segregation and apartheid on South Africa is poignant. In 1994, infant mortality rate amongst Africans was 54.3 percent and 36.3 percent among Coloreds, compared to 9.9 percent among Indians and 7.3 percent among White (Health System Trust 1996, May 2000, Woolard & Klasen 2000). Using the South African lower bound poverty line of R515, poverty rate was 56 percent in 1993 (Leibbrandt et al. 2010). What makes poverty and inequality rate more poignant in South Africa is the racial tone they carry. Table 10.1 shows poverty rate by racial groups in the early post-apartheid period.

Table 10.1. Poverty Rate by Population Group

African	*Coloured*	*Indian*	*White*
60.7	38.2	5.4	1.0

Source: Woolard & Klasen, (2000); Central Statistical Service, (1995).

Poverty pattern in South Africa also bears a strong gender mark, with the most affected being African women as indicated in table 10.2. This undoubtedly has implication in how this population gains access to many social and economic utilities. Geographical location also shows a strong bearing on pattern of poverty. In 1993, 70 percent of the national poverty rate was in the rural areas, while urban poverty was 30 percent. Although, this rate is slowing down, it was 62 percent in 2000, and 57 percent in 2008, poverty in South Africa is still concentrated in the rural areas. One major reason for the reduction in rural poverty from 1993 to 2008 is arguably the demographic shifts in population. Rural population decreased from 51 percent in 1993 to 40 percent in 2008, incidentally the urban poverty increased from 30 percent in 1993 to 43 percent in 2008 (Leibbrandt et al. 2010).

Data show the level of inequality in post-apartheid South Africa has not remitted, but actually increased. Fifteen years after the end of apartheid inequality continued to grow, measured by Gini coefficient, inequality rose from 0.64 to 0.67 in the period 1995 to 2008 (World Bank 2010). Undoubtedly the legacy of racial capitalism plays a huge role in the level of inequality, and the post-apartheid neoliberal policies have not been able to address this significantly. Income inequality is a very persistent economic problem in South Africa. Using a range of data sources Leibbrant et al. (2010) provide a trajectory of inequality and poverty over the course of the twentieth century in South Africa. These are presented in table 10.3.

Table 10.2. Poverty Level by Race and Gender in Percentages (Poverty Line R515 Per Capita Per Month)

	Population Share			*Poverty Share*		
	1993	*2000*	*2008*	*1993*	*2000*	*2008*
African female	40	41	42	51	50	52
African male	36	38	38	42	48	41
Coloured female	04	05	05	02	03	03
Coloured male	04	04	04	02	02	03
Indian/ Asian female	01	01	01	00	00	00
Indian/ Asian male	01	01	01	00	00	00
White female	06	05	05	01	01	00
White male	06	05	04	01	01	00

Source: Leibbrandt et al., 2010; Statistics SA-IES 2000, and SALDRU (NIDS) 2008 data sets.

Table 10.3. A Compilation of Estimates of Annual Per Capita Personal Income by Race Group in 2000 Rands and Relative to White Levels, 1917–2008

Year	White	Coloured	Asian	African	Average
Per Capita Income in Constant 2000 Rands:					
1917	13,069	2,875	2,894	1,184	3,946
1924	13,853	2,770	2,694	1,099	4,137
1936	19,212	3,000	4,443	1,462	5,359
1946	26,252	4,280	6,037	2,331	7,556
1956	30,494	5,158	6,668	2,627	8,541
1960	31,230	4,977	5,340	2,532	8,378
1970	45,751	7,929	9,248	3,133	11,140
1975	49,877	9,688	12,687	4,289	12,696
1980	48,340	9,238	12,304	4,088	11,818
1987	45,828	9,572	13,823	3,879	10,661
1993	46,486	8,990	19,537	5,073	11,177
1995	48,387	9,668	23,424	6,525	12,572
2000	56,179	12,911	23,025	8,926	16,220
2008	75,297	16,567	51,457	9,790	17,475
Relative Per Capita Personal Incomes (% of White Level):					
1917	100	22.0	22.1	9.1	30.2
1924	100	20.0	19.4	7.9	29.9
1936	100	15.6	23.1	7.6	27.9
1946	100	16.3	23.0	8.9	28.8
1956	100	16.9	21.9	8.6	28.0
1960	100	15.9	17.1	8.1	26.8
1970	100	17.3	20.2	6.8	24.3
1975	100	19.4	25.4	8.6	25.5
1980	100	19.1	25.5	8.5	24.4
1987	100	20.9	30.2	8.5	23.3
1993	100	19.3	42.0	10.9	24.0
1995	100	20.0	48.4	13.5	26.0
2000	100	23.0	41.0	15.9	28.9
2008	100	22.0	60.0	13.0	23.2

Source: Leibbrandt et al. 2001; 2010.

The estimates from this data show a poignant and persistent income inequality across the racial demographics in South Africa. It shows that Africans, the largest population group, are the most affected by income inequality; they earn the least during the period of the twentieth century. These figures help to explain why this group has a trend of generational poverty. The findings from the 2004 General Household Survey, table 10.4, confirm the high level of inequality in South Africa, with the African population having the greatest within-race inequality.

Table 10.4. Gini Coefficients by Race and Location, 2004

	African	Coloured	Indian/Asian	White	Total
Rural	0.43	0.38	—	0.37	0.51
Urban	0.53	0.45	0.43	0.36	0.56
Overall	0.51	0.47	0.43	0.36	0.59

Source: Statistics SA-General Household Survey 2004; Leibbrandt, 2010.

Studying inequality and poverty from a money-metric perspective is very important, but it does not provide a holistic picture. As Sen (1992) argues, what we can achieve or cannot achieve do not just depend on income inequality. It also depends on many variations of physical and social characteristics that affect peoples' lives. Poverty and inequality can also be measured based on access to public and private assets, and access to social and economic resources. The initial challenge of post-apartheid South Africa in 1994 was to confront the highly skewed access to assets and resources inherited from years of racial capitalism, social and economic neglect.

Data from the 1996 and 2001 censuses provide a picture of the legacy of historical pattern of inequality, and the subsequent challenges that confront the "new" South Africa.

For instance, with regard to access to water, in 1996, slightly over a quarter of Africans had access to tap water in dwellings while Whites and Indians had universal access, see table 10.5. With regards to education, more Africans than any other groups received no schooling. In 1996, 24 percent of Africans received no schooling compared to 1 percent of Whites, and 10 percent of Coloreds, and 6.5 percent of Indian /Asian. More females (21 percent) received no schooling than male (17 percent).

Historically state spending on African education was extremely low. For example, by 1975, the per capita social spending, which includes education, for Africans was about 12 percent of that of Whites, and by 1982 the total spending on African education was less than half that on White education. This is alarming considering that the African population was more than 4.5 times larger than the White population. By 1992, however, after generations of neglect, spending on African education surpassed that of Whites (Van der Berg & Bhorat 1999: 17). The neglect has drastically damaged the structure and quality of African education.

Table 10.5. Access to Piped Water in Dwelling, 1996

Africans	Coloreds	Indians or Asians	Whites
26.7%	71.9%	97.2%	96%

Source: Statistics South Africa, Census 2001.

Besides the limited spending on African schools, the introduction of Bantu Education Act of 1953 had a debilitating effect on African education. Bantu education was designed to keep the African population subservient to the White minority. The curriculum was structured to train Africans as laborers and other elementary forms of occupation. Children went to school in shifts of three hours daily in overcrowded classrooms and dilapidated school buildings with inadequate resources (Hartshorne, 1992; Hlatshwayo, 2000; Hyslop, 1999; Kallaway, 1984). The then Minister of Native Affairs, Dr. Hendrik Verwoerd, explaining the rationale for Bantu Education, declared:

> There is no space for him [the "Native"] in the European Community above certain forms of labor. For this reason it is of no avail for him to receive training which has its aim in the absorption of the European Community, where he cannot be absorbed. Until now he has been subjected to a school system which drew him away from his community and misled him by showing him the greener pastures of European Society where he is not allowed to graze (cited in Kallaway 1984: 92).

Among other reasons, such as formalizing Afrikaans (which was perceived as the oppressor's language) as the language of instruction, the state of African education was a contributing factor to the 1976 Soweto Uprising, which turned the course of apartheid. In 1975, half of Soweto's population was under the age of twenty-five, there were 16,000 families for every high school compared to 1,300 families for every White high school. At Morris Isaacson High School in Soweto, which was central to the 1976 uprising, there were seventy students in each classroom (Clark & Worger 2004: 74).

Unemployment also provides another layer of inequality. South Africa's unemployment rate was one of the highest in the world in the late 1990s to the early 2000s, using broad definition it ranged between 36 percent to 42 percent since the year 2000 (GPRG 2005; Hoogeveen & Ozler 2005). Encouragingly, the unemployment rate has been slowing down, and is currently around 24 percent (Stat SA 2015). Also in typical pattern of inequality in South Africa, unemployment bears a racial and gender stamp. According to the census of 2001, 57 percent of African women were unemployed compared to 6 percent of white women, and 43 percent of African men were unemployed compared to 6 percent White men. Even the employment pattern reveals stark inequalities: For adults 35–64 years old, most employed Africans and Coloreds work in elementary occupation, compared to most employed Whites who work as professionals and managers. Only 7 percent of Africans were employed as professionals and managers compared to 39 percent of Whites employed in these categories. See table 10.6.

Table 10.6. Occupation of Employed Adults (35–64 Yrs) According to Population Group

	African	*Coloured*	*Indian / Asian*	*White*	*Total*
Elementary	37.6	34.2	5.7	2.8	28.9
Operators	13.3	10.0	10.4	2.2	10.5
Artisans	14.3	15.6	12.1	9.1	13.3
Skilled agric	3.0	2.7	0.6	3.0	2.9
Sales workers	8.6	7.5	12.9	9.9	8.9
Clerks	7.1	11.5	18.7	17.6	10.2
Technicians	9.1	9.8	12.1	16.3	10.8
Professionals	4.2	4.2	12.4	19.9	7.7
Managers	2.8	4.6	15.1	19.1	6.8

Source: Statistics South Africa (2005), census 2001.

With the huge legacy of inequalities, poverty and challenges with access to water, electricity, formal dwelling, employment, education, and so forth, the new government was confronted with a two-pronged challenge: on one hand is the need to address the important social issues of inequalities, which is particularly critical for most of the population, on the other hand, the new government had to confront the challenges and opportunities offered by the current trend of economic globalization for its economic growth.

The ruling party, the African National Congress (ANC) and its alliance adopted the Reconstruction and Development Program (RDP), a policy program focused on meeting basic needs, eradicating poverty and investing in human capacities. The RDP was thus compatible with the social development approach and consistent with its humanitarian and "people-centered" values. This is contrary to the prevailing neoliberal approaches in other parts of the world. It was argued that the new South African government resurrected the social development approach and elevated it to a position of prominence (Midgley 2001, Visser 2004).

The RDP program soon began to confront serious problems: The government lacked the capacity to implement it; it was too broadly formulated and ended as a wish list for many people with slow pace of economic growth, and the government could not mobilize sufficient funds to meet the RDP's objectives without redirecting allocations from the mainstream government departments. With the need to focus on economic growth, and calm domestic capital and foreign currency markets, the government embraced a new policy of Growth, Employment and Redistribution (GEAR) (Visser 2004).

The adoption of GEAR in 1996 signaled a big phase in the history of South Africa, it formalized the beginning of democratic capitalism. Democratic capitalism is an economic ideology that supports a neoliberal economic paradigm. It supports a free market economic system, a democratic state and a liberal social system that encourages social and cultural pluralism. In practice, it involves the basic elements of neoliberal economic agenda of privatization and liberalization of the economy. GEAR aimed at building a bridge toward a long-term economic growth by establishing a medium term growth record that would attract foreign investors and raise the balance of payments constraint (van der Berg & Bhorat 1999). Critics argue that GEAR was a move from "growth through redistribution" to redistribution through growth," and that poverty problem would be resolved through higher growth rates and alleged "trickle-down effect" (Visser 2004).

While the RDP expected the state to conduct a people-orientated developmental policy, GEAR saw South Africa's economic "salvation" in a high economic growth rate that would result from a sharp increase in private capital accumulation in an unbridled capitalist system (ibid.). The post-apartheid neoliberal economic policy based on the ideology of democratic capitalism has not successfully addressed the South African inequality. While the South African state has adopted many policies typical of a social democratic polity, particularly the intervention of the state in social-economic welfare of the citizens, the leaning toward the ideology of "liberal capitalism" reminiscent of "laissez-faire" capitalism has been of serious challenge to South Africa. The liberal ideology exalts "free marketism," the belief that a free market economy will empower the "individual" and provide the "freedom" to attain self-determined goals.

Free market ideology is believed to encourage competition, economic growth, and employment in the economy. Since the market is structured as self-regulating, the intervention of the state should be minimal. With the development in communication technologies and a rapid revolution in the growth of economic and cultural globalization, a neoliberal agenda became a dominant ideology of global capitalism. This ideology has been paraded as "best practice" around the world, and adopted by many nations of the global south, including South Africa. Neoliberal economic policy encompasses a set of policy guidelines, often referred to as 'Washington Consensus," and it includes, fiscal discipline, privatization, deregulation, and trade liberalization (Williamson 1990).

Complying with ideology of neoliberalism, and acknowledging the power of globalization, the post-apartheid government retracted from interventionist economic and social strategies (exemplified by the RDP program), to a strategy that stressed growth through the market. Privatization process became one of the dominant economic policies in order to open up the South African market to foreign investors and induced growth. As Terreblanche (2005) notes, the neoliberal ideology in the framework of global capitalism is the ideological cement that unites old White and new African elite, if this remains in tact, South Africa should expect an alarming increase in the unequal distribution of income between the top 20 percent and the poorer 40 percent of households.

Undoubtedly, there have been improvements in many areas in addressing legacy of inequalities. The economy has grown steadily until the global economic crisis hit South Africa in late 2008. The economic growth was steady from the first quarter of 1993 to the second quarter of 2008, a period that the country enjoyed an unprecedented sixty-two quarters of uninterrupted economic growth (Statistics SA, Key indicator 2011; South Africa.info 2011b).

In other areas, some of the policies developed to rectify the inequities of the past have achieved notable achievements. Between 1991 and 2008, net secondary school enrollment went up from 45 percent to 72 percent. Since 1994, 1.6 million free housing units have been constructed for low-income families. Access to electricity went up from 34 percent in 1993 to 85 percent in 2012 (Stats SA 2013). Improvements have also been achieved in other areas, such as water and sanitation. The social grant system has expanded coverage from 2.5 million beneficiaries in 1999 to over 16 million in 2014, although there are debates about the sustainability of the grant system, it has in some way contributed to poverty reduction.

Increasingly, many of the most affected by years of inequalities are beginning to gain access to many socioeconomic assets and their dignity restored. But in spite of these achievements and growth, pattern of systemic inequality still exists, and this raises critical questions regarding the economic policies of the post-apartheid South Africa. Income inequality is still very high, as indicated in table 10.3, there is high level of inequality between races, with Africans earning 13 percent of white income. The national measure of inequality has increased, using the Gini-coefficient measurement, inequality rose from .66 to .70 between 1993 and 2008. It increased more sharply within the African population from .54 to .62; one reason for this is the African share of the national population and the demographical shifts. For instance, African population grew from 70 percent of the national population in 1970 to 80 percent in 2001 and White population declined from 17 percent to 9 percent in the same time period (Leibbrandt et al. 2010). Besides income inequality, other layers of inequality still persist in South Africa. While recognizing the achievements that have been made in social service delivery in about two decades of post-apartheid South Africa, it is also critical to reveal the inequalities in access to public and private household services during this period. (See figure 10.1 and figure 10.2)

With the high rate of inequality and poverty, access to many basic assets will be skewed, and unfortunately this exacerbates the experience of inequality. Take access to motor vehicle for instance, in 2008, only 11.12 percent

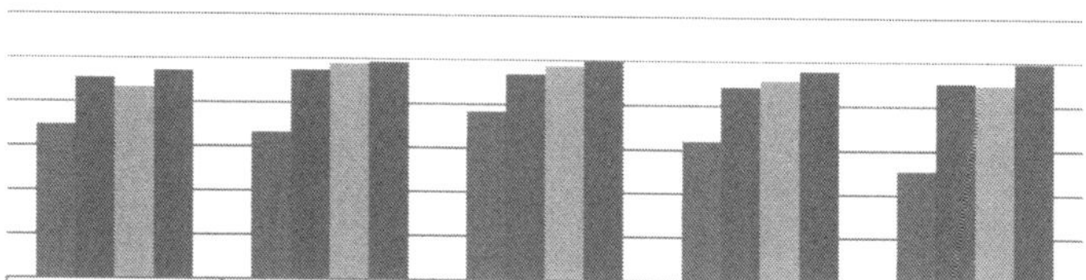

	Formal Dwelling	Piped water	Electricity (Lighting)	Electricity (cooking)	Chemical / Flush Toilet
African	69.5	66.48	76.63	63.88	50.9
Coloured	90.97	94.87	93.64	88.56	90.64
Indian/ Asian	86.59	98.02	97.37	91.6	89.59
White	94.41	98.66	99.77	95.93	99.23

Figure 10.1. Access to public assets by population group of household 2008.
NIDS 2008, (cited in Bhorat et al 2009)

of African households own a motor vehicle, compared to 78.42% of White households and 62.26 percent of Indian households, the Colored population ownership of motor vehicle is also low at 33.85 percent. Similarly, 30.03 percent of male-headed households own motor vehicles compared to 13.17 percent of female-headed households (NIDS 2008, Bhorat et al. 2009). This unequal access pattern is noticeable with regards to other assets, such as TV, radio, and other communication technologies. This analysis is the thrust of the subsequent section, it reveals how the pattern of inequality relates to access to communication technologies.

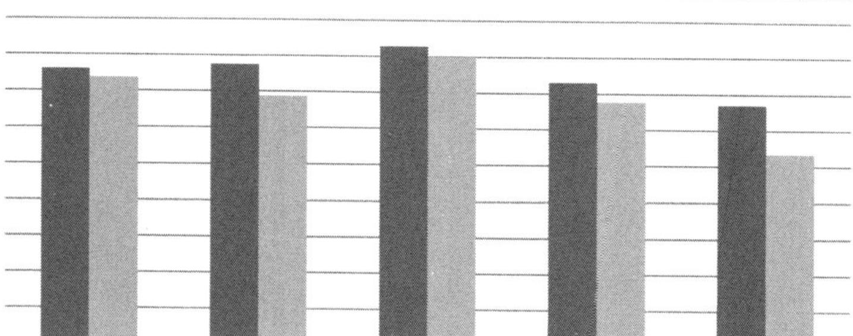

	Formal Dwelling	Piped water	Electricity (Lighting)	Electricity (cooking)	Chemical / Flush Toilet
Male	75.98	77.49	82.86	73.13	67.07
Female	73.71	68.78	79.91	67.72	53.54

Figure 10.2. Access to public assets by gender of household heads.
NIDS 2008, (cited in Bhorat et al, 2009)

Although one can confidently argue there have been huge achievements from the political-economic system of pre-1994, but the unremitting poverty is sobering. The poverty rate in 2002 is worse than apartheid era poverty of 1970 (Terreblanche 2005). Specifically for African women, poverty rate is worse in 2008 than 1993 (see table 10.2). Inequality has clearly fractured South Africa into five classes as seen in Figure 10.3 below.

Social Inequalities and Communication Technologies in the Era of Democratic Capitalism

The effect of a long history of inequality is very conspicuous in all the socio-economic sectors of South Africa. Inequalities exist in sectors such as health, transportation, education, and communications. The legacy of this historical pattern of inequality is also noted in the telecommunications sector. In the ideology of the Verwoerdian grand apartheid, the African townships around white South African cities were considered transient urban formations and financial investment into services were considered wasteful. The argument

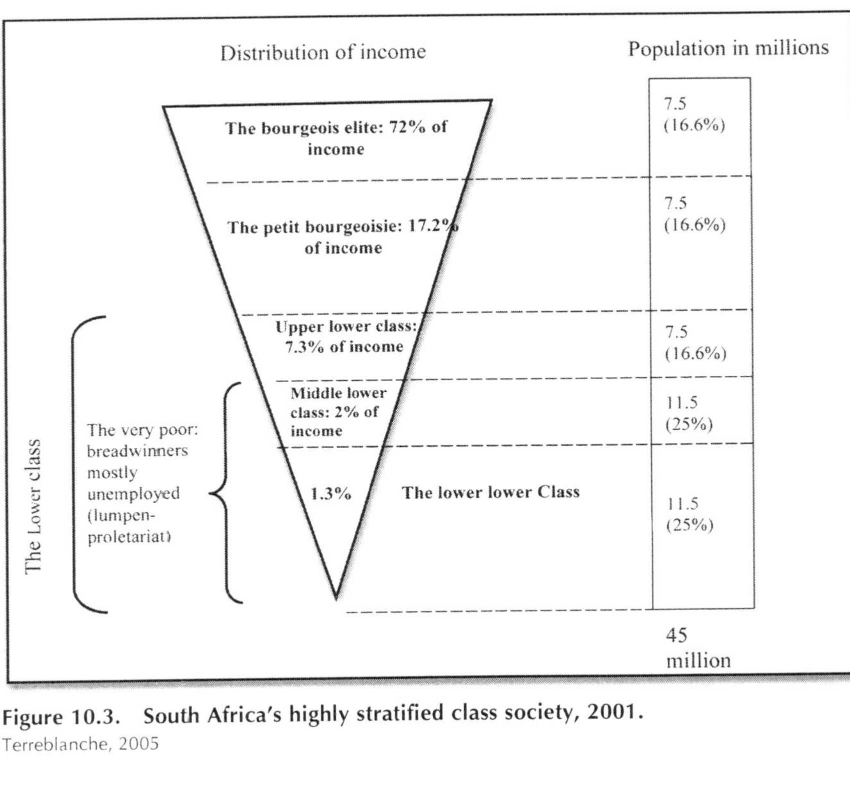

Figure 10.3. South Africa's highly stratified class society, 2001.
Terreblanche, 2005

was that any attempt to make these areas better places to live by providing services, including telecommunications, would lead to unwanted result of encouraging further African influx to white South African cities. Since the African homelands were considered independent (although their economic sustainability depended on handouts from the apartheid regime), many state parastatals had no jurisdiction to provide services in these areas. This began to change gradually when in the early 1980s, the South African Post and Telecommunications (SAPT) began to extend telephone services to Indian and Colored areas, and later to some African areas (Horwitz 2001).

The inequality in access to communications in the immediate years succeeding the end of apartheid was very stark. For instance, the 1996 census reported that only 11.4 percent of African households had telephone in dwelling or cell phone, compared to 43.6 percent of Coloreds, 77.2 percent of Indian / Asian, and Whites 89 percent. Considering that African population was about 80 percent of the national population, it explained the low penetration of 28.8 percent of all households with telephone in dwelling or a cell phone in the country. The 2001 census reported a higher access rate, but the inequality is still very stark, see Figure 4.

Besides limited household access to telephones, more than 50 percent of all schools, 30 percent of all libraries, and 15 percent of all hospitals and clinics did not have telephones (ibid). Less than 2 percent of African-headed households had a computer compared to 46 percent of White-headed households (Stats SA, Census 2001). Besides telecommunications, access to other communication technologies, such as radio and television sets, was skewed according to gender and race. Data from Statistics South Africa's General Household Survey (GHS) 2006 and the National Income Dynamics Study (NIDS) 2008, reveal the disparity in radio and TV penetration.

The extensive analysis of the historical context of inequality provided in this chapter offers a clear understanding of why certain groups, particularly the African population group, have very minimal access to public and private assets, including communication technologies. Realizing these inequalities in communications, the African National Congress' (ANC) government of post-apartheid South Africa embarked on a transformation and restructuring of the telecom sector. The South African Telecommunications Act was passed in 1996, and it highlighted the need to extend service across the country. In addition to this, it made provision for the establishment of an independent regulator, the creation of Universal Service Agency and a Universal Service Fund to extend telecommunications services to underserviced areas. With the rising wave of liberalization in South Africa, the 1996 Act was amended with the passing of the Telecommunications Amendment Act of 2001. Influential in this amendment was the adoption of a policy of "managed liberalization" (Skinner 2007). Key objects (among others) of the Act were the need to fur-

Table 10.7. Access to Radio and Television by Race and Gender 2006 and 2008 in Percent

	African Households	*White Households*	*Colored Households*	*Asian Households*	*Male-Headed Households*	*Female-Headed Households*
Radio:						
GHS 2006	74.98	95.63	82.74	88.44	80.01	75.87
NIDS 2008	75.20	94.71	83.6	83.59	81.29	74.84
TV:						
GHS 2006	56.41	96.67	84.05	93.06	66.09	61.61
NIDS 2008	61.13	92.00	83.19	90.4	69.56	65.33

Source: Statistics SA GHS 2007 and NIDS 2009, cited in Bhorat et al., 2009.

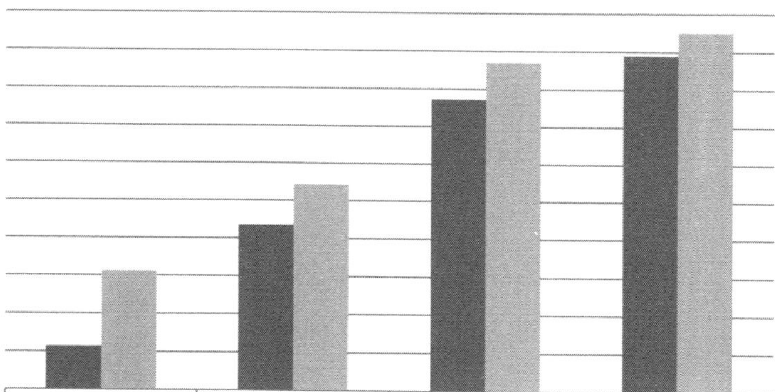

	African	Coloured	Indian /Asian	White
1996	11.4	43.6	77.2	89
2001	31.1	54.4	87.1	95.2

Figure 10.4. Percentage of household with telephone in dwelling or a cell phone by population group of the household head, Census 1996 and 2001.
Statistic South Africa, Census 2001

ther liberalize the sector, manage the convergence of telecommunications, broadcasting, information technologies and related service, and further the goal of universal access to communication.

At this juncture, it is critical to take a step back and engage the series of events that informed on the reform model of telecommunications in South Africa. Two core issues influenced the policy direction of South Africa's telecommunications reform process: the historical context of inequalities as discussed above, and the wave of global neoliberalism that impacted on the political economy of communication.

Horwitz (2001) observes that the deregulation reforms of the 1980s and the challenges to the rationale of natural monopoly in telecommunications created a wave of newly deregulated international telecommunications operators scouring the world for opportunities to extend their operations and serve the communication needs of large business users in other countries. These operators and their host governments began lobbying multilateral forums to break down the exclusivity of national monopolies in telecommunications. With regards to South Africa, indirect pressures for neoliberal agendas of liberalization and privatization were often orchestrated by the United States during the South African telecommunications reform process.

There were series of external pressures on the new government to adopt this "best practice" of liberalization of telecommunications. Many international telecoms operators submitted proposals and comments during the telecom reform process in South Africa, championing privatization, liberalization, and competition. AT&T floated a proposal to lay high bandwidth undersea cable ring around Africa to carry voice and data. Investment banks and consulting companies touted their successful roles in the restructuring and privatization of telecommunications in other countries. For instance, J. P Morgan Co. directly contacted the South African coordinator of the Telecommunications Policy Project. The US government posted a set of recommendations following the Green Paper and the US embassy made formal response to the White Paper on Telecommunications (ibid).

Horwitz (2001) notes the US submission reflected the policy of encouraging early privatization and competition, noting how these have worked in other countries. The arguments for pressurizing South Africa to liberalize its telecom sector were hinged on the typical rhetoric about neoliberalism, that "state intervention is counterproductive (if not bad in itself), and the free market and competition effectively harness new technologies and facilitate economic growth" (ibid: 35). But they did not acknowledge that neoliberalism and its elements tend to be a double-edge sword, that their implementation in telecommunications may induce job loss and expand inequality of access to telecommunications.

With the intention to open the South African market to global economy, increase foreign investment and grow the economy, the government eventually adopted the World Trade Organization's (WTO) *General Agreement on Trade in Services* (*GATS*). The WTO agreements basically made telecommunications services, which were historically considered domestic services within a national security analysis, tradable services. This agreement involving over one hundred countries pushed for liberalization of the telecommunications sector. The reform model of GATS agreement included privatization—with foreign direct investment in existing companies and cross-border transmission of telecoms services, competition, and the establishment of an independent regulator.

Gillwald (2005) notes that despite concerns about this model, particularly the privatization segment of the reform, this model was being pushed across the globe by telecom "experts" as "best practice model." In reality, South Africa "had little local expertise in the area of policy, regulation and specifically privatization, though this was not adequately acknowledged. It was highly dependent on the advice of its international financial and policy advisors who proposed the three pronged strategies that underlay the international reform model" (ibid: 474). With the intention of addressing its social objectives, the government eventually settled for a gradual privatization and competition process, the so-called "managed liberalization" strategy.

The "managed liberalization" involves the partial privatization of the state monopoly telecommunication corporation (Telkom), selling off 30 percent stake in the corporation to investors, and granting the corporation a five-year exclusivity period in which it has to roll out telephone lines to meet the social objective of the government by providing access to the millions who were unconnected. This process began the liberalization of the telecom sector in South Africa. In order to further address the social development goals, some policy agendas were implemented to tackle access issue, they include:

- License obligations and rollout targets attached to telecommunications licenses: This means that operators given license to operate in South Africa must meet extend services to the unconnected, usually in low-income and rural areas.
- Underserviced Area Licenses. This is a category of license to small and medium scale enterprises to provide services in mostly rural and semi-urban areas.
- The implementation of universal service and universal access program. The Universal Service Agency was established as directed by the Telecommunications Acts of 1996, and later renamed Universal Service and Access Agency of South Africa under the Electronic Act no. 36 of 2005. The goal of the agency is to manage the program of universal access to telecommunications in South Africa. Key in this program is the establishment of public access centers to telecommunications, such as telecenters, multipurpose community centers, and E-School cyber labs (to connect schools to the Internet).

One key success of this liberalization period is the introduction of competition in the mobile phone services. Cell phone penetration has grown tremendously in South Africa from a penetration of 32.3 percent in 2001 to currently over 100% penetration; one may therefore assert that the universal service goal has been achieved in the mobile phone sector, which is also a competitive market with five operators. One should not ascribe this success mainly to a particular policy program, the cellular technology and its unique character makes the mobile an attractive alternative to fixed line. Importantly, the pre-paid packages of mobile service make it attractive to many people. The development of the cellular network in South Africa eventually becomes very critical for Internet access, as mobile broadband Internet is currently the most popular form of connection to the Internet in the country.

Unfortunately, success has not been achieved in the fixed line sector. The privatization of the then state monopoly, Telkom, with the exclusivity benefit, and the roll out target to meet social obligation failed in extending access to the unconnected. It redlined areas considered uneconomical; these are areas where inequality and poverty are greatly concentrated, and where access to telecommunications could provide an opportunity to confront some of these social issues. For instance, Stavrou (2000) notes that Telkom's plan to meet its license obligation of extending network to the unconnected did not address inequality on geographical basis. The Gauteng Province, with 39 percent of existing telephones was earmarked for 30 percent of new lines in 1997. The Eastern Cape and Limpopo Province, which had 7 percent and 3 percent of all telephones, respectively, were allocated a percentage of the total number of lines to be rolled out.

Theoretically, the national operator (Telkom) initially met the network expansion target that was part of its social obligations (especially the extension of fixed line to selected underserviced areas). The massive disconnection of lines by the operator, due to non-payment of bills, resulted in the net effect that 75% of the license obligation for network extensions has not been fulfilled (Melody 2002). Given this massive disconnection, the policy of rollout targets for exclusivity was a failure, and social obligations were unmet.

The operator argued that the company had to clamp down on bad debt and enforce timely payment of bills, hence the massive disconnections. To identify the non-payment of service as the core reason for the massive disconnection is merely scraping the surface of the issue. In an attempt to re-balance telephone tariffs, Telkom had increased the prices of local telephone charges and reduced cost of international call considerably. This placed telephone access beyond the reach of a large part of the population. Argument can be made that this trend is typical of a privatization process in the economy, it has the tendency to lead to a rise in prices for domestic consumers. The argument is that privatized corporations operate stringently on the need for profit. This implies that services will be increasingly provided to those groups in the society who can afford to pay, those of the middle to high-income group. For the millions of the poor citizens that belong to the low-income group, or unemployed, and who bear the brunt of social inequalities, telephone access is priced out of their reach. This invariably affects the goal of universal service. But, the South African government had been encouraged by the benefits of foreign investments that the liberalization would bring and its impacts on the economic growth.

The policy reform that characterized the first decade of telecommunications reform in South Africa stands as a critical example of the dilemma that occurs with neoliberalism on one hand and addressing social issues on the other hand. The social issue of addressing the long history of inequality failed in regard to access to fixed line telephony. The impact of this failure is reverberating currently in South Africa's second decade of a post-apartheid polity. The limitations of fixed-line network penetration not only impacted on limited access to fixed line telephone, but it has significantly impacted on the roll-out of enhanced broadband services.

Data from Census 2001, ITU ICT 2015, reveal that the penetration rate of telecommunications in South Africa currently stands as follows:

- Fixed telephone 9.2 per hundred inhabitants
- Fixed broadband penetration: 3.1 per hundred inhabitants
- Internet users: 48.9 per hundred inhabitants
- Household with Internet: 39.4%

The major growth in the telecommunication sector is the cellular / mobile network penetration: mobile cellular penetration is 147.5 per hundred inhabitants and mobile broadband is 25.2 per hundred inhabitants.

Data from a 2007 Household ICT survey in South Africa by Research ICT Africa (RIA 2011) show only 15 percent of population 16 years and older use the Internet and only 12.6 percent of them have e-mail address. The data also reveal that 4.76 percent of households have home Internet and only 14.78 percent of households have home computer. The limited penetration of the Internet also implies that access and use will be skewed starkly at the disadvantage of those groups in the society who bear the brunt of inequality—that in most part is historical. For instance, a research study on Internet users in South Africa shows that the White population group in South Africa has 64 percent of the Internet penetration in the country, followed by the Black population with 24 percent, Coloreds with 7 percent and the Indian population with 5 percent (RIA 2011; Afrographique 2011; Muller 2011). This study also reveals that those with access are relatively affluent, there are more male users, at 69 percent, than female users at 31 percent. In terms of geography, the highest rate of Internet access (at 49 percent) is in Gauteng, the smallest but largely urbanized and most populated province in the country, also the economic "powerhouse" of the country.

A similar study conducted with students in ten South African universities, shows that 76.9 percent of African students do not have Internet access at home compared to 11.4 percent of White and Coloreds students, and 43.2 percent of Indian / Asian students (Oyedemi 2012). This study also shows that about half of African students, at 53 percent, have either a home desktop computer, a personal laptop or both. While almost all White students, at 98.3 percent, report to have either a home desktop computer, a laptop or both. Also, 60.9 percent of students that live in the cities have Internet access at home compared to 16.3 percent of those living in rural areas. The pattern of income inequality also reflects that students from low-income households tend to have the least access to home Internet. Poignantly, these students are from population groups that bear the brunt of social inequalities in South Africa, they are from families that experience high rate of poverty, less access to public and private resources, suffer the consequence of urban-rural inequalities, income and gender inequalities, which usually develop from a trajectory of historical inequalities, and often bear a racial stamp in South Africa (Oyedemi 2012).

CONCLUSION

This chapter explores a general and historical context of social inequalities in South Africa. This is an important task, because to engage social issues in South Africa, a discussion of social inequalities is imperative. The nature of social inequalities in South Africa is engaged from the perspective of the trajectory of capitalism from seventeenth century to the twenty-first century. The arrival of the Dutch East Indian Company, the discovery of gold and diamond, and the institutionalization of racism in apartheid system are all intertwined with racial capitalism. This form of capitalism, which manifested in the hugely exploitative structure of the labor force, the use of cheap (almost free) labor, and the ethnic ranking of population groups, created a generational pattern of poverty and inequality. The post-apartheid era of democratic capitalism and its neoliberal free market ideology has not sufficiently addressed this problem. The trajectories of these forms of capitalism and attendant political structures resulted in a generational pattern of inequality and poverty with resultant effects on limited and skewed access to many social resources. Eventually the historical legacies of inequalities based on racial capitalism will gradually diminish in explaining social inequalities in South Africa. The debate will be the (in)appropriateness of the post-apartheid policies in the era of democratic capitalism, and beyond.

NOTES

1. The 1847 "Springbok speech" by John Milford Bowker, a wealthy sheep commercial farmer was a poignant example. Stating the importance of the Cape wool to employment in England, he wrote:

"The day was when our plains were covered with tens of thousands of springboks; they are gone now, and who regrets it? Their place is now occupied with tens of thousands of merino sheep, whose fleece find employment to tens of thousands industrious men: are they not better than the springbok? Yet I must own that when I see two or three of them on wide plains, and know they are their last of their race, my heart yearns towards them, and I regret that so much innocent beauty, elegance and agility, must needs be swept from the earth. My feelings towards the Kafir (Africans) are not of that stamp. I know he has disregarded the zealous missionaries for years. I know that rapine and murder are all his thoughts, and I see them in his looks, and hate him accordingly . . . I begin to think that he too, the Kafir, as well as the springbok, must give place, and why not? Is it just that a few thousands of ruthless, worthless savages are to sit like a nightmare upon the land that would support millions of civilized happy men? Nay, Heavens forbids it . . . " (Cited in Magubane 2001: 11–12).

2. In South Africa, 'Coloreds' generally designates people of racially mixed parentage or descent.

REFERENCES

Afrographique. (2011). South African Internet users. Retrieved on September 01, 2011, from http://afrographique.tumblr.com/post/7697345304/an-infographic-depicting-the-breakdown-of-south.

Bhorat, H., van der Westhuizen, C., & Cassim, A. (2009). Access to household services and assets: Analysis using the NIDS Wave 1 Dataset. NIDS Discussion Paper no. 4. Retrieved June 10, 2011, from http://www.nids.uct.ac.za/home/index.php?/Nids-Documentation/discussion-papers.html.

Bundy, C. (1993). Challenging the past: South Africa in historical perspective. In Gentili (ed). *Sudafrica: procecessi di mutamento politico e constituzionale.* Rimini: Maggioli.

Clark, N. L. & Worger, W. (2004). *South Africa: The rise and fall of apartheid.* Harlow, England: Pearson Longman.

CSS (Central Statistical Service). (1995). *The income and expenditure survey.* Pretoria: Central Statistical Service.

Du Bois, W. E. B. (1903) *The souls of black folk.* H. L Gates., & T. H. Oliver (Eds.). (1999). New York: W.W. Norton & Co.

Gillwald, A. (2005). Good intentions, poor outcomes: Telecommunications reform in South Africa. *Telecommunications Policy* 29, 469–491.

Global Poverty Research Group (GPRG). (2005). Unemployment, race and poverty in South Africa. Retrieved March 11, 2011, from http://www.gprg.org/themes/t2–inc-ineq-poor/unem/unem-pov.htm.

Guelke, A. (2005). *Rethinking the rise and fall of apartheid.* New York: Palgrave Macmillan.

Hartshorne, K. B. (1992). *Crisis and challenge: Black education 1910–1990.* Cape Town: Oxford University Press.

Health System Trust (1996). *South African health review*, 1996. Health Systems Trust and Henry J. kaiser Family Foundation, Durban.

Hlatshwayo, S. A. (2000). *Education and independence: Education in South Africa, 1658–1988.* Westport, CT: Greenwood Press.

Hodge, J. (2004). Universal service through roll-out targets and license conditions: Lessons from telecommunications in South Africa. *Development South Africa* Vol. 21, no 1, 205–225.

Hoogeven, J. G., & Ozler, B. (2005). Not separate, not equal: poverty and inequality in post-apartheid South Africa. *The William Davidson Institute Working Paper* #739. Retrieved April 14, 2008, from http://www.wdi.umich.edu/files/publications/workingPapers/wp739.pdf.

Horwitz, R. (2001). *Communication and democratic reform in South Africa.* New York: Cambridge University Press.

Hyslop, J. (1999). *The classroom struggle: Policy and resistance in South Africa, 1940–1990.* Pietermaritzburg: University of Natal Press.

International Telecommunications Union (ITU). ICT Eye (2015). ICT penetration –country profile. Retrieved February 03, 2015, from http://www.itu.int/net4/itu-d/icteye/CountryProfile.aspx.

International Telecommunications Union, World Telecommunication/ICT Indicators Database (2011). Retrieved October 10, 2011, from http://www.itu.int/ITU-D/ict/statistics/.

International Telecommunications Union (ITU). ICT Statistics Newslog 2008. South Africa hits 1 million broadband users. Retrieved December 05, 2009, from http://www.itu.int/ITU-D/ict/newslog/South+Africa+Hits+1+Million+Broadband+Users.aspx.

International Telecommunications Union (ITU) The world in 2010—broadband speed affordability. Retrieved on May 16, 2011, from www.itu.int/ITU-D/ict/material/FactsFigures2010.pdf).

James, J. (2005). Technological blending in the age of the Internet: A developing country perspective. *Telecommunications Policy,* 29, pp. 285–296.

Kallaway, P. (Ed.). (1984). *Apartheid and education: The education of Black South Africans*. Johannesburg: Raven.

Leibbrandt, M., Woolard, I., Finn, A., & Argent. J. (2010). Trends in South African income distribution and poverty since the fall of apartheid," *OECD Social, Employment and Migration Working Papers*, No. 101, OECD Publishing.

Leipoldt, C. L (1936). *Jan van Riebeeck: A bibliographical study.* New York: Longman.

Lotter, H.H.P. (1997). *Injustice, violence, and peace: A case of South Africa.* Amsterdam: Radopi.

Louw, P. E. (2004) *The rise, fall, and legacy of apartheid.* Westport, CT: Praeger.

Magubane, B. (2001). *Social construction of race and citizenship in South Africa.* Paper presented at United Nations conference on racism and public policy, Durban, South Africa.

May, J. (2000). Growth, development, poverty and inequality. In May, J. *Poverty and inequality in South Africa: Meeting the challenge.* Cape Town: David Philip.

Mbeki, T. (1998). *Africa: the time has come*. Cape Town: Mafube.

Melody, W. H. (2002). Assessing Telkom's 2003 price increase proposal. *LINK Public Policy Research Paper.* No 2. Johannesburg: University of Witwatersrand.

Midgley, J. (2001). South Africa: the challenge of social development. *International Journal of Social Welfare*, 10 (4): 267–275.

Muller, R. (2011). SA's Internet users: Who are they really? Retrieved on September 1, 2011, from http://mybroadband.co.za/news/Internet/26869–sas-Internet-users-who-are-they-really.html.

Mybroadband, December 07 2011. SA's impressive wireless broadband numbers. Retrieved August 08, 2012 from http://mybroadband.co.za/news/broadband/39185–sa%E2%80%99s-impressive-wireless-broadband-numbers.html.

OECD Broadband Portal. (2010). Retrieved February 15, 2010, from http://www.oecd.org/document/36/0,3746,en_2649_33703_38690102_1_1_1_1,00.html.

Research ICT Africa (RIA). (2011). ICT indicator: South Africa. Retrieved 08/09/2011, from http://www.researchictafrica.net/countries.php?cid=19.

Sen, A. (1992). *Inequality reexamined*. Cambridge, MA: Harvard University Press.

Skinner, K. (2007). Meeting their public mandate: A macro assessment and analysis of the media and ICT sector in South Africa. In Open Society Foundation (2007) *Meeting their mandate? A critical analysis of South African media statutory bodies*. Cape Town: Open Society Foundation.

South Africa.info (2011b) South Africa: Economy overview. Retrieved March 10, 2011, from http://www.southafrica.info/business/economy/econoverview.htm.

South African Institute of Race Relations (SAIRR). (2008). Income inequality in South Africa has increased. Retrieved on December 16, 2008, from http://www.sairr.org.za/press-office/archive/news_item.2008–11–27.4978531658.

South African Institute of Race Relations. (2011). Fast Facts no 04. Fractured families: A crisis for South Africa. Retrieved 08/09/2011, from http://www.sairr.org.za/services/publications/fast-facts/fast-facts-2011.

Southern Africa Labour and Development Research Unit (SALDRU). (2010). National Income Dynamics Study (NIDS) 2008. University of Cape Town.

Southern African Regional Poverty Network (SARPN) (2004). Fact sheet: Poverty in South Africa. Retrieved April 12, 2008, from http://www.sarpn.org.za/documents/d0000990/.

Statistics South Africa. (1996). Population census 1996. Retrieved April 19, 2008, from http://www.statssa.gov.za/census01/Census96/HTML/default.htm.

Statistics South Africa (2001a). Education in South Africa: Selected findings from Census '96. Retrieved December 11, 2009, from http://www.info.gov.za/view/DownloadFileAction?id=70237.

Statistics South Africa (2001b). Census: Key Result. Retrieved April 19, 2008, from http://www.statssa.gov.za/census01/HTML/C2001publications.asp.

Statistics South Africa (2004). General Household Survey. Pretoria: Statistics South Africa.

Statistics South Africa. (2005) Census 2001: Stages in the life cycle of South Africans. Retrieved March 8, 2011, from http://www.statssa.gov.za/census01/html/C2001LifeStages.asp.

Statistics South Africa. (2008). *Community survey 2007*. Retrieved December 12, 2008, from http://www.statssa.gov.za/timeseriesdata/pxweb2006/Database/South%20Africa/databasetree.asp.

Statistics South Africa—General Household Survey (GHS) 2007. Pretoria: Statistics South Africa.

Statistics South Africa. (2009). Quarterly Labour Force Survey 2009. Retrieved December 07, 2009, from http://www.statssa.gov.za/publications/statsdownload.asp?PPN=P0211&SCH=4503.

Statistics South Africa. (2011a). Quarterly Labour Force Survey (QLFS), 4th Quarter 2010. Retrieved February 21, 2011, from http://www.statssa.gov.za/publications/statsdownload.asp?PPN=P0211&SCH=4852.

Statistics South Africa. (2011b). Key indicators: Gross Domestic Product (GDP). Retrieved March 10, 2011, from http://www.statssa.gov.za/keyindicators/gdp.asp.

Statistics South Africa—Income and Expenditure Survey (IES) (2000). Pretoria: Statistics South Africa. Retrieved June 23, 2015, from http://www.statssa.gov.za/publications/P0318/P03182012.pdf.

Statistics South Africa. General Household Survey (GHS) 2012. Pretoria: Statistics South Africa.

Statistics South Africa. (2015) Quarterly Labour Force Survey. Quarter 4 2014. Retrieved June 22, 2015, from http://www.statssa.gov.za/F5480D7C-DA71–46CC-9C66–8CF74979D211/FinalDownload/DownloadId-30A7476163096BED5ED-699318CBD3170/F5480D7C-DA71–46CC-9C66–8CF74979D211/publications/P0211/P02114thQuarter2014.pdf.

Stavrou, S (2000). Infrastructural services. In J. May, (Ed.). *Poverty and inequality in South Africa: Meeting the challenge*. Cape Town: David Philip.

Terreblanche, S. (2005). *A History of Inequality in South Africa 1652–2002.* Scottsville: University of Natal Press.

Van der Berg, S. and Bhorat, H. (1999). *The present as a legacy of the past: The labour market, inequality and poverty in South Africa.* Cape Town: University of Cape Town, Development Policy Research Unit.

Visser, W. (2004). Shifting RDP into GEAR. The ANC government's dilemma in providing an equitable system of social security for the "new" South Africa. In ITH-Tagungsberichte 39, "Mercy or Right". Development of Social Security Systems, Akademische Verlaganstalt, Wien, 2005, pp. 105–124.

Williamson, J. (1990). What Washington means by policy reform. In J. Williamson, (Ed.). *Latin American adjustmnet: How much has happened?* Washington, DC: Institute for International Economics.

Woolard, I., & Klasen, S. (2000). The nature and measurement of poverty and inequality. In J. May (Ed.). *Poverty and inequality in South Africa: Meeting the challenge*. Cape Town: David Philip.

World Bank. (2010). South Africa: Country brief. Retrieved February 20, 2011, from http://web.worldbank.org/WBSITE/EXTERNAL/COUNTRIES/AFRICAEXT/SOUTHAFRICAEXTN/0,,menuPK:368086~pagePK:141132~piPK:141107~theSitePK:368057,00.html.

Part IV

FROM THEORY TO PRAXIS (AND VICE VERSA)

Chapter Eleven

Reform and Vulnerability

Parsing Out the Cyclical Relationship of Praxis and Theory

Kala Ortwein, Sarah Rowe, and Olga Shapovalova

In this chapter we seek to explain the relationship between theory and praxis, and whether one initiates, facilitates, or impedes the other. In order to do so, we draw a distinction between academic institutions and the realm of bottom-up, grassroots activism situated outside of academia. For the sake of feasibility of this project, we investigate how the issue of various types of vulnerability can be observed, understood, explained, and reformed in academic and non-academic spheres. Using the example of vulnerability, we see three frames that scholars and activists frequently use to describe vulnerable bodies, namely Legitimate/Illegitimate, Recognized/Invisible, and Normal/Abnormal. Each dichotomy suggests an element of power versus powerlessness.

The opposition between theory and praxis stretches back to Aristotle and remains central to the work of Western scholars and philosophers today (Bernstein 1999). Our definitions of theory and praxis incorporate Aristotelian ideas on philosophical and practical wisdom, as expressed in his *Nichomachean Ethics* (Aristotle 1999). In Aristotle's explanation, philosophical wisdom appears as pure theoretical knowledge, which does not lead to any activities and ends in "products apart from the activities that produce [it]" (Aristotle 1999: 3). It preoccupies itself with matters "that are highest by nature, things invariable, which have not an end" (ibid.: 97). Although Aristotle recognizes philosophical wisdom as "remarkable, admirable, difficult, divine," he also treats it as "useless." In his view, those who "take refuge in theory" and do not apply their theories to influence social praxis do not produce any useful knowledge. To increase utility of any theoretical wisdom, a theorist needs to test it against the facts of life: "if it harmonizes with the facts we must accept it, but if it clashes with them we must suppose it to be mere theory" (ibid.: 177). This way, theory becomes praxis, whereby wisdom gains practicality both in terms of its intersection with action and doing, and with regards to its object of inquiry, which should be graspable and tangible.

This urge to look for a practical application of theory, which led Aristotle to discuss praxis, also guides Karl Marx to proclaim in his *Theses on Feuerbach,* "thinking isolated from practice" does not lead us anywhere, because any search for wisdom "is not a question of theory, but a practical question" (Marx 1994c: 99). Accordingly, Marx blurs the line between the purposes of theory and praxis. Instead of reinforcing the opposition between two notions, and treating theory as merely theoretical and praxis as exclusively practical, Marx unifies practice with theory, arguing praxis should be informed by theory during application.

Following Marx, we argue that the question—*does theory lead praxis or praxis lead theory?*—is a rhetorical one. Neither can exist without the other; rather, they correspond in unison. Without praxis, there can be no questions; without theory, there can be no answers—and vice versa. Massaging the dichotomy between theoretical and practical knowledge, we explore the issue of vulnerability within two modes of obtaining and producing knowledge. Theoretical knowledge is represented by academic institutions, in which theories are conscious products of the mind intended to describe and explain aspects of the world. Thus, the goal of theory is to conceptualize knowledge through its queries. According to this position, within academia, theory leads praxis.

The second approach, grassroots activism, exists outside of academia. Here, *grassroots philosophers* become producers of knowledge. We acknowledge that individuals in social movements and protests may be affiliated with an institution, whether it is academia, media, legislature, et cetera. What characterizes these individuals as grassroots philosophers is that their intent for praxis originates from their bodily experience. This praxis is enacted through alternative methods outside these institutions, whether on the streets or on the web. For grassroots philosophers, their being in the world and enacting action upon the world determines how their knowledge and theories are used and disseminated.

In the process of knowledge production in both academic and non-academic settings, scholars and grassroots activists either cause vulnerability to others or become vulnerable themselves. Our understanding of a vulnerable body stems from the works of Julia Kristeva (2006; 2010) and Judith Butler (2009). Kristeva maintains vulnerability as socially constructed, which she highlights by the term "person in a situation of handicap," where handicap becomes the "result of a limitation and a social response, a 'situation' created for the disabled person by society's reception of them" (Kristeva 2010: 259). Similar, Butler's conceptualization of vulnerability claims societal perception as a main construction force behind this notion of vulnerability. In our discussion, we argue that some practices in academic institutions contribute to vulnerability of those with physical or mental disability and those who experience racial, gender, sexual, and class marginalization. The examples we rely on are a collection of what we consider various manifestations of vulnerability of the body and self.

The examples of impediments that vulnerable bodies face while producing knowledge inside and outside academia can be separated into dichotomies: Legitimate/Illegitimate, Recognized/Invisible, and Normal/Abnormal. In the first part of our discussion, we explore situations when theory leads praxis, and focus specifically on academic institutions. The first category refers to the concept of gatekeeping and the process of institutionalization and legitimatization of knowledge. The category of Recognized/Invisible reveals the instances when the knowledge is produced predominantly by those who experience racial, gender, and class privilege. Finally, the category of Normal/Abnormal places under scrutiny the socially constructed notions of acceptability and pathology. These dichotomies are continued in the second part of our discussion, which is dedicated to grassroots philosophers and their ways to produce and disseminate knowledge.

ACADEMIA: THEORY LEADS PRAXIS

In *Economic and Philosophic Manuscripts*, Karl Marx argues that "[c]onceiving, thinking, and intellectual relationships of men [sic] appear as the direct result of their material behaviour" (Marx 1994b: 111). Further, he suggests, "The same applies to intellectual production as manifested in a people's language of politics, law, morality, religion, metaphysics, [among others]" (ibid.). Therefore, the scholar's intellect is never without societal and material influence. As we indicated earlier, theory cannot exist without praxis. However, Hans-Georg Gadamer, in his analysis of hermeneutical approach, argues that "the decisive function of the scholar" is imagination, because it "serves the ability to expose real, productive questions, something in which . . . only he [sic] who masters all the methods of his science succeeds" (Gadamer 2008: 12). In this manner, hermeneutical approach positions scholars and the theories they produce as influencing the way society functions. In what follows, we investigate this position, namely that theory leads and influences social praxis. More specifically, we approach the aforementioned three dichotomies to which theory influences social praxis regarding what we consider the most relevant impediments for vulnerable persons as both scholars and subjects of academic discourse.

Legitimate/Illegitimate

We argue that academia as an institution symbolizes this dichotomy of legitimacy versus illegitimacy through the regulation of knowledge. There is inherent power here. Who decides what knowledge is? Who decides who is knowledgeable? That is, whose ideologies, conceptions and theories are legitimate, and whose are not?

Academia is the mind of the liberal democratic body. Like any institution, academia legitimates its presence and its power by safeguarding its "products." As Marx (1994b: 118) states:

> The division of labour is a true division only from the moment a division of material and mental labour appears . . . From this moment on consciousness can really boast of being something other than consciousness of existing practice, or *really* representing something without representing something real.

Undoubtedly, in the case of academia, mental labor constitutes both the process and the products of theoretical accounts of knowledge. Further, the academic institution legitimizes scholars and their intellectual labors (largely in the form of lectures and/or publications) by various measures of gatekeeping. That is, accreditation processes apply value to individuals' intellectual capacity according to their products of labor. For those who acquire the designated qualifications of an academic career, the academy considers their theoretical analyses and perspectives to be credible (although discrepancies may exist within the institution). Thus, authorized intelligence has higher value or credibility than intelligence outside of academia. Consider online databases: online search engines are for the general public's use; yet, in most cases, research databases require paid membership or academic affiliation in order to access publications deemed credible. These products of labor (i.e., resources of knowledge in the form of academic publications) are safeguarded in secure communities that require fiscal membership.

Mental labor in the form of theory production or application is not a new concept, nor is the concept of gatekeeping. Historically, technological developments have increasingly permitted mass production and mass dispersal of information including theoretical texts, as Marshall McLuhan (1995) indicates in his book *Understanding Media*. Before the establishment of the printing press, acquiring and discussing theoretical knowledge was largely limited to the wealthy. According to Harold Innis (1943), it was not until the transition to pulp paper and the lithograph that documentation became affordable and efficient. Furthermore, prior to the invention of the telegraph, transportation of information was slow and unreliable. In this way, mental labor was a privilege to those who had the resources in economic wealth and time. As communication technology advanced, information became more accessible to a wider range of people: print allowed for mass production of books, magazines, and newspapers; radio, television, and satellites allowed for mass audio communication; and, the Internet enabled easy and relatively inexpensive access to a plethora of information.[1]

This rise in technology has encouraged the *commodification of information and knowledge*. Yet, the two are not synonymous. Information is readily produced and accessible; knowledge is not. This point of view distinguishes knowledge from information in terms of social status, but also in terms of legitimization. Once again, we consider the Internet: individuals may go online and study a wealth of different theoretical perspectives of Political Science. In fact, they might acquire as much information as necessary to understand the main premises of Political Science. However, this does not make them a Political Scientist, nor would anyone consider these individuals credible sources of "knowledge." They might accumulate information, but to be considered knowledgeable or reliable, they must earn this status through an accredited institution.

Another strategy of the legitimization of knowledge arises when we consider scientific validity in terms of the perceived limitations of emotion and subjectivity in academia. *Autoethnography*—a methodology that relies on the researcher's own lived experiences in some capacity—is a notable example of how academic backlash can occur when researchers attempt to interweave their own personal experiences or emotion into their academic work. Because autoethnography embraces personal insights in to their work, there is a tendency to criticize this work as being biased, self-indulgent, and has been described as "a form of public masturbation" (Sparkes 2002: 212). Although we appreciate the concept of validity in principle, we question the presumption that a researcher can ever be unbiased. Robert Rinehart in his article *Fictional Methods in Ethnography* has suggested this disparagement is due to the research community having a "deep mistrust of the worth of the self" and that researchers are expected to "check themselves and their work against some higher authority" (Rinehart 1998: 212). In other words, the presence of our *selves* might damage the credibility of science. Certainly, even the most pragmatic researchers have not found a way to tear the *self* from their body and leave it somewhere to be gathered after their research is completed. Rather, the researcher is somehow omniscient. Using the example of autoethnography, the researchers who tell someone else's story (imposing their theoretical principles and legitimized interpretations) are unbiased and praised, yet the researchers describing their own story (drawing largely from their own experiences and interpretations) are illegitimate researchers. In this way, these academic standards act as an additional gatekeeper in terms of what kinds of research is produced, published, and taken seriously.

In many ways, knowledge (as opposed to information) is conceptualized as a power tool; professional communities, including academia, rely on the possession of formal or specialized knowledge, termed expertise. In his analysis of professionalism, Elliott Friedson (1986) distinguishes expertise from common knowledge in which limited access to formal knowledge makes it a sole possession of the professional elites. Friedson describes professionals as "the agents of formal knowledge," who enjoy "prestige and respect" from those who are not identified within the particular professional community (Friedson 1986: 16). Magali S. Larson (1990) develops this notion and asserts that professionals often proclaim scarcity of (and monopoly over) the knowledge they possess in an attempt to maintain "control over access to the credential." Further, she suggests that because professional training programs are made available to the broadest public, this expertise can easily be distinguished from "other forms of scarce and esoteric knowledge" (Larson 1990: 137). Yet, it is worthwhile to point out how professional communities and institutions maintain a number of barriers that restrict or at very least limit access and participation for particular groups of people. This is problematic in terms of the role that professionals (in this case, theorists) play in constructing, authorizing and therefore legitimizing social and political praxis (Johnson 2007). Yet, as Michel Foucault points out, this form of legitimization does not come from explicit supremacy on behalf of some institution or power structure; rather this power is solidified because of the expected compliance of the lay public (Evetts 2003). In academia, then, knowledge and its social effects are legitimized twice: first by the gatekeeping strategies within the institution and second by the acceptance of these truths outside the institution. Yet, without a diverse array of participants with varying degrees of experience, this process of normalization legitimizes narrow understandings of knowledge.

Recognized/Invisible

The foundation of academic theory is laden with the work of privileged white men. This alone is representative of our second dichotomous frame, recognized versus invisible. These academic texts aim to generalize to *the people* while using the male pronoun and speaking about *man*. Indeed, *mankind* refers to humankind (Goffman 1977; Derrida 2005); yet, during the time of these classical texts, society hardly considered women, racial minorities, and people with disabilities as *human*. Although contemporary society has allegedly progressed, there are explicit markers of heteronormative principles and expectations. One example of this is the glorification of those who do transcend the boundaries of physical to mental labor, as Angela P. Harris (1991: 111), an African American female law professor in the 1990s, discusses in the following narrative:

> A colleague approached me once at a faculty dinner. He had read an article of mine in which I quoted both Jorge Luis Borges and Toni Morrison. He described the article as "literate." Then he shook his head. "I didn't think you could do it," he said. I didn't know what to say.

Harris describes her experience in an American university, which was largely comprised of upper-class white men. The above language is comparable to Barbara Schneider and Chaseten Remillard's (2013) finding that when talking about the homeless, individuals often used the term *human beings* in attempt to show compassion. However, terms like "human being" to describe people with unstable housing and "literate" to describe a female academic seems both arbitrary and condescending. Regardless of the attempt to acknowledge a marginalized group, superficial indicators of compassion perpetuate the expectation of a group's invisibility and vulnerability in a particular sector. Surely, terms like "human being" and "literate" are reserved for those who seemingly require legitimization or recognition.

A number of theorists discuss the frame of recognition versus invisibility. For example, Kristeva discusses the difference between *integration* and *interaction*. She speaks of policies regarding persons of disability, and says, "I had been witness to a *process*, perhaps even to a procedure, but not to a *rebirth*—to an *integration*, but not to an *interaction*" (Kristeva 2006: 220). She talks about disability, but we extend this concept to all underrepresented groups, specifically within academia. In this way, we consider the integration of women, racial minorities, and people with disabilities or illness in academic roles, but we question the visibility of—or the interaction with—these individuals. Another theorist, Nancy Fraser (2008) also questions the degree of transformability of theoretical remedies of social justice. For example, Elizabeth Anderson (2008) states that affirmative action in post-secondary institutions intends to provide subordinated groups access to post-secondary education and networking opportunities upon graduation. Yet, both authors question the success of these remedies: Do they represent integration without interaction? Do these policies intensify social inequalities and subordination? Further, do affirmative action strategies merely offer higher representation of subordinated groups into an existing social framework without actually considering their unique voices, ideas, and identities to form a new, diverse status quo?

In terms of recognition within theory, we turn to Gadamer's (2008) concept of scholastic imagination in relation to standpoint theory. Without the experience of a particular standpoint, how will a theorist know which questions to ask? For example, classical published texts talked about man because, for the most part, men wrote them. As representatives of the normative class, male scholars asked questions relative to their material experience. Subordinated classes are invisible in these texts when they do not have the opportunity to pose questions, raise concerns, and provide descriptions of their experience. Walter Brogan (2011) discusses two voices of humankind: the silent inner voice and the public voice. He describes Heidegger's conception of the public voice as "the everyday voice that is all around us and always ready to tell us who we are and what to say" (Brogan 2011: 169). Not surprisingly, Heidegger termed this public voice of humankind as the voice of *das Man*. If individuals' public voice is an echo of society—that is, a predominantly white, heteronormative and patriarchal society—then how do individuals assert their identities as something alternative? For example, in an attempt to make classical texts more inclusive and politically correct, editors replace descriptions like *mankind* with *humankind*. We argue these translations are not enough. Changing the language of a theoretical text merely implies recognition without these texts actually being more inclusive. Another example is the inclusion of women's studies in academic departments and into curriculum, where a mere week is spent to cover a so-called specialized subject area. We argue that though these curriculum additions might suggest *integration*, these texts continue to limit the *interaction* of originally invisible groups. White upper-class men theorize on a particular set of questions that bias against subordinated groups. According to standpoint theory, these men cannot answer questions outside their experience; but then, if the precariat—a term for the class of subordinated and precarious groups—never have the opportunity to ask their own questions, will there ever be answers?

Considering this idea of invisibility, we question how recognizable subordinate groups are in contemporary academia. As we have stated, affirmative action strategies attempt to provide opportunities to the less privileged. But even with this *integration*, there is little opportunity given for *interaction* and therefore little change in the structure to accommodate these differing identities; women are shoehorned into the Old Boys' Club, which remains unchanged. With limited representation and integration of vulnerable populations in academia, it is difficult to consider these perspectives when we may not face these same vulnerabilities. Without an eye to these vulnerabilities, how may we change the heteronormative discourse of *das Man*?

Normal/Abnormal

The normal versus abnormal dichotomy refers to theoretical work that discusses specific markers of the body that denote either social acceptability or social pathology. In this way, we argue that vulnerable or subordinated groups are regularly identified in terms of deviance. We suggest, then, that this framework is an extension of the recognized versus invisible dichotomy.

What society considers appropriate behavior can be determined by what it outlaws. We extend this concept to include what society deems pathological, as per Foucault's *Panopticism* where he explains that "all the authorities exercising individual control function according to a double mode[,] that of binary division and branding (mad/sane; dangerous/harmless; normal/abnormal)" (Foucault 1977). Of course, societal deviance and perceived abnormalities change over time. Do certain behaviors suddenly become more or less dangerous or abnormal? More importantly, how does theory encourage or prohibit these societal changes? We have previously established that social environment precedes theory (Marx 1994b), and it is the role of the theorist to ask theoretical questions to determine praxis in order to describe, explain, or reform society (Gadamer 2008). We have also recognized that social context dictates who is in a position to ask questions and whom their questions address. Our final consideration, then, is one of social reform. Specifically, we posit how theoretical structures inform or challenge societal norms.

We consider the concept of homelessness (i.e., housing insecurity) as an example of what society considers normal versus abnormal experience. We see this dichotomy being demonstrated by our example in two distinct ways. First, the socially constructed label *homeless* inevitably implies the abnormality of those who live on the streets, in temporary housing, or overnight shelters. Accordingly, individuals who are experiencing this material reality are made to be the "other" or the abnormal counterpart to the "housed." Not only is this language problematic in terms of the "us versus them" mentality, it is also problematic when we consider what "home" denotes and thus what being "homeless" implies. If home equates to familial support, comfort, and community, maintaining that an individual is "homeless" implies that these positive conditions must not exist in their lives. This postulation can lead to multifarious modes of discrimination and maltreatment, such as the case in the 2012 Vancouver Olympics when "the poor, homeless and marginalized [were treated as] . . . objects to be removed" in an attempt to manage the city's impressions (Porter et al. 2009). Using this example, we can see how theoretical discourse has the potential to lead praxis regarding the public perception and treatment of those experiencing chronic poverty. Specifically, we refer to constructionist research that attempts to deconstruct problematic social labels and alter the negative implications they have on particular groups of people. For example, in her participatory action research regarding the experiences of those with schizophrenia, Barbara Schneider (2010) uses terminology such as *housing security* and *unstable housing* rather than using the term "homeless." By altering this language, there is the potential to also change the perception that those without stable housing are somehow less normal than those with secure housing.

The second way the abnormal versus normal dichotomy is perpetuated in homeless discourse is among those with housing insecurities themselves. That is, there are clear distinctions of the *worthy* and *unworthy* poor. According to Gerhard Falk (2001), society reacts to such individuals either with *achieved stigma* or with *existential stigma.* That is, individuals are considered to blame or not to blame, respectively, for their behavior and resulting negative attention. With this in mind, there is particular social prejudice against the "dishonest poor" who seemingly deserve "punishment for [their] moral failing" (Pimpare 2008). Put another way, there are individuals who society deems worthy of sympathy and social aid, and those who are not. We consider, then, how the literature differentiates various degrees of housing security and how this might inform future research as well as social praxis. But research is only considered legitimate and visible if it garners funding, reaches publication, or earns favorable recognition for the institution. As a result, we question the effectiveness theory has in terms of social praxis regarding those who are seemingly considered to be abnormal or pathologized.

Alternative examples that demonstrate how theory initiates a conversation leading to praxis is Kristeva's work on disability, and Butler's performance studies that challenges heteronormative standards of identity. These works are reformist in the sense that there is an intention to alter public perceptions of ability and gender, respectively. It is difficult, if not impossible, to measure the direct impact that theory has on altering societal norms. Nonetheless, academia is the mind of society's active body; neither can exist without the other. The mind (academia) is conscious in that there is an attempt to understand and better the body (society). Yet, as Marx explains, "consciousness can never be anything else except conscious existence, and the existence of men [sic] is their actual life-process" (Marx 1994b: 111). In other words, the mind is a product of the environment. Whether it is in discordance or compliance, the mind does not exist alone. Thus, theory—the product of human consciousness—cannot exist prior to praxis. Theory aims to explain the world and to change it. Yet, we argue that in a liberal democracy, where institutional legitimization is necessary, social change requires empirical and theoretical action. To this end, the questions and suggestions that are posed by theory do not necessarily lead praxis. Rather, theory *authenticates* it.

GRASSROOTS PHILOSOPHERS: PRAXIS LEADS THEORY[2]

Individuals encounter vulnerability through their embodied experiences. As defined earlier, the phrase *grassroots philosophers* refers to those individuals enacting praxis outside academia. These individuals may be affiliated with institutions like academia, media, and legislature, however their methods for reform are what characterize them as grassroots philosophers. That is, praxis enacted through alternative means, either on the streets or on the web, indicates a grassroots initiative, as opposed to an institutionally-approved initiative. The efforts of praxis face the full brunt of institutional outrage over such illegitimated methods; yet, these grassroots philosophers have the power during protest. Enacting their vulnerability through bodily praxis both online and offline, grassroots philosophers call attention to their injustices. Such efforts, as well as the experiential knowledge informing them, are largely deemed illegitimate methods by institutions. Further, those in power assert that such emotionally charged praxis cannot be valid or logical, arguing that if the motivation behind such efforts are illegitimate then so are the efforts. The web-mediated praxis is better able to spread and allows grassroots philosophers to subvert knowledge gatekeepers by creating and sharing "illegitimate" and "unrecognized" knowledge. For grassroots philosophers, their being in the world and enacting action upon the world determines how their knowledge and theories are used and disseminated. As Mark Johnson (2007: 91) adds, "all our meaning, all our creativity, all our knowledge are grounded in our bodily engagement with our environment." We argue praxis engages with and from the vulnerability that grassroots philosophers' experience.

Paolo Gerbaudo (2012: 12) asserts social movements become successful through social media only when there is what he terms a "choreography of assembly." Success in social media occurs through a "sense of togetherness," and a "fueling of emotional tension extending from distant mediated connections to the 'effervescence' of physical proximity" (ibid.: 14). When these "emotional conduits" and a "shared sense of victimhood" bring individuals together online, there occurs a "convergence of disparate individuals around common symbols and places, signifying their unity *despite* diversity" (original emphasis). Gerbaudo's concept illuminates how the "Hands Up, Don't Shoot!" phrase and the protesters' physical movement of raising their hands originating in Ferguson, Missouri, can spread to Palestinian protests in Gaza, and to the Umbrella Revolution in Hong Kong in globalized acts of solidarity against injustice. A gesture originating out of a particular bodily experience and praxis in a certain time and space has gained traction and become a symbol signifying the vulnerable experience. Vulnerability encompasses grassroots philosophers' own being in the world, their inequalities, and their invisibility to institutions, whilst also motivating grassroots philosophers to enact praxis. To speak against the vulnerability of their bodies, grassroots philosophers deploy praxis in defense against gatekeepers; gatekeepers, in their turn, deem the philosophers' bodies, praxis, and ways of knowing illegitimate, unintelligent, invisible, and abnormal.

Legitimate/Illegitimate

When academia does not authorize or sanction certain ways of knowing, it deems them illegitimate. Such is the case for activists citing personal experience, social trends, even personal or communal histories as evidence of their vulnerability, when institutions like academia disregard "unverifiable" information. These so-called illegitimate knowledges develop from the philosophers' experiences and their reflexes reacting to injustice. Acting in the world, according to Maurice Merleau-Ponty (2012: 81), is a result of unconscious reflexes toward a conscious end: "reflexes themselves are never blind processes, they adjust the 'sense' of the situation." These reflexes create a "knowledge relation" or behavioral shift in ourselves and are an "intention of our total being" and a "pre-objective perspective that we call 'being in the world.'" That is, such reflexes enable and facilitate praxis. For example, the protests and outcry when Michael Brown was killed in Ferguson, MO, was an instantaneous, reflexive, emotional reaction. A mere five days after Brown's death on August 9, 2014, @FeministaJones organized a National Moment of Silence across the country. Within a week after Brown's death, the protests calling for Officer Darren Wilson's indictment began, countless vigils were set up. Academic theory does not motivate these unconscious reflexes, and Merleau-Ponty acknowledges the reflexes' conscious goal: to alleviate vulnerability.

This does not mean theory is separate from grassroots philosophers' praxis. If embodied vulnerability inspires praxis, we argue that praxis leads to theoretical understandings of these vulnerabilities. Take, for example, Moya Bailey's (2010) creation of the term, "misogynoir" in her blog entry to the *Crunk Feminist Collective* blog on March 3, 2010. Misogynoir, she writes, is a "word I made up to describe the particular brand of hatred directed at black women in American visual & popular culture." Though a graduate student at the time, Bailey discussed misogynoir outside the academy on a blog; therefore, we consider her a grassroots philosopher. Since the term's creation in 2010, countless online activists use this term to speak about anti-blackness and misogyny in patriarchal society. Of note is one activist named Trudy who writes the Tumblr blog *Gradient Lair*. While Bailey chose to work within academia while publishing outside it, Trudy left the academy while working on her second master's degree. The content she publishes on *Gradient Lair* comes from her embodied knowledge and praxis, and she argues that as a result, her content is judged as illegitimate in academia. This has not stopped academic researchers claiming her content as their own and incorporating it into their work. In her vehement opposition to academia, she states outright in a content use policy that she does not consent to formal academic use.[3] She objects that, when she attempted to use her content in an academic context it was deemed illegitimate, yet her content becomes legitimated when other researchers claim her words as their own. This is where her anger at academia stems from.

Trudy relies on social media (her blog and Twitter) as means of voicing her praxis and vulnerability. In contrast, while Michael Keren (2006) in *Blogosphere* describes blogs generally as a "global political arena that ostensibly frees individuals, allowing them a voice in the public sphere," (ibid.: 145) he also argues that political discourse is "trivialized" when done informally. What makes political discourse, specifically feminism, trivial online is the multiplicity of both political and apolitical statements in a single blog. For example, Keren analyzes one feminist blog in particular, and claims that the author's message is diluted and made apolitical by her posting culinary recipes alongside calls for action: "The online outpourings bloggers get in response to their posts can put the death of an aging cat on the same emotional level as the earthquake in Pakistan" (ibid.: 151). Applying Keren's thoughts to Trudy's blog *Gradient Lair*, he would consider Trudy's pairing of womanist manifestos alongside shared pictures of her hair, or of prominent African American celebrities just as trivial. While Keren's points are salient, he overlooks that these grassroots philosophers create this content as expression of their vulnerability. These blogs, Twitter accounts, et cetera, are of a personal nature, and while they convey the authors' vulnerability, the use is not solely a political one.[4] Individuals are multifaceted, and we cannot characterize their praxis as illegitimate just because we see more than one aspect of their lives.

Emotion is considered an illegitimate method of engaging in praxis, yet for grassroots philosophers, emotion is a key avenue in voicing their vulnerability. According to Paul McGinley (2008: 221), the act of crying can "tell [us] what is important, what matters to [us]. It is both expression and speech." For him, this "essence and art of being human," as embodied in crying, is a "performative essence." Crying is a connection between the body and the mind, which articulates vulnerability. Crying is also considered an irrational and unnecessary bodily function. For grassroots philosophers, crying, anger, and other emotions are avenues connecting life experience and praxis, as seen in Trudy's anger at academia, and Bailey's term to describe the "hatred" she felt from popular culture. Bringing together praxis and vulnerability into an act of crying allows a philosopher to "come closer to the real ideal of knowledge," (Gadamer 2008: 93) despite such avenues deemed illegitimate by academia.

Hermeneutics develops through a "process [that] is repeated continually throughout our familiar experience," (Gadamer 2008: 15) a process similar to the grassroots praxis of these philosophers outside academia. Gadamer (ibid.) explains how hermeneutics—and by extension grassroots praxis—offer a new perspective to the academic world:

> There is always a world already interpreted, already organized in its basic relations, into which experience steps as something new … Only the support of a familiar and common understanding makes possible the venture in the alien, the lifting up of something out of the alien, and thus the broadening and enrichment of our own experience of the world.

Grassroots praxis operates outside academia, but offers a new understanding of vulnerability that can enhance everyone's experience with and understanding of the world. Gadamer goes so far to say that knowledge can *only* be legitimated through an experiential, praxis-led grassroots process—though by and large the academic institution is wary of such processes. Critiquing the status quo is best done outside of it, seen through use of Bailey's misogynoir. In this way, following Gadamer (ibid.: 63), we argue that grassroots philosophers and their praxis better facilitate reform. Far from being illegitimate, grassroots praxis is better positioned to initiate change. When knowledge develops through informed vulnerability and praxis, theoretical approaches are more productive.

Recognized/Invisible

Gadamer states that the "knowledge of the universal is the unity of experience." Further, this knowledge and unity develop out of "accumulating recognitions that we call experience."

This knowledge of the universal is synonymous with the experience of vulnerability. Grassroots philosophers gain a connection to vulnerability through recognizing their bodily experiences, yet these methods of applying their grassroots praxis to enact change goes unrecognized by institutions. Jacques Derrida (2005: 141), in alluding to Franz Kafka's *The Trial*, claims, "if the Law is the condition of the institution, [and] if the institution is the Law, then the guardians of the institution are also the guardians of the Law." In his lecture Derrida is speaking of women's studies addition into academia, acknowledging its inclusion yet invisibility at large, concluding that individuals become vulnerable when unrecognized by the institution. Extending this to our grassroots philosophers, when unrecognized by the Law, both their praxis and bodies become vulnerable.

The lack of recognition by the Law is clearly seen in the Ferguson unrest since the fatal shooting of an African American Ferguson resident Michael Brown by Officer Darren Wilson. The circumstances around the shooting are contested: local residents assert Brown was unarmed and killed without cause, while the police department claims Officer Wilson was threatened. Residents, activists, and grassroots philosophers perceive Brown as yet another victim of institutionalized racism within the United States. The Every

36 Hours Campaign (2013), who produced a 2012 annual report on extrajudicial killings of African Americans, states that an African American is killed by police, vigilantes, or security guards *every 28 hours* nationwide. Further, "After more than three months of marathon Internet searching, we are sure that the actual number is closer to one state-sanctioned killing of a Black person *every 24 hours*" (original emphasis). The phrase "state-sanctioned" indicates the lack of recognition from the Law faced by African Americans. These injustices spark outrage, despair, and fear within this marginalized community. Most of the on-the-ground coverage on Ferguson came from alternative sources like *Al Jazeera America* or individual Twitter users—users organized by others into several lists, such as "STL [St Louis] Journalists" and "Ferguson Locals and Journos [Journalists]." As @SarahKendzior writes in a November 10, 2014, tweet, the "Media [is] waiting for #STL [St Louis] violence like vultures. Meanwhile everyday racism and repression in other regions goes uncovered and ignored." Because mainstream media failed to recognize the issues facing the community, there was a need for alternative means of journalism. Grassroots philosophers tweeted, collected, and disseminated information because of the bodily and emotionally reflexive need for justice. Theory does not inform their actions; they enact praxis because of the vulnerability, anger, and pain felt by residents and activists who are vulnerable from the police state and from inaccurate media institutions.

Derrida (1997: 142) discusses the paradox of grassroots philosophers' situation: if they are recognized and accepted by institutions, they "risk being just another cell in the university beehive." Grassroots philosophers are either invisible or, upon recognition, considered "reactionary, dangerous, only limiting the progress" of the status quo. The Ferguson grassroots philosophers resisting police action and media misinformation remained unrecognized by institutions. Similarly, Butler (2009: iv) notes how recognition by the Law, by academia, by institutions, determines "who will count as a subject, and who will not." She perceives "those who do not live their genders [or bodies, or praxis] in intelligible ways [are] at heightened risk for harassment and violence." This lack of recognition characterizes philosophers' vulnerability and motivates grassroots praxis. In *The Right to Philosophy*, Derrida (1997) also perceives invisibility and vulnerability motivating praxis toward theory. Theory that underlies praxis, he states, should result from a "sense of responsibility for the neighbour and the stranger" (Derrida 1997: 52). Rather than a "sitting judge," theory should facilitate praxis, theory should be "a wanderer and nomad, on the move, on call, without the wherewithal to lay down its head, hastening hither and yon whenever the call of the 'other' [the unrecognized] summons it into action" (ibid.: 51). Similarly, Brogan (2011: 173) describes the "ability to speak [to implement praxis] is beholden to a fundamental condition of speechlessness."

This was seen, again, in Ferguson's unrest and the lack of quality discussion between protesters and institutional representatives.

Twitter user @FeministaJones organized the National Moment of Silence across the United States in the days following Michael Brown's death in Ferguson, MO. Stating on Twitter her disappointment at vigils for Brown were taking place outside of where racially motivated violence typically occurs, she created the hashtag #NMOS14 (National Moment of Silence 2014) to build a movement across physical space. Through a decentralized network and a non-hierarchical structure, volunteers in almost every major city organized nationwide vigils through #NMOS14 in the few days after Brown's death. She describes the archived Twitter movement as exemplifying "how social media helped facilitate a national moment of silence to honour victims of police brutality, show solidarity with their families, and allow communities to come together in a moment of mourning and support." Within four days of initiating her praxis, @FeministaJones and volunteers created national peaceful protests. As Butler (2009: iv) states, vulnerable individuals must "exercise freedom" so freedom can "come into being." @FeministaJones managed this through her technologically mediated praxis on social media. Unfortunately, such exercising of freedom and praxis by on-the-ground Ferguson protesters has been more difficult to come by. This is perhaps because the Internet is not as *visibly* policed as the streets; in certain ways, grassroots philosophers are less vulnerable while online because it is a space with some independence from institutions.

Normal/Abnormal

As discussed, we can tell what society considers abnormal by what it outlaws. Protests without proper permits are outlawed. Similarly, "walking while Black,"[5] transgender, or any other identity deemed abnormal is considered a risk to society and such individuals are under threat of violence. Normalcy necessitates regulation of what is normal, and what lies outside of the standard. Those who are considered abnormal may receive recognition from the Law, but are merely recognized as deviant and experience violence from the institutions. This violence, ironically, occurs while largely invisible to the general public; in this way, we can see how our divisions of normal/abnormal, recognized/invisible, and legitimate/illegitimate flow and interconnect together. While these vulnerable bodies may challenge this invisibility, Butler (2009) argues that even this challenge reproduces the powers-that-be. In enforcing or challenging a hierarchy or dichotomy, power, norms, and standardizations can reproduce themselves. The grassroots philosophers and their emotionally charged praxis undermine institutional norms by working outside the normalized systems; yet, this still reproduces institutional power. Butler asserts, "There is no reproduction of the social world that is not at the same time a reproduction of those norms that govern the intelligibility of the body in space and time" (ibid.: x). This is true with dichotomies that define themselves against each other: legitimate versus illegitimate, normal versus abnormal.

Academic institutions deem grassroots philosophers abnormal for their reliance on embodied praxis, on alternative theories and practices, and their emotional responses. The nonacademics, in this case, are regarded as outsiders to the standard order. For those within academia who are informed by the grassroots and embodied motivations of praxis, they are *integrated* but their methods do not *interact*. There are times when grassroots praxis is considered so far removed from the norm that it goes unrecognized and appears as a surprise when tensions burst. This was the case for the four Indigenous women who initiated #IdleNoMore across Canada: "Ultimately, these efforts often go unnoticed—even ignored—until flash-point events, culminations or times of crisis occur. . . . most Indigenous peoples have never been idle in their efforts to protect what is meaningful to our communities—nor will we ever be" (Kino-nda-niimi Collective 2014: 21). For many Indigenous activists, #IdleNoMore created a visible space for their praxis. The Kino-nda-niimi Collective (2014) unites the different threads of #IdleNoMore together in *The Winter We Danced*, acknowledging #IdleNoMore's idiosyncracies and harmonies. Groups took on the #IdleNoMore mantle to discuss any and every issue facing Indigenous peoples, and used the grassroots movement to open a space for dialogue about the vulnerability felt by the First Nations. Indigenous activists felt like outsiders, considered deviant and abnormal in the context of a colonial Canada. There remains a question as to whether normalized praxis is at the least respectability politics and at the worst, assimilation in disguise.

Abnormality refers to something being wrong or out of place: a neurosis or a defect. The general public prefers these abnormalities to remain unseen. Far from repressing this abnormality, grassroots philosophers embrace it and integrate it into their bodily experiences, allowing them to confront the institutions that dictate their vulnerability. The imposed abnormality onto bodily experiences motivates praxis, as seen in Emma Sulkowicz's performative piece at Columbia University in protest of her rape in a residence hall, and the university's lack of disciplinary action against her rapist. Sulkowicz began to carry her mattress across campus to signify the weight she carries from her experience, and to give visibility to the injustice of this burden being placed on her and not on her rapist. Her praxis led to a National Day of Action on October 29, 2014, where Sulkowicz calls for students to march in solidarity for survivors and victims of sexual assault.

In response to this solidarity march, activist Abby discusses her attempt to join in the march on her blog *Leave A Trail*.[6] Abby notes how Sulkowicz specifically asked protestors to carry mattresses to stand in solidarity with her original conception of carrying a large weight. But, as Abby replies, she experiences rheumatoid arthritis and therefore cannot carry a mattress. Further, she cites statistics revealing women with disabilities having a greater risk of sexual violence than women without disabilities. In her response, Abby acknowledges how she is not part of the norm of those in activism around sexual assault, and this imposed abnormality and invisibility is felt in almost all elements of feminist protests: "disability is the often forgotten intersection in feminist activism, and I was disappointed to see her [Sulkowicz] lack of consideration for those of us who cannot carry the physical weight, but are at a much greater risk to be forced to carry it emotionally."[7] Grassroots philosophers connect their bodily experience and emotion with their intellectual knowledge, a connection Brogan (2011: 166) describes as a "silent voice that murmurs and vibrates but only as a sort of trace that occurs alongside the voice that I am and am not." This voice, and experientially informed praxis, succeeds only when it interacts with other vulnerable bodies in an intersectional, communal effort against institutionalized norms: "it is a question of recovering our connection to this 'lost voice' [in order to] experience ourselves as a whole, both wholly attuned to our existential being and wholly present in the world around us" (ibid.: 170). This is not to say that Abby's critical voice took away from Sulkowicz's message, but rather it allowed a discussion within a moment of praxis; a true moment of intersectionality. This is the wholeness Brogan describes, and is also similar to Gerbaudo's (2012: 12) "choreography of assembly." Gerbaudo acknowledges social media's role in facilitating the unifying of voices and social mobilization as "a process (rather than a state) of spatial *assemblaging*, with its own choreography" (original emphasis). Social media allows alternative and grassroots praxis a space to organize and grow.

These movements that social media like Twitter have facilitated could never occur offline in the same capacity. For many grassroots philosophers, the academy is yet another monolithic organization impressing institutionalized vulnerability upon them. On Twitter on November 9, 2014, @_Indigenista offers a welcome critique of academia: "Higher Ed actually education in general is settler colonial agenda, teach[ing] universal truth according to . . . their forefathers. So impt [important] for Natives and PoC [people of color] to challenge it. However, it is oppressive." In this critique, @_Indigenista has made space for her own voice, her own "wholeness" for her grassroots praxis through social media.

We assert that Johnson's (2007: 91) "embodied theory of meaning" and bodily experiences of vulnerability informing praxis should become the standard process for enacting praxis. But as the academic institution disregards grassroots philosophers and their emotional efforts, these philosophers' methods are considered abnormal. Butler (2009: x) advocates those who are vulnerable, unrecognized, and abnormal to "negotiate the right to speak, and [to] make sure that the voiceless are given a right to speak." However, Butler argues that by enacting freedom, freedom comes into being. In this way, vulnerable bodies will become recognized and accepted. Grassroots philosophers and their praxis as informed by the embodiment of theory has the ability to be effective in claiming recognition and legitimacy into what institutions consider normal; that is if the institutions choose to *interact*—not just *integrate*—with such philosophers. In a November 6, 2014, tweet, @Blackamazon adds "Feminists and orgs [organizations] needs [sic] to move from the 'look how awful it is for black women' to the 'this is how we are prioritizing FIXING IT'." In other words, reform rather description is a priority of social praxis.

@FeministaJones has intitated previous hashtag movements on Twitter, and of note is #YouOkSis. This hashtag allowed Twitter users to voice their experiences of catcalling as African American women, to critique the misogynoir that these women encounter everyday, and to offer support and solidarity to each other.[8] She announced on Twitter her intent to expand #YouOkSis into a program in the Bronx, New York. In her November 7, 2014, tweets, @FeministaJones writes about the passion and exuberance in this new avenue for her grassroots praxis: "I was thinking ahead, unsure of the best way to make use of it [#YouOkSis]. Now I know. Whewwww [sic] the fire in my bones!" Online-mediated praxis by grassroots philosophers can lead to offline change. While this may not always be the case—the individual initiating such praxis must have resources at hand—at the very least it allows communicative and educative lines to be opened. Though the #IdleNoMore protests in 2013 did not instigate tangible change, the Kino-nda-niimi Collective affirm #IdleNoMore's value as a "forum for how we can come up with solutions together . . . about how to live together meaningfully and peacefully, as nations and neighbours" (Kino-nda-niimi Collective 2014: 23). We describe grassroots praxis as productively bridging the vulnerability, emotions and bodily experience of individuals into protest against large institutions. Social media helps facilitate this process by sharing vulnerability and emotional tension to different individuals acrcss time and space. Through these alternative means of coming together, grassroots philosophers can achieve the recognition in order to begin legitimatizing their praxis.

CONCLUSION

From our discussion, we suggest that praxis initially leads theory, yet theory is required to legitimize praxis; thus, theory too leads praxis. In terms of defining and understanding the concepts of theory and praxis, we maintain that theory is a product of academic institutions, whereas praxis is a demonstration of the knowledge and experience from grassroots activism, situated outside of academia. By relying on examples of theoretical works by recognized scholars and blog posts by grassroots activists, we explore the interconnection between academia, the grassroots philosophers, and vulnerability. We suggest that recognizing the connection between theory and praxis allows us to see society as both, a product and determinant of theory. Nevertheless, it is evident that academic gatekeeping and the processes of legitimization and certification of knowledge, which are mandatory for recognition in the academic sphere, limit the access to theoretical knowledge. Therefore, society still controls whom and what is legitimate to study.

We recognize that a sharp distinction between theory and praxis is somewhat arbitrary, as Marx (1994b) asserts that theoretical knowledge is neither inherent nor pure. Consider our example of vulnerability. We argue it is not adequate to rewrite foundational theoretical texts to hereby include the precariat (i.e., through symbolic language like "humankind" or "s/he"). This act is mere abstraction without revolution, mere integration without interaction. Alternatively, it is equally insufficient to protest social reform without institutional legitimization. Thus, it is irrelevant whether theory or praxis leads the other; the pursuit to alleviate vulnerability requires mind (academia) and body (praxis).

NOTES

1. We do acknowledge the digital divide. While the Internet may be inexpensive, access through providers and the necessary technology is not. Acknowledging this, our point still stands that the Internet facilitated unlimited access to information hindered by the amount of time a user had.

2. A statement about our intent: we rely almost solely on African American women's activism throughout this section, mainly due to our own Twitter activity in following these particular activists. We do not intend a kind of academic colonialism, and instead attempt to act as allies by acknowledging these women's contributions to the field and their importance regardless of an academic connection or not. We wish to voice our privilege in this situation in talking about these women's experiences while being free from experiencing it ourselves as white women. In adding this note, and throughout this section's attempts to respect these women's original work, we strive to bolster their voices whilst avoiding colonizing their work.

3. It is for these reasons that we do not cite any of *Gradient Lair*'s original work, and only paraphrase Trudy's About page and Content Policy page. In this way, we respect her consent while acknowledging her as a grassroots philosopher in this chapter.

4. However, according to second-wave feminists, the personal is political (Carol Hanisch, "The Personal is Political," *Notes from the Second Year: Women's Liberation*, 1970).

5. This phrase comes from the colloquialism "Driving while Black," and indicates the vulnerability of African Americans who are considered deviant based on the color of their skin.

6. Abby, blog post, "[Picture shows 19 year old woman, standing with use of a cane…." *Leave a Trail* blog, October 29, 2014.

7. Ibid.

8. "#YouOkSis." Last modified June 2014. https://storify.com/FeministaJones/youoksis-a-small-effort-to-thwart-streetharassmen.

REFERENCES

Anderson, Elizabeth. (2008). "Affirmative Action and Fraser's Redstribution-Recognition Dilemma." In *Adding Insult to Injury: Nancy Fraser Debates Her Critics*, edited by Kevin Olson, 164–175. Brooklyn: Verso.

Aristotle. (1999). *Nicomachean Ethics*. Translated by W. D. Ross. Kitchener: Batoche Books.

Bernstein, Richard J. (1999). *Praxis and Action: Contemporary Philosophies of Human Activity*. Philadelphia: University of Pennsylvania Press.

Brogan, Walter. (2011). "The Voices That I Am." *Mosaic* 44.1: 165–175.

Butler, Judith. (2009). "Performativity, Precarity and Sexual Politics." *AIBR: Revista de Antropología Iberoamericana*, 4.3: i-xiii.

Crunk Feminist Collective, http://www.crunkfeministcollective.com/2010/03/14/they-arent-talking-about-me/.

Derrida, Jacques. (1997). "The Right to Philosophy." In *Deconstruction in a Nut Shell*, edited by J.D. Caputo, 49–70. New York: Fordham University Press.

Derrida, Jacques. (2005). Women in the beehive: A seminar with Jacques Derrida. *Differences: A Journal of Feminist Cultural Studies* 16.3: 138–157.

Every 36 Hours Campaign (2013). *Operation Ghetto Storm*. Malcolm X Grassroots Movement. Accessed November 4, 2014, https://mxgm.org/operation-ghetto-storm-2012–annual-report-on-the-extrajudicial-killing-of-313–black-people/.

Evetts, Julia. (2003). "Explaining the Construction of Professionalism in the Military: History, Concepts and Theories." *Revue Française De Sociologie* 44.4: 759–776.

Falk, Gerhard. (2001). *Stigma: How We Treat Outsiders*. Amherst: Prometheus Books.

@FeministaJones. "#NMOS14." Last modified August 2014. https://storify.com/FeministaJones/national-moment-of-silence-nmos14.

Foucault, Michel. (1977). "Discipline and punish, Panopticism." In *Discipline & Punish: The Birth of the Prison*, edited by A. Sheridan, 195–228. New York: Vintage Books. http://foucault.info/documents/disciplineandpunish/foucault.disciplineand

punish.panopticism.htmlhttp://foucault.info/documents/disciplineandpunish/foucault.disciplineandpunish.panopticism.html.

Fraser, Nancy. (2008). "Abnormal Justice." In *Scales of Justice: Reimaging Political Space in a Globalizing World*, 48–75. New York: Columbia University Press.

Friedson, Elliot. (1986). *Professional Powers: A Study of the Institutionalization of Formal Knowledge*. Chicago: University of Chicago Press.

Gadamer, Hans-Georg. (2008). *Philosophic Hermeneutics*. Translated by D. Linge. Los Angeles: University of California Press.

Gerbaudo, Paolo. (2012). *Tweets and the Streets*. London: Pluto.

Goffman, Erving. (1977). "An Arrangement Between Sexes." *Theory and Society* 4.3: 301 -331.

Gradient Lair, "About." Accessed October 29, 2014. http://www.gradientlair.com/about/.

Gradient Lair, "Content Use Policy." Accessed October 29, 2014. http://www.gradientlair.com/content-use-policy/.

Harris, Angela P. (1991). "Women of Color in Legal Education: Representing La Mestiza." *Berkeley Women's Law Journal* 6.1: 107–112.

Innis, Harold. (1943). "The Crisis of Public Opinion." *Canadian Journal of Communication* 31.2: 307–325.

Johnson, Mark. (2007). "'The Stone That Was Cast Out Shall Become the Cornerstone': The Bodily Aesthetics of Human Meaning." *Journal of Visual Art Practice* 6.2: 89–103.

Keren, Michael. (2006). *Blogosphere*. New York: Lexington.

Kino-nda-niimi Collective. (2014). *The Winter We Danced*. Winnipeg: ARP Books.

Kristeva, Julia. (2006). "At the Limits of Living: To Joseph Grigely." *Journal of Visual Culture* 5.2: 219–225.

Kristeva, Julia. (2010). "Liberty, Equality, Fraternity, and … Vulnerability." *Women's Studies Quarterly* 38.1/2: 251–268.

Larson, Magali S. (1990). "In the Matter of Experts and Professionals, or How Impossible It Is to Leave Nothing Unsaid." In *The Formation of Professions*, edited by R. Torstendahl and M. Burrage, 24–50. London: SAGE Publications.

Marx, Karl. (1994a). "Economic and Philosophic Manuscripts." In *Selected Writings*, edited by L.K. Simon, 54–97. Indianapolis: Hackett Publishing Company.

Marx, Karl. (1994b). "The German Ideology. Part I (Selections)." In *Selected Writings*, edited by L.K. Simon, 102–147. Indianapolis: Hackett Publishing Company.

Marx, Karl. (1994c). "Theses on Feuerbach." In *Selected Writings*, edited by L.K. Simon, 98–101. Indianapolis: Hackett Publishing Company.

McGinley, Paul. (2008). On Crying. *Existential Analysis* 19.2: 210–223.

McLuhan, Marshall. (1995). *Understanding Media.* Cambridge, MI: MIT press.

Merleau-Ponty, Maurice. (2012). *Phenomenology of Perception*. Translated by D.A. Landes. New York: Routledge.

Pimpare, Stephen. (2008). *A People's History of Poverty in America*. New York: New Press.

Porter, Libby, Jaconelli, Margaret, Cheyne, Julian, Eby, David, & Wagenaar, Hendrik. (2009). "Planning Displacement: The Real Legacy of Major Sporting Events

"Just a person in a wee flat": Being Displaced by the Commonwealth Games in Glasgow's East End Olympian Masterplanning in London Closing Ceremonies: How Law, Policy and the Winter Olympics Are Displacing an Inconveniently Located Low-Income Community in Vancouver Commentary: Recovering Public Ethos: Critical Analysis for Policy and Planning." *Planning Theory & Practice* 10.3:395–418.

Rinehart, Robert. (1998). "Fictional Methods in Ethnography: Believability, Specks of Glass, and Chekhov." *Qualitative Inquiry* 4:200–24.

Schneider, Barbara (2010). *Hearing (Our) Voices: Participatory Research in Mental Health*. Calgary: University of Toronto Press.

Schneider, Barbara, and Chaseten Remillard. (2013). "Caring about Homelessness: How Identity Work Maintains the Stigma of Homelessness." *Text & Talk* 33.1:95–112.

Sparkes, Andrew C. (2002). "Autoethnography: Self-Indulgence or Something More?" In *Ethnographically Speaking: Autoethnography, Literature, and Aesthetics*. Editied by C. Ellis and A. Bochner, 209–232. New York: Alta Mira Press.

Annex 1

Personal Resources

At-risk Indicators and Characteristics of Social and Digital Exclusion

Annex nr. 1. Personal Resources: At-Risk Indicators and Characteristics of Social and Digital Exclusion

	Characteristics	
At-Risk Indicators	*Social Exclusion*	*Digital Exclusion*
Psychological & physical well-being	• Lack of availability and access to care infrastructure and support • Limited ability to engage with better diets, exercise habits, collaborative treatments… • Lack of support due to social security status • Subject to substance abuse, cf. drugs, alcohol… • Higher poverty risk amongst chronically and terminally ill, and those with stigmatized diseases	• Design inequalities (cf. not in line with usability standards) • Lack of availability, affordability and awareness of adaptive technologies • Limited awareness, attitude and take-up of ICT-solutions for health problems
Values, attitudes, opinions	• Defiant social identity • Defiant symbolic references • Lack of self-determination • Lack of life satisfaction • Subject to a criminal, chaotic or unstructured lifestyle • Lack of awareness about the benefits of social, cultural, economic, educational participation	• Indirect effects of offline behavior, life stage and lifestyle on ICT-access and use, cf. daily wants & needs, personal affordances, creative lifestyle, development creative content online • Negative personal perception of ICTs • Lack of perceived usefulness of ICTs • Lack of interest in ICTs • Lack of awareness about the potential personal benefits of ICTs • Lack of awareness about the necessity of additional ICT-courses due to under or overestimation of skills level • Limited willingness to engage in additional ICT-related courses

Social and soft skills	• Limited ability and confidence to interact with others, with institutions, in social activities due to lack of social intelligence, lack of communication skills, low self-esteem… • Lack of confidence and competences to deal with difficulties in an autonomous and independent way due to lack of self-efficacy, lack of problem-solving capability	• Limited ability and confidence to interact with ICT-tools and services due to a lack of soft skills • Limited ability and confidence to interact with others and with institutions when dealing with ICT-problems • Lack of ability to deal with ICTs and their dynamic nature (constant processes of renewal, rapid evolution, new services…) in an autonomous and independent way due to lack of self-efficacy and lack of problem-solving capability • Subject to button anxiety • Limited ability to develop a professional online identity • Lack of communication skills for online interaction
Cognitive skills	• Limited educational potential & attainment within formal education • Limited ability to engage in lifelong learning courses	• Limited educational potential & attainment within formal education • Lack of ability to develop digital skills autonomously through practice or self-study (e.g., trial-by-error) • Limited ability to deal with the multilayered set-up of ICTs • Stringent need of support when engaging with ICTs • Lack of skills to determine when and what type of help is needed, and where to get that specific help

Sources: Barzilai-Nahon, 2006; Bianchi et al., 2006; Brandtzaeg et al., 2010; Brants and Frissen, 2003; Brotcorne et al., 2010; Communities and Local Government, 2008a, 2008b; Costa, 1998; Daly et al., 2008; Dekkers and Kegels, 2003; Donat et al., 2009; Haché and Centeno, 2011; Haché and Cullen, 2010; Hargittai, 2003, 2007; Heeley and Damodaran, 2009; Helsper, 2008; Husing, 2006; Jehoel-Gijsbers and Vrooman, 2007; Lankshear and Knobel, 2008; Levitas et al., 2007; Liamputtong, 2007; Livingstone and Helsper, 2007; Mossberger et al., 2003; Newhome et al., 2008; Schurmans and Mariën, 2013; Selwyn et al., 2005; Steyn and Johanson, 2011; van Deursen, 2010; van Dijk, 1999; 2003, 2005; Warren, 2007; Zillien and Hargittai, 2009.

Annex 2

Social Resources

At-risk Indicators and Characteristics of Social and Digital Exclusion

Annex nr. 2. Social Resources: At-Risk Indicators and Characteristics of Social and Digital Exclusion

	Characteristics	
At-Risk Indicators	*Social Exclusion*	*Digital Exclusion*
Family composition	• Family breakdown, cf. violence, divorce, abuse… • Constraining family obligations • Teenage pregnancy • Poverty-risk amongst single-parent families • Higher poverty risk amongst children placed within child care systems	• Negative ICT-attitude or low digital skills amongst family members • Low or no media richness within household • Limited freedom of use due to shared access to ICTs • Limited ability to practice ICT-use • Less ICT-access amongst singles due to access elsewhere, more financial constraints…
Social support networks	• Limited embedding in social capital communities • Lack of intensified social interactions • Limited participation in formal and informal networks, cf. local associations, leisure… • Lack of positive stimuli to engage and participate within society • Lack of social support within immediate social environment (cf. family, friends, colleagues...)	• Limited participation in formal and informal networks, cf. local associations, leisure… • Low or no media richness, limited skills levels and lack of opportunities of use within surrounding communities and networks • Lack of communities of practice • Lack of positive stimuli to use ICTs • Limited ability to enlarge social networks through the use of ICTs

	• Lack of available forms of human capital, due to negative consequences of neighborhood factors within poorer areas	• Lack of strong and weak ties, warm experts, local experts, proxy users within immediate social environment (cf. family, friends, colleagues...)
Societal norms	• Limited social integration • Rejection of common social norms • Lack of sense of belonging to society • Defiant view on norms of social citizenship (e.g. reciprocity, mutual obligations, social responsibilities) • Inability to live according to common societal norms • Defiant moral and social literacy	• Limited willingness or ability to engage with services that are digital by default • Lack of compliance with digital by defaults as the overall norm within society

Sources: Bakardjieva, 2005; Bianchi et al., 2006; Brotcorne et al., 2009; Costa 1998; Crang et al., 2006, 2007; Donat et al., 2009; Gilbert, 2010; Haché and Centeno, 2011; Haché and Cullen, 2010; Haddon, 2004; Hargittai, 2003; Heeley and Domodaran, 2009; Helsper, 2008; Jehoel-Gijsbers and Vrooman, 2007; Jin and Cheong, 2008; Kennedy et al., 2008; Lanskhear and Knobel, 2008; Liamputtong, 2007; Manueli et al., 2007; Naughton 2013; Notley and Foth, 2008; Sinclair and Bramley, 2010; Steyn and Johanson, 2011; Stewart, 2007; Tsatsou, 2011; Vandenbroeck et al., 2007; van Deursen, 2010; van Dijk, 2003; Verdegem, 2009; Warren, 2007; Witte and Mannon, 2010; Wright and Wadhwa, 2010; Zillien and Hargittai, 2009.

Annex 3

Cultural Resources

At-risk Indicators and Characteristics of Social and Digital Exclusion

Annex nr. 3. Cultural Resources: At-Risk Indicators and Characteristics of Social and Digital Exclusion

	Characteristics	
At-Risk Indicators	*Social Exclusion*	*Digital Exclusion*
Gender	• Gender defined and limited participation of women in labor market • Gender biased role patterns within society / household dynamics	• Gender defined ICT-use patterns due to gender-related content preferences, wants & needs, daily practices & routines • Male-driven design of ICTs • Limited participation of women in IT-training and IT-labor market • Low take-up of ICTs by women due to household dynamics and power relations within the home
Age	• Age-related position in the labor market, cf. youth unemployment, high cost of elderly employees… • Social isolation amongst elderly • Health issues amongst elderly	• Age defined ICT-use patterns due to age-related content preferences, wants & needs, daily practices & routines, cf. influence of life stages, lifestyles, social and cultural habitat and attitude… • Specific ICT-learning needs amongst elderly, cf. small groups, low pace, 1-on-1 coaching… • Button anxiety amongst elderly • Negative attitude toward ICTs, technology & innovation amongst elderly
Ethnicity	• Lack of employment opportunities • Reproduction of inequalities amongst ethnic minorities by the educational system	• Culturally defined ICT-use patterns due to culture-related content preferences, wants & needs, daily practices & routines • Dominant language schemes of ICTs versus ethnic minority languages

	• Confrontation with discrimination and racism • Limited societal participation due to type/status of immigration	• Limited participation in additional ICT-courses and training • Gender unbalance in ICT-access and use
Language	• Lack of general literacy and numeracy skills • Limited command of national language	• Lack of general literacy and numeracy skills • Limited access to ICT-content because of dominant languages schemes of ICTs • Lack of accessible and easy-to-understand language schemes (cf. *klare taal*) • Inability to deal with the communication schemes of specific ICTs/platforms
Cultural norms	• Defiant normative/cultural framework of reference (cf. weak work ethic, abuse of social security system, delinquent behavior, crime unstructured lifestyle, gun and knife culture…) • Defiant cultural identity • Defiant gender norms • Rejection by society	• Influence of deviated gender norms on ICT-access and use • Influence of deviated cultural norms on ICT-access and use • Lack of added value of ICT-use because of game and leisure oriented use patterns

Sources: Brandtzaeg, 2010; Brants and Frissen, 2003; Brotcorne et al., 2009; Communities and Local Government, 2008a; Costa, 1998; Cuervo and Menéndez, 2003; Dekkers and Kegels, 2003; Donat et al., 2009; Gee, 2007; Haché and Cullen, 2010; Hargittai, 2007; Hargittai and Hinnant, 2008; Helsper, 2008; Husing, 2006; Jehoel-Gijsbers and Vrooman, 2007; Jenkins, 2009; Mossberger et al., 2003; Moura de Holanda and Dall'Antionia, 2006; Selwyn et al., 2005; Sinclair and Bramley, 2010; Steyaert and Gould, 2009; Steyn and Johanson, 2011; Tsatsou, 2011; van Deursen, 2010; van Dijk, 2003; Warren, 2007.

Annex 4

Economic Resources

At-risk Indicators and Characteristics of Social and Digital Exclusion

Annex nr. 4. Economic Resources: At-Risk Indicators and Characteristics of Social and Digital Exclusion

	Characteristics	
At-Risk Indicators	*Social Exclusion*	*Digital Exclusion*
Employment	• Lack of financial means and economic independence • Lack of education and training opportunities at work environment • Inability to develop skills, cf. communication, social, soft… • Higher poverty risk amongst (long-term) unemployed	• Limited opportunities of access and use, cf. no/low integration of ICT-practices within daily routines • Limited access to weak ties • Lack of ICT education and training opportunities within work environment
Income	• Limited capacity to purchase goods and services • Limited capacity to participate in social and cultural activities	• Limited capacity to acquire home access to ICTs • Secondary cost of ICTs, cf. ink, software, cables, memory devices… too high • Low quality of access, no or few places of access, old ICTs, low connectivity speed, low quality of equipment…
Economic opportunities	• Lack of saving opportunities • Problematic debts • Limited access to wage premiums, cheaper products, participate in group purchases…	• Lack of access to advantages of package deals, bundling of services, monthly subscriptions • Limited ability to obtain economic benefits from use of ICTs, cf. price comparison, cross-border orders…

Financial skills	• Lack of capacity to manage budgets • Limited advertising literacy	• Limited advertising literacy of ICTs • Lack of understanding of ICT business models / payment models
Education & Training	• Reproduction of inequalities by the educational system • Lack of lifelong learning opportunities • High school drop-out • Lack of compliance with formal education, cf. rejection of formal education, differing learning styles, differing learning needs… • Limited willingness to engage in additional education and training, cf. negative learning experiences, poor educational achievement…	• Lack of opportunities to develop digital skills, cf. button knowledge, information skills, strategic skills… • Lack of compliance with formal education, cf. rejection of formal ICT-education, differing learning styles, differing learning needs… • Limited availability and focus of ICT-courses in formal education • Lack of awareness of informal ICT-courses and training • Limited willingness and ability to engage in additional informal or formal ICT-related courses • Limited educational benefits from use of ICTs / online learning opportunities • Lack of recognition and certification schemes of ICT competences

Sources: Barzilai-Nahon, 2006; Bianchi et al., 2006; Brandtweiner et al., 2010; Brants and Frissen, 2003; Brotcorne et al., 2009; Communities and Local Government, 2008a, 2008b; Costa, 1998; Crang et al., 2006; Daly et al., 2008; Cuervo, 2005; Dekkers and Kegels, 2003; Gilbert et al., 2008; Gilbert, 2010; Gorski, 2008; Haché and Cullen, 2010; Hanafizadeh et al., 2007; Hargittai and Hinnant, 2008; Heeley and Damodaran, 2009; Helsper, 2008; Jehoel-Gijsbers and Vrooman, 2007; Livingstone and Helsper, 2007; Lohnes and Kinzer, 2007; Moreas, 2007; Pena-Lopez, 2009; Steyaert and Gould, 2009; Steyn and Johanson, 2011; Tsatsou, 2011; van Deursen, 2010; van Dijk, 2003, 2005; Vehovar et al., 2006; Verdegem, 2009; Warren, 2007; Wilson, 2007; Witte and Mannon, 2010, Zillien & Hargittai, 2009.

Annex 5

Political Resources

At-risk Indicators and Characteristics of Social and Digital Exclusion

Annex nr. 5. Political Resources: At-Risk Indicators and Characteristics of Social and Digital Exclusion

	Characteristics	
At-Risk Indicators	*Social Exclusion*	*Digital Exclusion*
Impact of regulatory framework	• Lack of horizontal policy approach • No implementation of *"poverty check,"* cf. poverty impact assessment alongside new regulatory measures • Lack of social security support mechanisms • Lack of low-skilled jobs within overall job market • Perverse effect of (dis)incentives to avoid poverty trap • Negative consequences of historical societal evolutions	• Lack of horizontal digital inclusion policy approach • Lack of regulatory frameworks of ICT platforms, cf. data protection, privacy… • Lack of regulatory framework for digitization of public and commercial services, cf. digital by default, universal service approach, implementation of *"digital exclusion check"*… • Perverse effects of market driven diffusion of ICTs • Limited compliance with usability and user friendly design due to a lack of integration of at-risk profiles in user-centred design processes of ICTs • Lack of relevant and easy-to-use ICTs and content
Participation in decision-making bodies	• Lack of structural participatory policy processes • Lack of engagement of at-risk groups in participatory policy actions and lack of mediation by professionals to enhance their participation • Limited involvement in local/national politics and organizations • Limited ability to present organized claims	• Lack of structural participatory digital inclusion policy processes • Lack of engagement of at-risk groups in participatory digital inclusion policy actions and lack of mediation by professionals to enhance their participation • Limited involvement in local/national politics and organizations through ICT-tools, cf. online pressure groups, online civil action groups… • Limited ability to use ICTs to present organized claims

Socio-spatial opportunities	• Low quality of housing and overall living area, cf. crime, illegal dumping, poor housing… • Lack of transport availability • Lack of public and private services and infrastructure • Socio-spatial inequalities, cf. ghettoization, rural underdevelopment…	• Lack of ICT-access in rural areas • Low connection quality • Lack of overall ICT-infrastructure • Cherry picking by IT-industries • Lack of public computer spaces • Limited availability of learning institutions (formal and informal)
Public service infrastructure	• Limited access to (online) public services and lack of structural mediation by professionals to enhance access to public services • Lack of social service infrastructure	• Perverse effects of public services that are digital by default and lack of structural mediation by professionals to ensure participation of digitally excluded groups, e.g., through informal learning infrastructure, accessible technical support…
Social rights	• Lack of access amongst at-risk groups to social security agencies • Limited mediation by professionals to enhance access to social security and health services • Limited accessibility and availability of information on social rights issues	• No implementation of a social tariff for ICTs, cf. e.g., Internet access, mobile… • Lack of recognition of access to ICTs as social/human right
Agency	• Limited capability to make life choices and personal decisions • Limited capacity to determine needs • Limited capacity to maintain independence	• Limited capacity to control content and nature of ICT use • Limited influence on digitization of society • Lack of free digital choice

Sources: Bianchi et al., 2006; Bouwman and Van Der Duin, 2007; Communities and Local Government, 2008b; Costa, 1998; Cuervo, 2005; Damy et al., 2008; Emmel et al., 2006; Haché and Cullen, 2010; Helsper, 2008; Jehoel-Gijsbers and Vrooman, 2007; Lankshear and Knobel, 2008; Liamputtong, 2007; Notley and Foth, 2008; Olshansky, 2008; Selwyn, 2004; Steyn and Johanson, 2011; van Deursen, 2010; van Deursen and van Dijk, 2009; van Dijk, 2003, 2005; Warren, 2007.

Index

About the Contributors

EDITORS

Jan Servaes (PhD, 1987, Catholic University of Louvain, Belgium) is Chair Professor at the Department of Media and Communication, City University of Hong Kong, UNESCO Chair in Communication for Sustainable Social Change at the University of Massachusetts Amherst; Honorary Guest Professor at the Huazhong University of Science and Technology (HUST), Wuhan, China; Researcher at the "Brussels Center for Journalism Studies" (BCJS), Belgium; Editor-in-Chief of the Elsevier journal "Telematics and Informatics: An Interdisciplinary Journal on the Social Impacts of New Technologies"; Editor of the Southbound Book Series "Communication for Development and Social Change"; Editor of the Springer Book Series "Communication, Culture and Change in Asia"; and Editor of the Lexington Book Series "Communication, Globalization and Cultural Identity." He has been President of the European Consortium for Communications Research (ECCR, www.ecrea.eu) and Vice-President of the International Association of Media and Communication Research (IAMCR, www.iamcr.org), in charge of Academic Publications and Research, from 2000 to 2004. He chaired the Scientific Committee for the World Congress on Communication for Development (Rome, October 25-27, 2006), organized by the World Bank, FAO and the Communication Initiative. Servaes has taught International Communication and Development Communication in Australia (Brisbane), Belgium (Brussels and Antwerp), the USA (Cornell), The Netherlands (Nijmegen), and Thailand (Thammasat, Bangkok) in addition to several teaching stints at about 100 universities in forty-three countries. He has undertaken research, development, and advisory work around the world and is known as the author of journal articles and books on such topics as international and development communication; ICT & media policies; intercultural communication and language; participation and social change; and human rights and conflict management. Some of his most recent book titles, include: (2014) Jan Servaes (Ed.). *Technological Determinism and Social Change*. Lanham: Lexington Books; (2014) Jan Servaes and Patchanee Malikhao. Communication for Social Change (in Chinese). Wuhan: Wuhan University Press; (2013) Jan Servaes (Ed.). *Sustainable Development and Green Communication. African and Asian Perspectives*, London/New York: Palgrave / MacMillan; (2013) J. Servaes (Ed.). *Sustainability, Participation and Culture in Communication. Theory and Praxis*. Bristol-Chicago: Intellect-University of Chicago Press; (2008) J. Servaes. *Communication for Development and Social Change*. Los Angeles, London, New Delhi, Singapore: Sage; (2007) J. Servaes & Liu S. (Eds.). *Moving Targets. Mapping the Paths Between Communication, Technology and Social Change in Communities*. Penang: Southbound; (2006) P. Thomas & J. Servaes (Eds.). *Intellectual Property Rights and Communications in Asia*. New Delhi: Sage; (2006) J. Servaes & N. Carpentier (Eds.). *Towards A Sustainable European Information Society*, ECCR Book Series. Bristol: Intellect; (2005) Shi -Xu, Kienpointner M. & J. Servaes (Eds.). *Read the Cultural Other. Forms of Otherness in the Discourses of Hong Kong's Decolonisation*. Berlin: Mouton De Gruyter; (2003) J. Servaes (Ed.). *The European Information Society: A Reality Check*, ECCR Book Series. Bristol: Intellect; (2003) J. Servaes (Ed.). *Approaches to Development. Studies on Communication for Development*, Paris: Unesco Publishing House; and (2002) J. Servaes. *Communication for Development. One World, Multiple Cultures*, Cresskill NJ: Hampton Press. E-mail: 9cssc9@gmail.com

Toks Oyedemi (PhD Communication, University of Massachusetts, Amherst, USA) engages sociological questions around media and communication. His research examines communication, media, culture and society, digital culture, pattern of marginalization and exclusion in the communication and technology environment, communication for social change, and the intersection of social inequalities, citizenship and technology. He serves as editorial board member of the Elsevier journal *Telematics and Informatics*: *An Interdisciplinary Journal on the Social Impacts of New Technologies*, he also serves as a grant review panel member for the South African National Research Foundation. He was a fellow at the Center for Communication for Sustainable Social Change (CSSC) and at the National Center for Digital Government (NCDG) both at the University of Massachusetts, USA. He was an academic member of NetTel@Africa: a transnational network of international academics and institutions for capacity building and knowledge exchange in the Telecom/ICT Sector in Africa. His research publications have appeared in international journals, such as *International Journal of Communication,* and *Citizenship Studies.* His chapter contributions are in books such as J. Servaes (Ed.). *Sustainability and Culture in Communication: Theory and Praxis.* Bristol-Chicago: Intellect-University of Chicago Press; and Z. Lesame (Ed) 2005. *New Media: Technology and Policy in Developing Countries.* Pretoria: Van Schaik. He has taught at colleges and universities both in the United States of America and South Africa. He is currently at the University of Limpopo, South Africa. E-mail: Toyedemi@gmail.com / toks.oyedemi@ul.ac.za

AUTHORS

Debra M. Clarke is an associate professor in the Department of Sociology at Trent University in Canada. She is the author of *Journalism and Political Exclusion: Social Conditions of News Production and Reception* (McGill-Queen's University Press, 2014) and other publications addressed to her research interests in political communication, news production, and news reception. She also serves on the editorial boards of the *Canadian Journal of Communication* and the *Electronic Journal of Communication.*

Banu Durdağ is a Ph.D. candidate and research assistant in the Faculty of Communication, at Ankara University, Turkey. Her research interests focus on the political economy of communication, digital media, the relationship between technology and social change, social inequalities, ICT policies, critical information society studies, alternative media, and social movements.

Nova M. Gordon-Bell, Ph.D. is a senior lecturer in Communication and Media at the University of Technology, Jamaica. Head of the School of Humanities and Social Sciences, she has spearheaded the introduction of media and communication courses, and a degree in Communication Arts and Technology, in Jamaica's national university. A creative writer and university teacher, she has published award-winning fiction and poetry in several journals and magazines.

Rob Heyman is a PhD student in the department of communication sciences of Vrije Universiteit Brussel, at iMinds-SMIT. He researches how social media users' autonomy and lifeworld is shaped and limited by social media technologies to generate profit. His research combines user research with ANT and critical theory of technology.

Ilse Mariën started working as a junior researcher at iMinds SMIT, a research center attached to Communication Science Department of the Vrije Universiteit Brussel (VUB), in 2007. She had been leading several policy-oriented projects related to digital inequalities, the social consequences of the digitization processes and digital inclusion policies. She is also on the verge of finishing her doctoral thesis that focuses on the development of (1) a renewed theoretical framework for digital inequalities; and (2) a comprehensive digital inclusion policy framework.

Glenn W. Muschert is professor in the Sociology and Social Justice Studies, and faculty affiliate in Comparative Media Studies, at Miami University (USA). His research has appeared in over three dozen articles and chapters, and he has edited six volumes or special issues in the fields of media studies, sociology, and criminology. His research has focused on mass media framing of mass violence, and more recently on the sociological aspects of inequality in the digital sphere.

Kala Ortwein is a Master's of Arts student at the University of Calgary with a Bachelor's of Arts in Psychology from the University of British Columbia. Her primary research interests regard the public perception of homelessness, mental illness, and addictions. Relying on narrative inquiry and Arthur Frank's (1995) *Wounded Storyteller* model, her current autoethnographic work examines the life stories of daughters of men who have experienced chronic homelessness. In her spare time, Kala enjoys wandering in the Canadian Rocky Mountains and writing poetry.

Massimo Ragnedda is a Senior Lecturer in Mass Communication at Northumbria University, Newcastle. His research interests include new media studies, surveillance and web 2.0, and digital inequalities. He is author of six books and his publications have appeared as numerous book chapters and articles in peer-reviewed journals in English, Spanish, and Italian. He has been Affiliated Visitor at the Department of Sociology, University of Cambridge and an Academic Visiting Scholar at Oxford Internet Institute.

Sarah Rowe is completing her Master's of Arts at the University of Calgary Communications and Culture Department. Her thesis examines the role of identity performances in online communities, and the contestation of fan and geek identities along gender lines. Sarah's research includes gender and performance studies, feminism, and online activism. She spends her free time reading comics, playing video games, and arguing with misogynists on Twitter.

Ruth Sanz Sabido is Senior Lecturer in Media and Communications at Canterbury Christ Church University (UK). She is coeditor of *Contemporary Protest and the Legacy of Dissent* (2015) and author of a number of chapters and articles on media discourse, memory and the Spanish Civil War, and social movements. She is coeditor, with Professor Stuart Price, of the book series "Protest, Media and Culture" (Rowman and Littlefield).

Koen Salemink is a Ph.D Candidate and Project Researcher at the Faculty of Spatial Sciences, University of Groningen. He researches the effects of a lack of digital developments in the margins; either spatial margins such as rural areas, or social margins such as vulnerable groups. In this he touches upon debates in rural development and social exclusion.

Eunice Castro Seixas holds a Ph.D in sociology (specialization in "Post-colonialisms and Global Citizenship"), a Master in social psychology and a degree in health psychology. She has worked as psychologist, as assistant professor and research assistant and is currently affiliated with the Communication and Society Research Centre (CECS) at the University of Minho, Portugal, as an integrated researcher. Her research interests comprise: global governance; democratization; development aid; peacebuilding; human rights; civil society; environmental discourses; climate change; media analysis; post-colonial and decolonial theories and critical discourse analysis.

A. Fulya Sen studied MSc (Public Relations and Publicity) at the Institute of Social Sciences, Gazi University, Turkey. She received her doctorate in Public Relations and Publicity from the Institute of Social Sciences, Ankara University, Turkey. Her research interests include media representations, media and ideology, the discourse of news, social movements and media, social media activism, the issues of participation and democracy. Currently, she is an Associate Professor in the Faculty of Communication in Firat University, Turkey. She is working on a book about the representation of the working class in Turkish news media.

Y. Furkan Sen earned MSc and Ph.D. degrees in Political Science from Gazi University, Turkey. His research interests include nationalism, globalization, security, terrorism, human trafficking and smuggling. He is the author of seven books and many journal articles. In his latest book entitled *Nation Perception and Nationalism in Turkish Political Culture*, he has examined how Turkish people comprehend nationalism. Some of his other books are: *Nationalism Trends and Nation-States in Globalization Process*, *Old Discussions in the New Period: Migration, Ethnicity, Nationalism, Kurdism, and*

Laicism, and *Human Smuggling, Human Trafficking and Organ-Tissue Trafficking from the Perspectives of Turkey and the World.*

Olga Shapovalova is a graduate student at the University of Calgary, Communication and Culture Department, with background in political science and international relations (MA in European, Russian, and Eurasian Studies, from Carleton University, Ottawa). Her current research lies in organizational communication, with a specific focus on the concepts of organizational identity, culture and their production, contestation, and reproduction in informal online communication of organizational members. In her free time, Olga is learning her fifth language and enjoys reading an occasional spy novel.

Leo Van Audenhove is professor at the Department of Communication Studies at the Vrije Universiteit Brussels. He lectures International Communication, Policy Analysis, and Globalisation and the Information Society. He is also a senior researcher at iMinds-SMIT where his main areas of interest are international media and communication, the information society and ICT policies, the political economy of Internet media and Internet governance. He has published in international journals such as *Third World Quarterly, International Review on Education, Communicatio, Political Communication, Journal of Media Business Studies, Gazette*, etc. and has coauthored two books on the digital divide.